A new genre for television?

Manchester University Press

A new genre for television?

Creativity in historical drama documentary

Justin Hardy

MANCHESTER UNIVERSITY PRESS

Copyright © Justin Hardy 2024

The right of Justin Hardy to be identified as the author of this work has been asserted in accordance with the Copyright, Designs and Patents Act 1988.

Published by Manchester University Press
Oxford Road, Manchester, M13 9PL

www.manchesteruniversitypress.co.uk

British Library Cataloguing-in-Publication Data
A catalogue record for this book is available from the British Library

ISBN   978 1 5261 7953 1   hardback

First published 2025

The publisher has no responsibility for the persistence or accuracy of URLs for any external or third-party internet websites referred to in this book, and does not guarantee that any content on such websites is, or will remain, accurate or appropriate.

EU authorised representative for GPSR:
Easy Access System Europe, Mustamäe tee 50, 10621 Tallinn, Estonia
gpsr.requests@easproject.com

Typeset
by Deanta Global Publishing Services, Chennai, India

I dedicate this book to my wife, Larissa, who supported me through the whole writing process when I should have been making films and earning money.

Contents

Preface		*page* viii
Acknowledgements		ix
Introduction		1
1	2000: Emergence of a new kind of history television for the millennium	15
2	2000–2002: From vignettes to fuller dramatisation	37
3	1960s–1990s: Looking for progenitors	56
4	2001–2003: Was the flowering of dramatised history documentary led by auteurs?	76
5	2003–2005: Working towards fuller dramatisation and a new genre?	116
6	2006–2008: Confirming a new genre	157
7	2008–2010: Decline and fall of a genre	170
Conclusion		198
Bibliography		207
Interviews		214
Index		215

Preface

In the first decade of the new millennium, amidst a commonly accepted 'history boom', over four hundred dramatisations of the past were commissioned by the documentary departments at the BBC and Channel 4. Not to be confused with the hitherto more-studied dramas based on true stories (commissioned by the *drama* departments), these dramatised documentaries have never been examined in toto. This is surprising given that it contains such well-known televisual works as Simon Schama's *A History of Britain* (BBC, 2000–2002) and the Oscar-winning *Man on Wire* (BBC, 2008). This book intends to redress this oversight, re-evaluating the reputation of works of international importance – the significance of which, it argues, has been neglected by public historians and television scholars. This book aims, furthermore, to answer the question of whether this hybrid model was indeed the 'bastard genre' of contemporary criticism. Not only does this body of work deserve classification as a genre, but, far from being belittled, it should be seen as a stylistic mode that enabled innovation, creative ambition, and value-for-money television-making in a way that was uniquely of its time. It was, indeed, the very blurring of boundaries between drama and documentary that created fertile ground for originality. For the limitations set by the hybrid state were its strength, as Orson Welles concurred, when he famously proclaimed that 'the enemy of art is the absence of limitations'.

I aim to submit this corpus to media theories that surround drama documentary, auteurism, and genre in order to determine if and how the material has characteristics that can be shown to be consistent. This media excavation will also reach back to the inspirational dramatised documentaries of the 1960s such as *Culloden* (BBC, 1964) and look forward to more recent factual drama inheritors, such as *Chernobyl* (HBO, 2019), to highlight a golden thread that links drama documentaries across more than fifty years of British television.

Acknowledgements

This book has derived from a time of putting my practice into theory, under the kind supervision of Professor Stella Bruzzi (Film and TV Studies) and Professor Melvyn Stokes (History). I would like to thank Caitlin Hyland, Stevie Doran, my former history tutor at Magdalen College, Oxford, Professor Laurence Brockliss, and the insight of Dr Derek Paget, an inspiration from first to last. I would also like to thank my contacts in television, who very kindly gave up their time to help me define this underexplored corner of television commissioning, especially Hamish Mykura who very sadly died in 2023.

Introduction

While the turn of the millennium was a golden era for the dramatisation of history documentaries, these films were not universally popular with television critics and scholars. Traditional historians were affronted by the non-traditional approaches to the telling of history through dramatic narrative and overtly contemporary resonance. The television historian Tristram Hunt, director of the Victoria and Albert Museum (V&A) since 2017, wrote scathingly in 2006 of television's various attempts to make history more populist. Re-enactments, like *The Trench* (BBC, 2002), were disparaged as 'dumbed down, drum and trumpet' appeals to the masses, the author going further to call them 'bastard genres'.[1] He was following a well-trodden academic path that objected particularly to the hybrid of dramatisation with the pure documentary of history. For many years, television studies had also ridiculed what they termed 'docudramas'; one of the most prominent critics of the genre was the producer Jerome Kuehl, who complained in the late 1980s that 'many docudramas are produced with little regard for historical truth, or psychological plausibility, but with every regard for pecuniary advantage'.[2] Another pre-millennium condemnation from *The New York Times* added fuel to the fire: 'the only good docudrama is the unproduced docudrama'.[3] The hostility towards docudrama's inherent hybridity has continued from television scholars and critics alike, and is best characterised by Derek Paget's description of the genre as an 'impure, mongrel element in an already mongrel medium'.[4]

This book aims to do three things.

The first is to explore this negative attitude towards the mix of historical drama and documentary, focusing particularly on the key years of 2000–2010, when over four hundred hybrid films were screened on Britain's public service television. It will often draw on the scholarship of Paget and his fellow scholar in the United States, Stephen Lipkin. Paget provides one of this book's foundational axioms: 'Frequently portrayed as bad documentary, bad drama, or both these things simultaneously, dramadoc/docudrama is best understood first of all as itself – a form in its own right rather than some kind of "mongrel", "hybrid" or even "bastard" form.'[5] As a practitioner of historical drama and documentary myself, I shall not explore this televisual mode simply out of defensiveness but because I firmly believe that one can show how creative many of these films could be, especially with less money available than the makers of conventional period drama ever had at their disposal.

The second aim is to properly define the scholarly terms at use here. Proper definition will be welcomed by a film and television industry that often fails to communicate clearly, even within itself. Paget helps to show the dilemmas faced by scholars and critics alike when he refers to a variety of concepts inherent:

> 'Blurring the boundaries', 'The "truth" of fiction is stranger than the facts', 'Friction over faction', 'Dubious drama', 'Drama out of suffering', 'Fact or fiction?', 'True to the facts?', 'An unsuitable case for television treatment?', 'Making a documentary drama out of a crisis'.[6]

And Paget was only really referring to drama that was based on documentary sources but was only being commissioned from the drama departments. He was focusing on dramas that were primarily being made by ITV during the 1980s and 1990s and also stretched into the 2000s, such as *Hostages* (ITV, 1992), and hence their work should be distinguished from the films that are the key focus for this book. *A New Genre?* is looking specifically at films commissioned by British documentary departments during this period that just happened to use drama to tell their narratives, such as *Pyramid* (BBC, 2000). The terms 'dramadoc' versus 'docudrama' must therefore be properly understood in order to progress with distinct scholarships. It is intended that this series of clear definitions shall be achieved for the first time.

Finally, the book will thoroughly address the question of the title: *A New Genre?* It is acknowledged that the form is a mix of two forms: drama and documentary. That is not under debate. But do the four hundred films selected for consideration actually support the call for a genre to be created for the very first time? If so, it will need to be proven that the films share a generic set of rules, have similar antecedents and follow the rise and fall of a genre in much the same way as other television genres have done in the past. Thus, the book will aim to tread fresh ground for the newly created studies across media and the recent representation of history.

Contemporary resonance

Why does the question of establishing a genre for historical drama documentary matter? The answer is quite simple: because according to Tristram

Hunt, while dramatising history is a medium often unsuited to a nuanced deciphering of the past, popular TV history is a vital component of how millions interact with the past. The question, Hunt continues, is not whether TV history is a good thing, but how we can make it better, by which he means balancing the nuances of historical sources with the less nuanced demands of narrative. Most historian filmmakers would agree with this call to arms. History-telling on screen, especially in the 2020s, needs to continue to adapt so that it can remain relevant and, more importantly, can appeal to each new generation of viewers, readers, and thinkers, acting as a potential anchor in turbulent times.

While the scope of this book ends in 2010, it is important to determine that the drama documentary hybrid has continued to influence some of the best modern dramatisation of true stories, right up to the time of writing. The now-iconic nuclear disaster drama *Chernobyl* (HBO, 2019), starring Jared Harris and Emily Watson, is a provable direct heir to no less than two dramadocs of the 2000s, as shall be shown in Chapter 5. Indeed, looking forward, it will not be long before the benighted people of Ukraine are going to want to know how best to define their recent history of war at the hands of Russia. This book will hopefully become a template for their broadcasters to choose how to televise their story. Will they tell it as a straight documentary with a presenter, albeit their televisually sophisticated President Zelensky in contrast to Putin's obsession with Russia's historical legacy? Will they select members of the public to re-enact various key moments of hardship brought on by the invasion: a *Trench* in the Donbas region – too much factual documentary? Or will huge budgets be siphoned off to pay for a drama with well-known, even Hollywood, actors to play real-life characters: a *Braveheart* for the Ukraine – too much contrived drama? Or, as this book suggests, will Ukraine choose the most balanced view of history told in the form of a documentary made more engaging with a dramatic narrative? All the more reason to understand the genre at stake here, and the definitions that might go to build it.

The two-pronged approach of practice and theory

> I try [...] to bridge what is often seen as a gap between the academy and the entertainment industry; people from both worlds have been helpful to me in my attempt to combine theory and practice.[7]

This is one of the opening statements of Derek Paget's work on dramadocs and docudramas, *No Other Way to Tell It*, and articulates an approach with which I emphatically concur. Combining theory and practice is key to the methodology of this work. But whereas Paget is a longstanding scholar, I have come from the entertainment industry into academia late in my career. As a writer, director, and producer of television history dramatisation during the period of this 'history boom', I hope to put my practice into theory, offering an insight into the industrial and aesthetic processes of television production. I spent three years studying modern history at Oxford in the 1980s and have spent three years from 2018 to 2021 studying Film/Television Studies at UCL, which has led to the writing of this work. But six years of academic research must be balanced against thirty years in the film and television industry, during which I made more than one hundred films. At the turn of the millennium, specifically, I was involved in the production of more than twenty history dramatisations, concentrating on turning primary sources into narrative structures that befit television commissions and budgets. I may not (as yet) be a professional historian-filmmaker, but in the words of Natalie Zemon Davis about Steven Spielberg, I could be defined as an 'artist for whom history matters'.[8] Hence, a cross-disciplinary approach involving history and screen studies, and a combination of academic research and practice, will inform this book.

Practice and theory

Throughout the first decade of this century, I witnessed first-hand the ratings and critical battle between the two public service broadcasters, BBC and Channel 4; competition will remain a threat throughout the work. It is worth noting that ITV specialised in docudramas, not in drama documentaries, and therefore sits outside the scope of this work. This work has, therefore, benefitted from privileged access to many of the decision-makers at Channel 4 and the BBC, whose personal tastes were reputed to have shaped the decisions to invest heavily in dramatised documentary, beginning with the most powerful partnership in this arena: Janice Hadlow, Head of History at Channel 4, and subsequently until 2016, Controller of BBC Four and BBC Two; and Martin Davidson, executive producer before becoming Head of History at the BBC until 2017. According to independent producer and latterly Chairman of the BBC, Samir Shah, Hadlow and Davidson acted as 'the Medici in terms of their patronage, and success' (Shah, 2019).[9] Furthermore, I have interviewed the heads of relevant independent production companies, born out of the Broadcasting Acts of the 1980s and 1990s, that changed the face of British television, primarily through their rejection of a BBC 'silo' system which had kept drama and documentary departments physically and metaphorically separate. The CEO of the powerful indie production company Wall to Wall TV, Alex Graham, has contributed considerable insight over the course of many interviews, so it has been decided that the story of the company's rise to a frequently recognised dominance in all modes of television history should become the sole focus of Chapter 4. Through this single independent production company, the structures of institutional power and aesthetic progress can be intriguingly combined and challenged.

The limitations of this privileged access and close textual analysis should be evident. One must approach the perspectives of those who commissioned or produced the fabric of these films with some circumspection, since their memory of creating a genre of critical significance needs to be corroborated. Furthermore, if unchecked, the book might contain too much subjectivity from the present writer, who was involved in the production teams of some of the films under consideration. This involvement could potentially lead to outright bias. Conversely, it is argued that the specific approach towards every level of production will sufficiently contribute to a greater objectivity that benefits from intimate knowledge and relationships within this sphere.

The greater limitation of this period must be mentioned at the outset. In 2024, the eleventh year of Black Lives Matter, it is pertinent to wonder whether the stories of the United Kingdom's multicultural heritage were adequately represented by the BBC and Channel 4 during this period. In brief, the answer is that this history content was targeted mostly at an educated class, and in televisual terms, white men over fifty years old. Indeed, much of the boom in historical commissioning in the early 2000s emanated from a white, Oxbridge hegemony. Jane Root and Janice Hadlow aside, the commissioners were often men, highly educated, and entirely white. Although industry leaders Hadlow, Michael Jackson and Alex Graham were not educated at Oxford or Cambridge, many of the commissioners and controllers were, and most were educated beyond first degree status – so too TV historians such as Dan Snow and Tristram Hunt, and even independent producer/directors such as Richard Bradley and Sue Horth. Samir Shah aside, very few historians/filmmakers/commissioners at any level of this chain of command were from an ethnic minority, and much of the history subject matter commissioned on Britain was founded on a white island story that looked not dissimilar to the world depicted by Trevelyan or Macaulay. As will be seen, the lens of the history boom gradually becomes more focused, first onto the participation of women – aside from queens and courtesans – and the beginnings of social history on television. Actually, this focus was largely begun by *Out of the Dolls' House* (BBC, 1987), but it took some time before it was followed by a genuine wave of feminist history. This evolution will be further explored in Chapter 5, as will the participation of ethnic minorities in the imperial story, something that began in earnest with *Bloody Foreigners* (Channel 4, 2015) and David Olusoga's *The World's War: Forgotten Soldiers of the Empire* (BBC, 2014). In the five years prior to the time of writing, the new mode of presenter, represented by Anita Rani and Yasmin Khan, among others, owes a great deal to those trailblazers.

Speaking of trailblazers, this book complies with the notion put forward by the extraordinary 1960s drama documentarian Peter Watkins (the subject of Chapter 3) that films are not the product of a single auteur; it has been decided, therefore, to break with the film and television studies convention in which a film referred to in a scholarly context should be accompanied by the name of the director. Any film, especially one as complex as a drama documentary, is to be assumed to be the collective work of many creatives under the banner of the production company who hired them and/or the broadcaster who supplied the investment. Also, the production teams behind the films, from the camera assistant to the sound designer, should always be acknowledged for their aesthetic contribution. By means of my additional access as a director, interviews have also been conducted across the entire spectrum of the production and the post-production arena to include directors of photography, sound designers, and visual-effects artists at the micro level, a working contingent that has been unfortunately neglected by many students of television studies. It is to be hoped that this will fulfil the request of Ann Gray, Emerita Professor of Cultural Studies at Lincoln University, that this present author make 'an invaluable contribution to the knowledge of micro-production, which is so underexplored' (Gray, 2019).

Finally, the book conducts an attempted survey of every historical drama documentary commissioned between 2000 and 2010, which will involve a data set compiled by key witnesses at the BBC, Channel 4, the History Channel, National Geographic, and the most successful independent production companies. Hamish Mykura, of both Channel 4 and National Geographic, accepts that the primary statistics centre upon the battle between the BBC and Channel 4. National Geographic, the History Channel, and Channel 5 at this stage were minnows by comparison, and their films did not 'move the dial of the genre' (Mykura, 2020). With Mykura's guiding hand, amongst other BBC and Channel 4 commissioners, I have been encouraged to pursue such a survey, bearing in mind that this hybrid is, at its best, a truly inventive mode of representation that could be regarded as a genre of its own – which I believe worth keeping alive for the benefit of filmmakers, historians, and observers of history. Hence one of the key aims of this book is to argue for the creation of a new genre, one that connects history, drama, and documentary in a hitherto-unexplained framework.

From the perspective of critical theory, this book hopes to bring academic enquiry to an industry that rarely pauses to consider the cycles of storytelling aesthetics in a larger context. It will be enlightening for many practitioners to hear discussion of some of the best fundamental questions that underlie history drama documentary. What aesthetic best enables the viewer to feel as if they have actually travelled in time? How does the simplicity of narrative allow for the complexity of history's *ad hoc* sources? Why is a primary source often more compelling than a secondary source? Critical theory has answers to many of these questions, from historians, philosophers, and television studies researchers alike.

History boom on television

The boom in history programming on British television was identified by academics and people working within the industry alike soon after the millennium, and yet quite long after the industry had become aware of the phenomenon. This is confirmed by Sir David Cannadine, who chaired a symposium at which the phenomenon was discussed. He observed: 'in Britain, the late 1990s and early 2000s witnessed what was widely regarded as an unprecedented interest in history: among publishers, in the newspapers, on radio and on film, and (especially) on television; and from the general public, who it seemed, could not get enough of it'.[10]

There are many causes for the boom, ranging from a more educated viewership after Blair's education reforms of the 1990s to a millennial need for confirmation of who and what the British had become a thousand years after the Norman invasion. Historians like Felipe Fernandez-Armesto noted that there had been an increase in consumer demand for screen and print media products dealing with historical subjects,[11] while Williams cited wider social changes, which triggered a search for personal and community origins and identities, supported by the growing confidence of TV commissioners in the ability of the genre to deliver large audiences. Further exploration of this millennial impulse will be found in Chapter 1.

Meanwhile, Cannadine brought together the thoughts of Simon Schama, Jeremy Isaacs, Tristram Hunt, Ian Kershaw, Melvyn Bragg, David Puttnam, John Tusa, and Max Hastings, revealing that both industry and academia were well represented at the symposium. The subject of history and the media continued to draw attention for another five years, and in 2010, the former BBC Director-General, Greg Dyke, hosted the Institute for the Public Understanding of the Past (IPUP) at the University of York (where he was Chancellor) to define the genesis, legacy, and impact of Simon Schama's *A History of Britain*, a defining series that will be explored in Chapter 1.

In the 2010s, Paget's collaboration with his colleague Tobias Ebbrecht-Hartmann culminated in a broader, Europe-wide consideration of the drama documentary mix on television: *Docudrama on European Television* (2016). They acknowledge that while the history boom has not been as vigorous in continental Europe as it has been in Britain over the past decade and a half, each European country has needed to confront the events of the twentieth century, when the ebbing tides of fascism and communism fought for control of the continent.

Paget has a further theory that the production of factual dramas is a form of 'cultural tourism' in which the British, initially, enjoy visiting the cultural tourist sites of their own perceived heritage.[12] This is a hugely pertinent concept for the history boom, and it frames very clearly the British devotion to its monarchy in particular. 'Cultural tourism' is a concept that also embraces the international power of the history boom, when British production companies were providing the world with drama documentaries on Ancient Egypt, the Italian Renaissance, and the intersections of the Middle East, as well as a carefully considered presentation of China's heritage. Paget knew who the buyers would be – for his specialist area, docudrama, and especially so for the genre analysed in this work: history dramatisations. They were Americans, quickly followed by the Japanese, for, as he pointed out, 'tourism is an expression particularly of American and Japanese economic supremacy'.[13] Mostly, Paget used the term 'cultural tourism' critically. He was confirming that a tourist never gets to know the place they are visiting; they are just passing through. This suggests that dramatisation helps history to be visited more thoroughly because the traveller gets to know the drama's characters and their contexts. So, if this tourism was a strong idea for docudramas like *Hostages* (ITV, 1992), set in Beirut, it is immensely so for a film about the building of the pyramids, *Pyramid* (BBC, 2002). It provides an elemental judgement call by which to define a historical film; that is, do we really get to visit the past properly and witness its own rules – and evoke its own smells – or do we take photos from the jeep, with what Hayden White calls a 'presentist' understanding, holding our noses upwind?[14] This issue will be further developed in Chapter 2's discussion of dramatised history films such as *Pyramid* and *Plague*.

Drama and documentary

In a similar vein, American scholar Steven Lipkin, who was to exchange ideas with Paget for the next decade or so, crystallises the notion that the combination of drama and documentary is 'little explored in film scholarship',[15] and he begins to correct that lack with his contribution to the field: *Real Emotional Logic: Film and Television Docudrama as Persuasive Practice* (2002). It becomes clear that he admires Paget and, referencing Hayden White, argues that it is perfectly acceptable to introduce narrative to facts. He creates three key terms as aids for analysis: 'approximation', 'emplotment', and 'melodrama'. Each of these introduces a potent concept and will be further articulated here in the approach to case studies. Lipkin really consolidated his own conceptual thesis in 2011 with the impressive *Docudrama Performs the Past*, in which he asserts that since drama documentary 'performs a memory', it has an obligation to the past. Furthermore, he takes issue with docudrama (dramas based on fact) being considered a genre, and instead recasts it as a 'mode of presentation'.[16]

I intend to test that theory (amongst others) against the drama docs that are the subject of this book. It will be proposed, in the following chapters, that there might well be reason to call this corpus more than a 'mode of presentation' and to go as far as to call it a genre. Before attending to the concept of genre, I have been lucky enough to stumble upon a potentially new way to describe the conflict of drama and documentary, using the terms 'sense' and 'sensuousness'. It has been very much assisted by Lipkin, who draws attention to a variety of aesthetic terms whose definitions he shares with Robert Burgoyne, arguing that 'in order to recover the "sensible" dimensions of history, film will address necessarily the tactile, the visceral and the affective'.[17] The term 'sensible' is an important early reference for this new idea, and so it is worth pausing here to better define it. Having touched upon the senses, Lipkin quotes Burgoyne, who

> recognises what he terms 'sensuous' ways of understanding history, strategies for gaining access to the literal 'sense' of social memory as the cultural desire to reexperience the past in a sensuous form [that] has become an important, perhaps decisive, factor in the struggle to lay claim to what and how the nation remembers.[18]

Burgoyne claims, and Lipkin agrees, that there is a widespread cultural desire to re-experience the past sensuously, whether in film, in museums, in theme parks.[19] It reveals that the affective power of the moving image, with sight and sound combined, has been acknowledged by film scholars.

These Austenesque terms, 'sense' and 'sensuous', have led me to what is hoped might be a new approach to the discussion of historical drama documentary – to test the corpus of work under consideration in terms of its 'sense and sensuousness'. Such an approach might resonate within the industry as well as within academia, and this notion will be expanded upon in Chapter 2.

History on film

Little has been written on British history on film, and less on television, that might help with the televisual study of how the past is represented.

American history on film has been well documented, however, and the most prolific writer on that subject is Robert Rosenstone. In his celebrated book *History on Film/Film on History* (2013), Rosenstone crystallises the notion of the moving image's contribution to the communication of the past by means of analogy with Buddhist painting in Japan, which, he observes, 'arrived in the 6th century to help people feel the story of Buddhism. Not to fully explain, but to get them started. It was called the Mandala. It has now replaced many of the Buddhist texts'.[20] Rosenstone asserts that this story draws a neat parallel with how history in the West was newly represented on film; film helps audiences to piece together 'the traces of the past'.[21] It is a thoughtful evocation of what it is to be a historian, and particularly a historian-filmmaker. For anyone who has delved into primary sources and tried to fit those into the image already established by the secondary sources that have, in turn, wrung dry their own primary sources, one will recognise the sense of helplessness. For what one has in front of one with a primary source is no complete picture. It is simply a series of minute 'traces of the past' – an imprint of a life once lived and put away in an attic, with the infinitesimal chance that one day, unintended by its author, a modern-day history archaeologist will find it and use it to illuminate the author's time and place of life. It could be the diary of an important person or the shopping list of an ordinary one; a Royal Charter or an account of a Poor Law dispensation. They are all 'traces of the past', and often of equal value to the historian-filmmaker.

Thus, Rosenstone goes on to post the question: 'why not investigate their [historian-filmmakers'] rules of engagement with the traces of the past, rules of engagement that come out of the possibilities and practices of the medium in which they work?'[22] Rosenstone is realistic about what the historian-filmmaker may achieve with these traces of the past. One cannot create a window onto the past 'but the construction of a simulated past, not a literal reality but a metaphorical one'.[23]

One cannot discuss history on film without recourse to the great Canadian scholar Natalie Zemon Davis, who famously advised on the historically steeped film, *Le Retour de Martin Guerre* (1982). She has a strategy for considering historical films in three parts, which could prove useful for the case studies of television dramatisations that follow:

1. Genesis – who had the idea?
2. Synopsis – the story – and deviations from the truth.
3. Judgement – what does the film contain that makes us think seriously about the past – and 'how might it be changed to make it more valuable as a historical work?'[24]

Spartacus (1960) gets a mixed report. She is much more in favour of *Beloved* (1998), a film about the scars of slavery, which Davis believes contains the 'spirit of the truth' despite being fictional. What is most interesting here is Davis's contention that the production team should be more honest in the credits. Indeed, she goes so far as to recommend that the example of *Rashomon* (1950) should be more often followed, that is, that sources often conflict, and so films based on them should show alternative versions. This may, of course, not follow the dramatic nor the commercial imperative, but respecters of history should consider this as an option.

However, as Rosenstone acknowledges, what to show and what to leave out presents a dilemma to filmmakers who are also amateur historians. Drama, according to Alfred Hitchcock, is, after all, life with the boring parts left out. Rosenstone accepts that filmmakers must use 'compression or condensation', 'displacements', 'alterations', 'dialogue', and 'characters', all of which come together in a 'drama' which aims to 'contribute to the larger discourse of history'.[25] He chooses as a case study, *October* (1928), in which he includes a quote about Sergei Eisenstein's preparation for the film, which means more to a practitioner than Rosenstone might imagine: 'for weeks, perhaps months, he did as much research as a pressured filmmaker can do'.[26] A 'pressured filmmaker' is an admission, rare within the academy, that filmmakers do not always have the time allotted to research as thoroughly as a professional historian.

If this is true of filmmakers, with considerable budgets affording prep time, it is even more applicable for TV makers in the budget-sensitive documentary field, where it aspires to dramatise. In general, across the ten-year life span of the history boom, dramatised documentary budgets plateaued out at £400–600k/hour. This figure does not include foreign locations or considerable amounts of computer-generated imagery (CGI), which in co-productions could take the budget to £1 million/hour. Both examples were less than the average period drama budget of the time, at between £1.2–2 million/hour. (These numbers have now been exceeded by the Netflix era, in which a period drama such as *The Crown* is reputed to cost in the region of £5 million/hour.) These figures go to show how austere the economy of a £500k/hour dramatised documentary of the mid-2000s decade must have been. Scripts were being developed, written and edited in months, where drama would have spent years. Fully scripted dramatised documentaries such as the *Trial of the King Killers* (Channel 4, 2005) and *Trafalgar Battle Surgeon* (Channel 4, 2005) were hurriedly written by their directors and producers from primary source records, yet they are, broadly speaking, historically accurate. But the key point to remember is that there was no luxury of time here. With this context in mind, Rosenstone's words resonate more clearly: production teams did as much research as 'pressured filmmakers' can do.

Auteur and genre theories

A New Genre? examines two academic theories in particular; these are the writings that inform criticism surrounding auteurism and genre studies. Oddly, perhaps, as a director myself, I believe that directors receive too much deference for their filmic contributions, and this book will point up evidence of considerable and repeatable creative teamwork across the works under scrutiny. Chapter 4 offers a case study of one production company whose influence on the television history ecology was so significant that it is pertinent to ask whether the CEO could be considered the true auteur of this period; adopting an unusual approach to auteurism, this chapter ties the story of a fascinating creative professional to underlying questions of ownership.

Auteur theory was constructed and supported by key essays from the 1940s to the 1960s, notably Alexandre Astruc's 'Camera Stylo' (1948), François Truffaut's 'A Certain Tendency in French Cinema' (1954), and Andrew Sarris's 'Auteur Theory and the Perils of Pauline' (1963). It then drew fire from its detractors: Rolande Barthes' 'The Death of the Author' (1967), Michel Foucault's 'What is an Author?' (1969) and Peter Wollen's *Signs and Meanings* (1969). Happily, I have discovered a more recent contribution from Eric Knudsen at Bournemouth Film School, which better fits my own middle ground view on auteurism. This likens the concept of 'total football' as exemplified by the Dutch team of the 1970s, under Johann Cruyff, to a notion of 'total filmmaking', where the auteurism is necessarily shared with the rest of the crew[27] – a democratic realisation that resonates very well with my years of practice.

Finally, we reach the central question driving this book, which is whether the films under discussion, from this period of history dramatisation, constitute a genre of their own. Much of this question is answered by a never before attempted quantitative evaluation of the films under consideration. Seeing the works categorised year by year has revealed a pattern that seems most generic in its rise and fall and has enabled industrial colleagues to derive a proper overview of the programming landscape. But this is not sufficient to establish a new genre that will satisfy academics. Therefore, to inform that pursuit, it will be necessary to draw on genre theory, including the much-adapted works of French film theorist Christian Metz in *Language and Cinema* (1947), and those of his more recent American counterpart, Thomas Schatz, in *Hollywood Genres* (1981), along with the essays by Steve Neale and Rick Altman in *Genre and Hollywood* (1988). Chapters 1, 2, 3, and 4 will look through these critical prisms at the various characteristics revealed by both the early adopters and the progenitors of the dramatisation of history documentary. Chapters 5, 6, and 7 will attempt to apply four stages of a genre's rise and fall (Experimental, Classical, Parody, and Deconstruction) to examine whether this corpus of work can fit a pattern, find a home within academia and the industry, and acquire a name by which it might henceforth be known.

Notes

1 Tristram Hunt, 'Reality, Identity and Empathy: The Changing Face of Social History Television', *Journal of Social History*, 39:3 (2006), pp. 843–858.
2 Jerome Kuehl, quoted in Alan Rosenthal (ed.), *Why Docudrama? Fact-Fiction on Film and TV* (Carbondale, IL: Southern Illinois University Press, 1999), p. 7.
3 Walter Goodman, 'The Basic Crookedness of Docudramas', *New York Times* (2 November 1989), p. 10 (Goodman, cited in Rosenthal, 1999, pp. 7–8).
4 Derek Paget, 'Introduction: A New Europe, the Post-Documentary Turn and Docudrama', in Derek Paget and Tobias Ebbrecht-Hartman (eds), *Docudrama on European Television: A Selective Survey* (London: Palgrave Macmillan, 2016), p. 7.
5 Derek Paget, *No Other Way to Tell It: Dramadoc/Docudrama on Television* (Manchester: Manchester University Press, 1998), p. 3.
6 *Ibid.*, p. 2.
7 *Ibid.*, p. viii.
8 Natalie Zemon Davis, *Slaves on the Screen* (Cambridge, MA: Harvard University Press, 2000), p. 11.
9 The many interviews with industry figures will be referenced by interviewee and date; the references will not subsequently be repeated with each quotation unless needed for clarity. Please look to the appendix at the end for more detail.
10 David Cannadine, *History and the Media* (London: Palgrave Macmillan, 2006), p. 1.
11 Felipe Fernández-Armesto, 'Epilogue: What is History *Now*?' in David Cannadine (ed.), *What is History Now?* (London: Palgrave Macmillan, 2002), p. 159.
12 Derek Paget, *True Stories: Documentary Drama on Radio, Screen and Stage* (Manchester: Manchester University Press, 1990), p. 88.
13 *Ibid.*, p. 89.
14 Hayden White, *Metahistory: The Historical Imagination in Nineteenth-Century Europe* (Baltimore, MD: Johns Hopkins University Press, 1973), p. 4.
15 Stephen Lipkin, *Docudrama Performs the Past: Arenas of Argument in Films Based on True Stories* (Newcastle: Cambridge Scholars Publishing, 2011), p. 2.
16 *Ibid.*, p. 91.

17 *Ibid.*, p. 92.
18 Lipkin, *Docudrama Performs the Past*, p. 91.
19 Robert Burgoyne, *Film Nation: Hollywood Looks at U.S. History* (London: University of Minneapolis Press, 1997), pp. 104–105.
20 Robert Rosenstone, *History on Film/Film on History,* 2nd edition (Abingdon: Routledge, 2013), p. 175.
21 *Ibid.*, p. 176.
22 *Ibid.*, p. 180.
23 *Ibid.*, p. 183.
24 Natalie Zemon Davis cited by Rosenstone, *History on Film/Film on History*, p. 30.
25 Rosenstone, *History on Film/Film on History*, p. 45.
26 *Ibid.*, p. 66.
27 Erik Knudsen, 'The Total Filmmaker: Thinking of Screenwriting, Directing and Editing as One Role', *New Writing: The International Journal for the Practice and Theory of Creative Writing*, 13:1, pp. 109–129 (p. 110).

1

2000: Emergence of a new kind of history television for the millennium

Introduction

On 4 May 2000, Channel 4 transmitted a documentary on the life and times of Queen Elizabeth I that surprised the television executives at the channel with extraordinarily high viewer ratings for a history programme. The numbers would have been well received at 2 million. A figure of 2.5 million would have been considered a 'hit'. The actual viewing figures for *Elizabeth* (Channel 4) were 3.7 million. The IMDb rating was a very high 8.2/10, indicating that viewers were actively posting their approval.[1] The plaudits were duly accepted with good grace by David Starkey, the Tudor historian who presented the four-part series.

Six months later, after five years of development and production, and therefore not in direct response to Channel 4's commissioning, the BBC transmitted the first episode of Simon Schama's *A History of Britain*. The viewing figures for BBC Two were the highest for a factual show that year at 3.5 million, and the IMDb rating was an astonishing 8.7. Again, Simon Schama, with his name sometimes in the title, was the focus of the media's attention. Soon, the media created a post-rationalised battle between what Janice Hadlow calls 'the sages on the stage' (Hadlow, 2019). The two public service broadcasters were launching what we have described in the Introduction as the 'history boom'. But this current writer sees these shows as more than presenter-led documentaries. Their storytelling power is very much personified by the two sages, but their popular success is attributable to more than the appeal of seeing an academic declaiming in front of a castle. It is the introduction of what this book calls sensuous drama techniques that also brings history to life. It is the Reithian principle of entertainment combined with education and information that is on offer in both these shows, a combination that could not be described fully by critics or viewers at the time, but that can now, with twenty years' hindsight, be placed into a theoretical structure. Schama and Starkey had presented programmes before, but both without much success (as will be explained), so it would be difficult to assert that their presenting techniques were the key variable. No, the variable was the introduction of dramatisation into the portfolio of techniques.

The first case study will be Simon Schama's *A History of Britain*, which did not transmit first, but was the first of the films to be developed, and therefore has much to contribute to our understanding of the institutional context.

A History of Britain (BBC, 2000–2003)

> Brief summary: *A fifteen-part series on Britain's history from pre-Conquest to Churchill. It was presented by Simon Schama, but featured impressionistic elements of visual dramatisation and actors reading primary sources. It was part of the BBC's celebration of the millennium, but at the time was regarded as a very high-risk project.*

There is no better place to begin to discuss the institutional context of the dramatised history boom than an interview with Martin Davidson, one of the enduring drivers of the history boom, both in terms of dramatisation and the two other modes, presenter-led and living history. Davidson's value to this book is underlined by his proximity to the hugely influential, groundbreaking, and landmark BBC series *A History of Britain*, of which he was, by the time of transmission, executive producer. Davidson explains the making of *A History of Britain* from his point of view inside the BBC History Unit, as it was then called. 'History was an ugly duckling genre in the early-mid '90s', notes Davidson, 'it was a default genre, never much loved. Never as much as Arts, which was championed by Alan Yentob and Michael Jackson' (Davidson, 2019). Then in 1993–1994, as Michael Jackson took over as Controller of BBC Two, Davidson, Hadlow, Tim Kirby and Liz Hartford moved from *The Late Show* to the History Unit, where Laurence Rees was already encamped.[2]

The competition between the emerging Hadlow and Rees was marked. 'It was like Buda and Pest, we were in the same office space, but we did not talk to each other', recalls Davidson. This competition brought about an explosion in ambition and scale. Jackson had seen *Schindler's List* (1993) and wanted a history of the Nazis. 'Rees kept it under wraps, like Voldemort, and when *Nazis: A Warning from History* (BBC, 1997) came out, it had an epochal impact. Despite this series being mostly the intellectual product of Professor Ian Kershaw, at Sheffield, it launched a thousand Rees ships.' Alongside his interest in the Nazis, Jackson was also keen on better understanding how the history of the British Isles could be charted from beginning to end. 'It was blindingly obvious to me', explains Davidson; 'we knew Rees would not be interested, as it wasn't about Nazis at all', but Hadlow and her team were keen to take on the challenge. Both sides of the History Unit were buoyed by ambition since the influx of enhanced budgets from across the Atlantic via the Arts and Entertainment Channel, which was launching the History Channel. For the next few years, Hadlow and her team developed the series' scope and shape, and hunted for a presenter worthy of such a landmark event. '1994/5 was the beginning; we had a symposium at Orsino's, a dinner for 15 academics. Presenter versus not? Bits of drama reconstruction or not? What did Britain mean? That sort of thing', explains Hadlow in a rare interview given to this current writer (Hadlow, 2019). According to Hadlow, before real thoughts about dramatisation took place, her activity in 1995–1997 centred on the hunt for a presenter. There was a shortlist, and Hadlow and Jackson agreed on an English presenter who meant something in the United States, particularly for the History Channel. Schama was a polymath professor, previously at Harvard and latterly at Columbia, who specialised in Dutch and French history, with an expertise in history of art. In 1995, he had presented *Landscape and Memory* (BBC, 1995), a series that had won more plaudits than viewers, and so would have been considered a risk. So too, Hadlow was regarded as a risk as executive producer, confides Michael Jackson in an even rarer private interview (Jackson, 2020). Hadlow and Davidson went to New York to meet Schama in 1997, and by 1999 they were filming – with transmission in August–September 2000. 'This makes it sound easy. Long but easy; it wasn't', confides Davidson.

The filming had focused on Schama's pieces to camera, with some days allotted to general views of landscapes and scudding clouds. Only one day of the ten-day shoot allowed for some very elemental dramatisation, which shall be described in greater detail shortly. Drama reconstruction was believed to be expensive, and the team was not experienced in the budgeting nor the aesthetics of dramatisation.

In 1999, another major change came from the United States that would affect the budget. The Discovery Channel outbid the History Channel for the BBC co-production deal, known internally as the Joint Venture – and 'it changed everything', says Davidson. Discovery was not interested in history but favoured the internationally saleable subject of science. Internally at the BBC, all talk was focused on the rise of the Science Department. The Documentary Department had collapsed, and the History Department could only survive if it could persuade 'Discovery to do history if it didn't look like history', continues Davidson. For ten years, during the 1990s, science was central to specialist factual commissions. This period is also when the History Channel started to pretend that it was not about history. In

2000, Hadlow left *A History of Britain* and the BBC History Department for Channel 4, with support from Jackson, who was then CEO of Channel 4. 'She kicked off history at Channel 4 for the next five years', explains Jackson.

Where did this leave *A History of Britain*? On the one hand, its budgets were up, but institutionally, Davidson admits that the series no longer had the support it once had. The word in the corridor, according to Liz Hartford, a director/producer on the series, was that 'we were walking with a dinosaur' (Hartford, 2020).[3] She recalls that Mark Thompson, the new Controller of BBC Two, was not a supporter of the series. At the UK launch in the Barbican, Thompson appeared at Hartford's shoulder and said 'three words: "well, it's happening", which were not exactly words of encouragement', she recalls.

In the battle between two BBC Specialist Factual Departments, Science and History, Science was in the ascendant: 'Science stories are broad, really internationally saleable, they are mystery-solving, plus spectacle. They did not need a presenter, and certainly no university professor, because they had CGI, a different type of dramatization', explains Davidson. *Walking with Dinosaurs* (BBC, 1999) and Robert Winston's *Human Body* (BBC, 1998) were huge successes. The former was a co-production with Discovery, the latter with the Learning Channel (part of the Discovery family).

The day that *A History of Britain* came out, Jane Root, now Controller of BBC Two, sent an email to the team, according to Hartford: 'it's a triumph. 3.5 million viewers. Number one show on BBC Two. It even beat *Cheers*.'[4] Davidson confirms that the viewers for *A History of Britain* declined slightly series by series, but it remained a critical and popular success nevertheless. Ten centuries of what it is to be British is told in fifteen episodes, not just from the royals' perspective, but in a genuine attempt to trace the country's evolution across the social spectrum. As far as BBC Science was concerned, *A History of Britain* gave the History Department some status, on which it traded for the next decade. According to Davidson, 'Science couldn't kill history, it would be like a python eating a sheep.' This must be one of the most curious determinants of success: *A History of Britain* had achieved the notable distinction of being a ruminant animal too substantial to be eaten whole.

Having established the industrial conditions at the time leading up to *A History of Britain*'s transmission in 2000, it is appropriate to move on to two further questions: what were the narrative and aesthetic characteristics of the series, and how well did *A History of Britain* contribute to the televisual representation of history? One of the clues about *A History of Britain*'s narrative characteristic lies in its indefinite article: it was only ever intended to be a version of this island's story, ostensibly as shaped by Schama, but in reality designed by Hadlow and, latterly, Davidson. The scope is from the Conquest to Churchill, and the programme was intended to be achieved in twenty-six episodes but was ultimately commissioned as fifteen, going out in three series between 2000 and 2003. Episode One was an add-on, a pilot, and went out a week before. This pilot encompassed history from the Stone Age to the Dark Ages, from the pre-Romans through to the increasing unification of 'England' under Alfred and the Normanisation of the island under Edward the Confessor, many years before William the Conqueror arrived in 1066 (in Episode Two).

An intellectually bold viewpoint is evident throughout the series and is, unbeknownst to the viewer, the result in no small part of a scholar like Schama coming to a subject on which he has freshness, since he is not a specific expert. He brings a broad perspective from his continental specialisms and, above all, he brings an understanding of iconography from his art-history background that aligns in an ideal way with this most visual of media, television. Although some might call it a 'rush through history', according to Hartford, director of Episode Two, 'Conquest', Schama himself told her that 'comprehensiveness is the enemy of understanding. Choices have to be made' (Hartford, 2020). Coverage of the Enlightenment in Scotland was reduced to five minutes, which was later a regret, since it smacked of the BBC's London-centric viewpoint. But the story of Thomas Beckett was told fully (as will be discussed later in the chapter) from the critical viewpoint of historian Justin Champion. 'We didn't do the Wars of the Roses, the Civil War left much more of a legacy', was how Hadlow described the narrative decisions when invited by Greg Dyke to commemorate the series at an academic forum at the University of York in 2010, on its tenth anniversary (Hadlow, 2019). She spoke of two overarching main aims: firstly, that the series demonstrate a healthy emphasis on the importance of chronology ('joining things up'); and secondly, that by doing so it would be capable of transmitting complex ideas in an accessible manner. Thus, each individual episode would be part of a longer and broader continuity, but they would also be stand-alone programmes that would tell the viewer why one particular moment or era was so significant in the wider span of British history.

Hadlow is not just proffering received wisdoms here. She studied history at King's College London, and has gone on to write extremely well-regarded histories since her impactful career in television.[5] This is to underline that Hadlow was not just the 'telly exec', with Schama as the 'sage', but rather that both were, and remain, experienced and interested in the intellectual shaping of history and the media through which it is transmitted. Like documentary meeting drama, Hadlow and Schama brought together complementary but not distinct pieces of the puzzle. Schama confirmed, at the same event, that he was attracted to the series precisely because it embodied

Reithian values and was very much in the spirit of a tradition of history from Tacitus to Macaulay. He accepted that the chronological approach to history had been out of fashion, but he was persuaded by Hadlow that being no expert in any of the periods could bring a restraint and diligence, and create better television. Calling to mind R. G. Collingwood's *The Idea of History* (1946), Schama reminded the audience that the role of the historian is not merely to be an anthologist of events, but rather that historians must intellectually re-enact in their minds that which has gone before. 'Joining things up' meant joining the past to the present as well as joining the dots of the past. Viewers were ready and willing to receive such an anthology. According to Jerome De Groot, 'one might argue that the phenomenal popularity of history in the late 1990s was a desire for comforting metanarrative in a post-modern, multicultural, directionless, fragmented United Kingdom'.[6] A similar perspective is offered by John Corner:

> Historical representation in the media, particularly in documentary television series, has had a remarkable run of success in Britain over the last few years. It is tempting to speculate that one of the deeper reasons for this is that as the promise of the future starts to seem more like a threat, the past takes on added allure both as a source of knowledge and of imaginative satisfaction.[7]

Further cultural context for the history boom will follow later in the chapter, but the key intent here is to discern how much the dramatisations contributed to this holistic Reithian delivery of the past. It is Schama who describes best the power of the dramatisation as a 'poetics of television history'.[8] 'Poetic reconstruction, if it is to work, needs to lose the characters, and by extension, us, who are watching them, entirely within their own world without any inkling of their return trip to the contemporary.'[9] Schama could very well be quoting filmmaker Alan Rosenthal: 'I want to tell a good story that will engage both the head and the intelligence, and the heart and the emotions. I want to put viewers in touch with the past in a way that academics can't do.'[10]

I suggest that putting 'viewers in touch with the past' is achieved by the aesthetic approach of the series, which includes a very early, and often crude, form of dramatisation. 'Aesthetics' in television are worth defining here. It is not a term that is employed in the industry and is one that carries a great deal of conflicting weight in academia, not least because Immanuel Kant triggered a whole debate about subjective beauty while defining the term. Television scholars have increasingly defined aesthetics as, quite simply put, film style. As David Bordwell argues in *Poetics of Cinema*:

> Film style matters because what people call content comes to us in and through the patterned use of the medium's techniques ... Style is the tangible texture of a film, the perceptual surface we encounter as we watch and listen, and that surface is our point of departure in moving to plot, theme, feeling – everything else that matters to us.[11]

The dangers of using the term 'aesthetics' too casually have been remarked upon by Dominic Lees and Max Sexton in *Televisuality and Aesthetics* (2021). They are concerned that one should not simply call something cinematic because it aspires to the cinema, when quite clearly, nowadays, that comparison no longer holds firm. Cinema is no more cinematic than high-end television. But in the first decade of the twenty-first century, this transition was yet to fully occur. *Band of Brothers* (HBO, 2001) was still not quite *Saving Private Ryan* (1998), and no drama documentary discussed in this work cost a fraction of *Band of Brothers*. Yet aesthetics should refer to a sense of innovation and even textual playfulness, all of which are appropriate to the imaginative films under consideration. One final theoretical observation is worth recalling, once more from Bordwell: 'Style is not simply window-dressing draped over a script; it is the very flesh of the work.'[12] I agree with this statement, not least as a narrative filmmaker. Style is part of the very essence of the filmmaking process. It marries storytelling choices with the look and feel of the story. It contains the key factor that defines whether a film feels right or not – the not insignificant matter of what in the industry is called 'tone'.

Returning to *A History of Britain*, Hartford recalls that there were big meetings about tone and dramatic re-constructions, which mostly served to confirm the expected pitfalls. 'We had a cheesy Monty Python alert, of two knights meeting on horseback', she remembers. Clare Beavan, director of Episode Three, avoided drama altogether and remains wary of the whole hybrid approach. 'Stick on beards, re-enactment societies', she states, 'don't believe in mixing the two. Unless you have a clever knowing way of doing it. Never bought an actor playing Henry VIII. Although Philippa Lowthorpe's hand-held *Other Boleyn Girl* [BBC, 2003], commissioned by the Drama Department was great – and held the spell. Otherwise, never the twain should meet' (Beavan, 2020). Hartford was less drama-averse and reconstructed the death of Edward the Confessor as a still tableau in a crypt.

Hartford went one step further when she filmed the re-enactors of Regia Anglorum bringing the Battle of Hastings to life.[13] The imagery is edited with a blurred step-frame motion that articulates the chaos of battle, but never allows the eye to rest on an image that would be considered inadequate if left untreated. This is a device that avoids the literal, and reminds one of Robert Rosenstone's remark: 'the past on screen is not meant to be literal but suggestive, symbolic, metaphoric'.[14]

Hartford recalls filming a rat in a Saxon village, outside York, to visually conjure the Harrying of the North. 'The rat wrangler presented the rat, a very furry, sweet-looking thing, not at all a sign of deprivation. So, we put some lip gloss on the rat and made its fur tangled and spikey', she recalls; 'it was a solution, of sorts'. The use of animals was extended by Beavan in her episodes. She decided that since the same species were present in the period, they were 'weirdly historically accurate'. Ravens, deer and wolves helped to evoke a sense of focus, violence and hunger in the Angevin episode, *Dynasty*. The battle between Church and State was represented by two foxes fighting over a red cloak. The episode on Elizabeth I utilised peacocks and hawks. 'The unit headed to a hawk sanctuary – in the North – but it rained', says Beavan; 'the wet hawk was barely behaving. So we bought in some helicopter archive of deer running, in which a stag stumbled – probably disturbed. A letter came in from a viewer, saying how dare you chase a herd of deer! I feel bad about buying in that footage to this day.'

Davidson maintains that the visual lexicon and grammar of the series were imitated for some years to come but have often been found wanting by an increased pace of editing, which pushes back against the audience's ability to take time to digest all they are seeing. A third director, Jamie Muir, who was introduced for the third series, dealing with the eighteenth century onwards, chose to avoid the literal by shooting on grainy, black-and-white Super 8 film, which 'as well as hiding or obscuring potentially telling anachronistic details, also endowed something of the sense of the visceral and immediate, giving the sense almost of a newsreel' (Muir, 2019). Muir was also inspired to seek out supporting artists with faces that were 'not like us', according to Hartford. They were filming Queen Victoria's visit to the North of England, showing her carriage as it passes three young waifs. 'We managed to get the carriage to Hampstead Heath and make up three rather pretty young girls', explains Hartford; 'we turned them into waifs by the application of Rice Krispies on their faces.'

Prosaic solutions abounded. Another avoidance of the literal was created by the adoption of hand-held techniques, since the films did not need to look 'smoothed out'. Beavan worked with Douglas Hartington, a cameraman from Manchester, on the episode about Elizabeth I. 'The trouble with cameramen', says Beavan, is 'we are dealing with harshness – why make it beautiful? Polanski's *Macbeth* was muddy and shit. Stop balancing the whites! Not interested in tracks and cranes. Never known them to be better than handheld. Cover more, keep the story focussed, immediate', she insists. Luke Cardiff, who filmed twelve out of fifteen of the episodes of the whole series, says that Muir had asked him what the trick was to the dramatisations, to which Cardiff's reply was 'see as little as possible' (Cardiff, 2020).

Cardiff has come from drama – as a focus puller and then operator on feature films, most notably *The Draughtsman's Contract* (1982) and *My Beautiful Laundrette* (1985). 'I learned my craft there – you are still cutting corners on a big-budget feature. Coverage is really important but so is lighting', he says, but on a series like *A History of Britain*, something would have to give. Cardiff believes that television had benefitted from a technological advance in the late 1970s, when the Swedes started using Super 16 mm. This was inherited by Directors of Photography, such as Curtis Clarke, for whom he clapper-loaded and focus-pulled on *Draughtsman's Contract*. He filmed *A History of Britain* on Super 16: 'It was good for drama doc – but the pressure was on to switch to tape, even though *A History of Britain* was expensive (the biggest event documentary since *Civilisation*,[15] but with no co-production money.' Cardiff continues: 'Halfway through the series the pressure for tape told, so I started shooting with a pro-mist to give tape a filmic look.'[16] The executives were nervous about many aesthetic choices made by many of their directors. Even Schama noticed what he calls 'a plastic look' of tape. Cardiff used smoke guns and haze machines to get the best out of tape but admits 'it was nowhere near as good as today's digital'.

Cardiff recalls working with Beavan on the Florence Nightingale episode. They were recreating Mary Wollstonecraft's death, and Beavan's animals would not fit the bill, so Beavan relented and brought in a woman in costume to approximate Wollstonecraft. 'We had to blur it', explains Beavan, 'confuse the viewer, but again it wasn't a trick we could always use. We were filming dormitories under the railway lines in Shoreditch. There were no health and safety issues. It was liberating really. You came up with ideas and nobody stopped you.'

Muir says that early impressionistic documentary dramas were personified by 'Steve Beckett – he had a van and would collect you from Heathrow. He would say to me: "I was a Roman senator last week. Had to pull a sheet over my tattoos."' The downside is that the ensembles that Beckett was in were never really directed. 'The Peasants Revolt is a line of utterly bored extras', admits Muir. It is worth noting that his view on early dramatisation in documentaries is, in essence, as antagonistic as Beavan's.

Dramatisation with dialogue that is recognisable as scripted drama was still a way off in the early 2000s, and what was being attempted might be referred to as 'impressionistic dramatisation' – images that give the impression of the past and are often made up of partial shapes (and sounds) in a way reminiscent of how impressionist painters used rapid brushwork strokes. Commissioners were always keen to distinguish between the less expensive 'impressionistic drama' and the full blown. The former was, on average, one half of the price of the latter. Yet it is still useful to obtain the view of those who worked on the impressionistic dramatisations of the very early 2000s, whose craft was rooted in documentary, and who had been responsible for one of the great early exemplars of the proto-genre. Ultimately, *A History of Britain* was about narrative storytelling, told by a master storyteller, and supported by the 'poetics of television'. Beavan sums it up:

> *A History of Britain* is Simon's and Janice's version, and we directors made it into a campfire story. We didn't know shit – just like Michael Jackson, running the channel. I went to Goldsmiths to do Communications B(Hum), and Michael Jackson went to central London Poly – now Westminster University. We are post-modern people, trained to question everything. When it comes to drama, we can't do pretend reality and corny feelings. (Beavan, 2020)

So, did the dramatisations work in *A History of Britain*? Not obviously, no. The series is famous for its presenter and his mellifluous delivery of emotionally charged scripts. But just because the drama is low-key and unobtrusive does not mean it is negligible in its impact. One simply could not fill fifteen BBC hours with visual material without a certain visual brio. Tim Kirby, one of the original producer/directors of the Hadlow/Davidson cabal, can recognise the green shoots of dramatisation emerging, and it is evident in his episodes. 'King Death', about the fourteenth century and the Black Death, creates an evocatively morbid mood. His colour grade of the raw material film shows true artistry, and he is one of the only directors to have used computer-generated imagery (CGI), causing the stripped-bare pillars of a church at Long Melford to return to the vibrant colours of their pre-Reformation life. 'This was very early for television CGI. I think Molinare[17] did it, a young man called Dimitri' (Kirby, 2020).

Sometimes, the amateur drama aesthetics were noticeable, sometimes less so, but they are all evident on retrospective viewing: limited performance, sketchy production design, embryonic make-up/costume, sound design and computer-generated imagery. In his article 'Seeing the Past: Simon Schama's "A History of Britain" and Public History', Justin Champion gives an appraisal of *A History of Britain* that would have encouraged the new mode if members of the television industry had been reading academic appraisals. The programme 'presents the viewer with the experience of the rich diversity of the passage of human time in the British islands', he begins, 'from the Stone Age coastal settlement on the west mainland of Orkney at Skara Brae … to Wigan Public Library, Schama leads the viewer by the hand through a first-class tour of "our" history'.[18] He remarks on the aesthetic of the series: 'Startling landscapes, brooding forests, stark ruins and tempestuous seas provide ample context for describing the development, evolution and confirmation of the geographic and imagined boundaries of tribal and national identities.' Clare Beavan's animals are especially praised: 'As well as the flora, the fauna of the land has a starring role. Deer, ravens, hawks, rats, horses and rather more exotic creatures like leopards provide illustration and metaphor for the dynamic of the stories.'[19] He even mentions the reconstructions, without a hint of sarcasm:

> In viewing *A History of Britain* we encounter kings and queens, princes and courtiers, ordinary peasants, foot-soldiers and generals, slaves and workers, priests and heretics, revolutionaries and dictators, fanatics and children. We see where they lived, worked, loved, played, plotted and died. At points we also see reconstructions of people actually doing these things too.[20]

Champion has an ear for the auditory content of the series as well: 'Welsh, Irish and Scottish voices, as well as regional accents from the north, south, east and west of England, [all] tell us about the past'.[21] Champion offers support for the representation of history by any means that enable the audience to hear, see, feel, smell, and ultimately to imagine:

> The knights are named, bells toll. Schama delivers his dramatic PTC, recounting the murder in the exact location (so he comments that, 'Becket was caught up with, [right] in here'). These passages of the films bring immediacy and authenticity. They tell us something of the 'truth' of the events, although they explicitly appeal to visual and aural senses.[22]

And so here, dramatically articulated, is an example of the effect that *A History of Britain* was having on television viewers up and down the country. Their visual and aural senses were being awakened to stories from the nation's past that had only been dimly filled with illustrations in Ladybird books and the Gradgrindian prose of O-Level facts.[23] It was not just the dramatisations that were attempting the dramatic but also the editing, music, narration and the voices from the past: Michael Kitchen, Jonathan Pryce, Bill Paterson, Lindsay Duncan, Prunella Scales, Juliet Stevenson. It is a list of who's who in British performance. And it was all contributing to the dramatisation of the past.

Michael Jackson has denied there was any dramatisation in the series, but when reminded of the above by the present writer, he relents. *A History of Britain* was regarded by the press and public in 2000 as a groundbreaker, even if that was mostly a nod to history emerging as a subject on the broadcasting agenda. Above all, the series became known by viewers and critics alike because of the popularly perceived 'head-to-head' of Schama versus his rival David Starkey: two television historians representing their channels,

BBC versus Channel 4. It made good headlines. So, what was the Starkey phenomenon?[24] What were its industrial origins? Was there a different drama aesthetic, and how well did it represent televisual history?

David Starkey's *Elizabeth* (Channel 4, 2000)

> Brief summary: *Dr David Starkey chronicles the story of Queen Elizabeth I, first broadcast in four parts on Channel 4. The series uses a combination of actors within tableaux, testimony from descendants, contemporary documents, and Starkey's own narration to tell the story of Elizabeth, who reigned for over forty tumultuous years.*

To understand the industrial origins of the Starkey-versus-Schama phenomenon, it is helpful to hear the viewpoint of Martin Davidson's direct rival, the executive producer of *Elizabeth* (Channel 4, 2000), Mark Fielder. Operating out of Bristol as opposed to London, he worked for an independent production company, United Productions. Fielder recalls the origins of the production: 'We had Elizabeth as an idea, but no presenter. We were looking for a woman, ideally. But kept stumbling over the word "gravitas"' (Fielder, 2020). Clearly, at the time of writing in the third decade of the twenty-first century, women are just as likely to be associated with 'gravitas' as men. But 2000 was a different era, and despite Fielder's reluctance about casting a man to describe a Queen's life, the decision was made by Peter Grimsdale, the commissioning editor at Channel 4. Fielder explains: 'Dr David Starkey was not the perfect choice. *Henry VIII* [Channel 4, 1998] had not done terribly well, it was full of modern analogies, using imagery from the 1980s Miners' Strikes to reimagine The Pilgrimage of Grace.'[25] Fielder felt that history had been experimenting with tricks to reinvent itself, and Starkey's *Henry VIII* was one such example. Also, Starkey approached the subject of Elizabeth I with a determined negativity; according to Fielder: 'she achieves nothing and leaves nothing' (Fielder, 2020), Starkey is reported to have concluded. Fielder faced a challenge if he was to launch David Starkey's *Elizabeth*.

Fielder had been at BBC Bristol, making history documentaries with foreign correspondent Charles Wheeler and military historian Richard Holmes. Then he received the call from United Productions in Bristol, a direct competitor to the BBC. Fielder recounts: 'BBC History in Bristol was not going to be possible while Laurence Rees was at BBC London. Then I was offered … a great chance to be based in Bristol, from the United production arm'. The partnership of Fielder and United was blessed by Grimsdale, the commissioning editor at Channel 4, who knew Fielder from Bristol, where they had worked in the same factual department at the BBC.

Fielder also had something original to offer Channel 4's history output. He had experience of dramatisations, having produced a series entitled *999* (BBC, 1982–2001) with recreations of various accidents of around eight to nine minutes each – two of them in a half-hour show. They had been popular with the audience, and Fielder had learnt the rudiments of how to direct actors, many of whom were, strictly speaking, amateurs. The part-time actors on *999* were often medically trained or had some skill in stunts. So, when Fielder pitched the *Elizabeth* idea to Channel 4, he was keen to add dramatisations to the presenter-led material. The warnings, however, were evident from the start. With budgets at £250k/hour (for four episodes), 'we could not do enough drama minutes'. He recalls that Channel 4 asked him, 'so how could we expand it?' Channel 4 wanted a good balance between presenter and representation of the past. In this writer's opinion, it is Fielder's imagination that determined the solution. That solution did not come directly from *999*, but from an imaginative leap that defines aesthetic choice. It was moment of inspiration that came while he was staring at the many portraits of Elizabeth and seeing them for the public relations coups that they were. In late-sixteenth-century England, all members of the gentry were expected to hang a portrait of the Queen in their halls as an indication of their loyalty. Gloriana, with all of the subtle encoded messages in her dress, was the equivalent of early propaganda films, he thought. So Fielder determined that 'portrait shots were the answer'. This simple and broadly economical solution turned out to be the hallmark of the series, partly because it was an aesthetic choice that introduced an audience to what Fielder calls 'untouchable majesty, onto which you could project moods'. It was not just what Bordwell calls 'window-dressing'; it was indeed 'the very flesh of the work'.

Although Fielder admits that the royal portrait shot was repeated too often, 'it was a constant reminder of the regal individual, and contained both magic and emotional flexibility to be reinterpreted at every turn of the narrative'. Fielder went beyond the amateur actors utilised in *999* and employed a casting director, Liz Stoll, who in turn, delivered professional actors, albeit outside the top level of recognised stars. 'Imogen Slaughter, who played the young queen, had a great face, she had presence and magic', notes Fielder. With Starkey delivering punch and storytelling power, the drama enabled the viewer to achieve a degree of emotional engagement.

Elizabeth transmitted to an even bigger audience than *A History of Britain*, 'consistently about 3.7 million', recollects Fielder, which was validation that the decision to spend his money on so many portrait shots had been well invested. Those shots involve, for example, the actress, Imogen Slaughter, dressed and made up in full drama scale, presented in a cavernous royal location, surrounded by hundreds of lit candles. Slaughter remains with a fixed expression, and she looks directly *into* the camera. The image delivers a neutral expression upon which the audience can place their own emotional response. Above all, the candle-light flatters, the whole image shimmers, there is a sensuousness of costume drama being delivered that rewards the longueurs of time spent looking and admiring, and that bears the weight of so many repeats. This is a royal portrait encased by a television screen.

Starkey soon became ubiquitous on Channel 4, as his series maintained its popularity. The *Six Wives of Henry VIII* (Channel 4, 2002) achieved similar audience ratings to *Elizabeth*, then the team moved onto *Monarchy* (Channel 4, 2003–2005). 'It was a golden era for us', notes Fielder; 'as we gained in confidence we introduced more dialogue into *Six Wives*, and we had more letters, determining longer sequences'. The introduction of increasing dialogue is an important evolution. *A History of Britain* did not follow suit, instead remaining strictly impressionistic, possibly thanks to the influence of its now leading director, Clare Beavan. But Starkey's royal histories provided the professional actors, cast by Liz Stoll, the opportunity to speak the recorded words of monarchs and their entourage.

According to Fielder, more directors joined, but much of the team remained consistent. Chris Openshaw was the Director of Photography, Roger Long the sound recordist. 'The costume designer went to the Bristol Old Vic to costume background artists, but Angels in London for the top end', recalls Fielder.[26] Dramatisations always involved a battle with the budget, and required hybrid solutions to be found. On *The Six Wives of Henry VIII*, Fielder and the United Productions team were pushing against the limits of budget. They had twenty-five people in the crew, representing about half to one third of a traditional period drama. They employed a First Assistant Director (AD) down to a Third AD, but the hybrid solution was to employ a Third AD with some experience.[27] This difficult choice can cause imbalance and inefficiency in a film set. Many observers look at a film set and see crew members sitting around without obvious employment. But they are not sitting idly; they are waiting for the critical moment when they are required. This has been proven, over years of experiments, to be the most cost-effective way to operate a drama. However, the drama documentary does not have this opportunity and must look to cut costs without shedding efficiency. This is one of many reasons why the makers of drama documentaries, such as Mark Fielder and his directors, such as Jamie Muir, deserve respect for their newly adopted craft, particularly when the subject matter has high ambition. As Fielder remarks, 'a Royal show needs a good look'.

The portraits were shot in a church in Somerset, utilising at least three hundred candles with bright-burning triple-wicks to replicate the illumination offered by a modern lightbulb. The wicks must be relit just before the camera switches on so they remain consistent and the wax candles do not burn down too fast. *Barry Lyndon* (1975) was notorious for its interiors having been filmed entirely by candlelight, utilising triple-wicks. But the film cost a considerable $12 million in 1975. *Elizabeth* was a dramatised documentary on £250k/hour and required a solution that recreated the *Barry Lyndon* effect but without the cost. The problem was solved by a small special-effects company from Bristol looking to compete with the special-effects house that supplied the metropolitan hub of London. Deep in the background of the portrait shots – which were often slightly out of focus, so that the candles achieved a halo effect glow – not all the candles were real. Fielder admits that 'some of the candles may have been Ikea-type nightlights'. As a practitioner, this present writer salutes that solution; re-examining the portraits with this in mind, it is not possible to see what is candle-lit and what is nightlight. Herein, one finds an example of the new dramatised documentary achieving a stellar movie effect for a low drama-equivalent budget.

Another of the dilemmas facing this new approach to history documentary was the casting and subsequent use of professional actors in a hybrid production. At this early stage of dramatisation, the enterprise could not be considered what the actors' union Equity would call television 'drama'. The hybrid production fell between the amateur and professional, and attempted to negotiate accordingly. The actors were hired as if to record their voices, or to be mannequins for the portrait shots. Many actors and agents would not wish to engage with such a deal, as it threatened the union's protection of their members. But there will always be actors who want to work, and who wish to raise their profile. This new employer, dramatised documentary, offered the opportunity to be dressed in period costumes, and the chance to play a world-famous royal. It was only two years earlier, in 1998, that Cate Blanchett had played Elizabeth I in the successful theatrical rendition, alongside Richard Attenborough. They had probably been fitted in the same costumes from Angels. The actors who played Catherine of Aragon and Anne Boleyn in Starkey's *Henry VIII* were Annabelle Dowler and Julia Marsen. Dowler had learned her craft on *The Archers* (BBC Radio) and Marsen on *Coronation Street* (ITV). Once dressed and escorted onto set by the inexperienced Third AD, the trained actors would approach the trained documentary-makers, such as Fielder; as he recalls, 'they want to know – what is my motivation? We asked them to improvise, we weren't recording live dialogue. You are courting the young Elizabeth and she's not sure of your advances', he continues. 'It was tricky.' This reminiscence offers clues as to the pitfalls of a part-drama, part-documentary culture, which would remain 'tricky' for all parties for many years to come. The learning curve was very steep for all concerned, and it is therefore particularly impressive that these impressionistic dramatisations are, in the judgement of a practitioner, well handled and certainly well photographed, with lush costumes in fine settings. Even when Fielder's team move the researched monologues from Starkey to the actors, the suspension of disbelief is retained. There are even moments when Annabelle Dowler recounts the recorded letters of Katharine of Aragon to her husband Henry VIII pleading for the continuance of their marriage, and it is possible to believe one has been transported into the past. The success of this aesthetic may have been responsible for the 3.5 million viewers that regularly watched *Henry VIII and his Six Wives*.

Behind the scenes, the tight budgets continued to affect every aspect of the production, according to Fielder. Any micro-level practitioner will relate that it is the reduced shooting schedule that most reflects the lack of money available. *Henry VIII and his Six Wives* enjoyed a proper drama location, the medieval Haddon Hall, in Derbyshire, but unlike a drama, the team had to conclude an hour of finished material on screen in only two or three days. If one calculates that there was twenty-five minutes of dramatisation in a forty-seven-minute Channel 4 episode, this requires eight to twelve minutes of edited material per day. A period drama would aim to complete four to five minutes a day, and a period feature film would aim for two minutes per day. The make-up team of two (a period drama would have many times that number) was particularly pushed for time, recalls Fielder, and there was frequently a state of tension, mostly because Haddon Hall was expensive, and there was a fear of the overtime bill. Fielder admits that the budget went over on both shows, but 'I decided it was a loss leader, which paid off because the *Monarchy* deal was a big one, at least we thought so at the time.'

Monarchy (Channel 4, 2004–2006) was a huge commission, in history drama documentary terms. Twenty episodes confirmed the new status of the potential genre, as the money was being redirected from other departments to fuel the viewers' appetite for their nation's regal history as well as their appetite for dramatised history. Fielder believes that the £5 million budget sounded like a drama-sized number, but the critical economy of scale that would allow him to create dramatisations of the same standard as the series' predecessors was no longer working to his advantage. He remembers that Starkey's agent had walked in to Channel 4 to discuss the *Monarchy* deal with the Head of History, who was now none other than Janice Hadlow. He recalls the meeting: 'The agent wanted £100k per ep, up from £15/20k for *Elizabeth*. Hadlow agreed to £50k.' £1 million would be taken from the production budget to pay for its presenter, before Starkey's demand for chauffeured cars and other expenses. The knock-on effect was a reduced amount for dramatic reconstruction. 'Some of them were good', he says, 'but others were simply underfunded. We could no longer even afford the portrait shots.'

In 2003, after six episodes of *Monarchy*, Fielder left. 'Starkey's unpleasant waspiness got to me in the end. He also thought that all forms of government naturally devolve to monarchy, and frankly, outside his period he was not great.' Jamie Muir, meanwhile, had moved from directing *A History of Britain* to *Monarchy*. Muir met Starkey, who greeted him with the following exchange: 'I'm a very professional man, I run myself as a business' (Muir, 2019). Muir recalls that he found the 'business' a bigger problem than he had expected, since somehow after paying the 'business', there was money left for two actors and two days of reconstruction. 'But people were expecting more, not less! So I went to a neighbour with two paintings – and asked: can we reconstruct these with sound?' The dramatisation needed a new solution, and sound was a very cost-effective and innovative aesthetic idea. 'The sound design was brilliant. Human voices [were] run backwards. The idea was all Bella Saer, a freelancer from next door. But the Exec Producer said, sorry, but we need to use our sound design in Bristol, and so it was the only episode I did.' Muir continues: 'By then, there were history programmes like *The Great Plague* (Channel 4, 2001) and *Seven Industrial Wonders of the World* (BBC, 2003).[28] That was where the visual innovation was.'

The success of Starkey on Channel 4 and Schama on BBC endured for half a decade, and their legacy for half a decade more. As John Willis, BBC's Head of Factual (2001–2004) commented to Fielder, 'the direct, personal style and the sheer narrative strength of Starkey and Schama pull the viewer in so that he or she starts to live the history'. The history boom and arguably, the boom in dramatisation, can be traced to their enormous viewing figures. Their presenters' public dislike of each other fuelled the appetite of the press and was reflected by their producers. As Fielder sums up: 'We thought that *A History of Britain* was a dog's dinner. It was a confused conception. Janice did not care about pictures. Clare Beavan's animals' conceit was a nice idea but then there would be another director with a different conceit. On one episode there was no director in the credits.' Beavan returns the insult: 'Starkey was all candles. Starkey's scripts were po-faced, unlike Schama's. Simon's history comes through because it's less like homework, less didactic. It can be a bit sentimental and dewy eyed, but he's a better writer and presenter than Starkey. It all falls out of him.' But despite this no doubt genuine animosity, the two 'sages on the stage' launched a new trend in history programming. Producers would reference these two juggernauts for years to come, as much for their dramatisations as for the presenters. As Fielder concludes: '*Elizabeth* was sufficiently new to make not just history but Channel 4 feel novel and original. By a degree or two. It was a golden era, and a wave went through the television pond, lasting five years maybe longer.' The reviews for *Elizabeth* were newsworthy. The front page of *The Telegraph* announced: 'the war of the television ratings delivered a surprise result yesterday. David Starkey's series about Elizabeth I attracted more viewers than *Friends, Frasier* and *Da Ali G Show*' (*The Telegraph*, 2000). The London *Evening Standard* concurred: '*Elizabeth* astounded C4 bosses. They were surprised it could wipe out popular comedy shows and its soap operas *Brookside* and *Hollyoaks*. Every episode peaked at over 3.5m viewers' (*Evening Standard*, 2000). Much of this success was down to the entertainment value brought both by Starkey and the dramatisation. 'History has broken out of its old dates and chalk-dust image and more and more adults are turning to it for entertainment and enlightenment' (*Sunday Telegraph*, 2000), wrote Andrew Roberts in *The Sunday Telegraph*. In the television industry magazine *Broadcast*, Granada Sky Broadcasting's Director of Programming, Gary Shoefield, added: 'Truly a mix of information and entertainment at its very best' (*Broadcast*, 2000). And thus, the winning combination of information and entertainment sketched a possible future for the dramatised history format.

Cultural context of the dramatised history boom

This is a moment to pause and reflect on the cultural context of the history boom in its generality and to also wonder, more specifically, how far did the dramatisation within Starkey's and Schama's multi-episodic series advance the cause of the televisualisation of history? In terms of being popular with controllers, commissioning editors, advertisers on Channel 4, and the AB 1 socio-economic audiences[29] that advertisers desperately sought, they helped immensely. The two public service broadcasters, BBC and Channel 4, were delivering exactly what the government required of them: educative programming that reached beyond the intellectual elite. This was achieved by two presenters who were considered engaging, aligned with the dramatic mode of image and sound that made history less dusty. John Willis, BBC's Director of Factual, announced in the *Guardian*: 'Now both Channel 4 and BBC2 are promising to increase history production by about a third, and BBC2 Controller Jane Root says "It's the absolute core of what we are doing."'[30] Willis believed there were underlying social and political changes that made the history boom so current: 'The millennium has forced us to focus on our past in order to make more sense of our present and future.' Fielder adds to this in the same article: 'in a secular society where religion is not as powerful as it once was, viewers turn to history to understand what it means to be English, Scottish or Welsh'.[31]

Hadlow says that 'every generation makes history in its own image' (Hadlow, 2019), and looking back twenty years later, it is striking how one can identify a millennial Britain that is very different from Britain in the early 2020s. One does not need to look at the subject matter very closely to become aware of Starkey's interest in the narrative of royalty, and while Schama's viewpoint is more democratic, it is still a story of Britain's heroic deeds, a tale of Empire, and racial homogeneity. Samir Shah, an independent producer, confirms this view: 'this is predominantly white history, presented by middle-aged white Oxbridge men' (Shah, 2019). Women presenters were not employed on equal terms with male presenters until Bettany Hughes received a commission to present *The Spartans* on Channel 4 in 2004; Mary Beard began her television career in earnest with *Pompeii* on the BBC as late as 2010. There was no David Olusoga for some time – until *The World's War, Britain's Forgotten Soldiers of Empire* on the BBC in 2014. The generation of the millennium can be judged by some of these viewing habits, but it might be worth remembering that they were perhaps more interested in their island history. Perhaps, too, the audience had become more interested in their past by dint of being more educated, since Tony Blair (and his education reforms) had come to power in 1997. Neither of these ideas are provable. What is more provable is that the nation was reading more history, and the boom was also occurring in the publishing industry.

Roland Phillips was a publisher at Hodder in the late 1990s. He confirms that, as the millennium approached, there was a collective fear about the end of the world. In many cases, it went no further than an obsession with Y2K, and Phillips was on a committee trying to mitigate the risk of computers failing and supermarkets emptying – a fear that the commercial world was coming to an end. He describes the ironies of the situation:

> In the 1990s, we were reading the book *The End of History* (1992) by Francis Fukuyama, about the collapse of Communism, but then that book *Georgiana: Duchess of Devonshire* (2001) came out, a perfect combination of subject matter and Amanda Foreman. It got five stars across the board, made tons of money and everybody piled in. (Phillips, 2019)

He goes on: 'Suddenly, William Dalrymple was getting a multi-million-pound advance for five books.' By the time Phillips arrived at John Murray, a more specialist high-brow publisher, he confirms that the history boom was well underway. He commissioned *Nathaniel's Nutmeg* (Hodder, 1999), a microcosmic world view that became a very popular sub-genre, in the style of *Longitude*.[32] 'Thereafter, we commissioned anything innocuous that changed the world. The potato, the tomato', Phillips adds. He goes onto explain that six-figure advances were standard in non-fiction as never before. 'Ultimately we commissioned a lot of history that we had to write off later', he admits.

Conclusion

Television is culturally very aligned to publishing, and it is no surprise to Phillips that there was a history boom in both industries simultaneously. Meanwhile, Channel 4 had done well since the millennium against its much bigger public service broadcasting rival, the BBC, and in the case of Starkey versus Schama, had overtaken it in viewing figures, as well as having poached Janice Hadlow. Hadlow's job was to increase spend in the history arena and to define Channel 4 as distinct from the BBC. Drawing bigger audiences was always going to be a tall order when the BBC could expect a third of the viewing population, and Channel 4 was hovering at 10 per cent. But in the arena of history, and in dramatised history especially, there were advances to be made.

Hadlow chose to package the century after Starkey's Tudors, despite the fact that historians generally proclaimed that the Stuarts were less popular, certainly in terms of book sales and exam choices. But Hadlow did not seek to call the series *The Stuarts* and instead sought to draw the century together under a very different banner: that of great disasters. Hadlow would have agreed with Jerome De Groot that texts like docudramas 'often stage within them discussions of pleasure and enjoyment, or of horror and disgust'.[33] Furthermore, she would have confirmed Steven Lipkin's idea that 'Docudrama offers effective television programming because it is "rootable", "relatable" and "promotable".'[34]

For Hadlow, the seventeenth century was, promotably, a century of troubles.

Notes

1. IMDb is an online database of information related to films, television programmes, home videos, video games, and streaming content online – including cast, production crew, and personal biographies, plot summaries, trivia, ratings, and fan and critical reviews.
2. Laurence Rees – Head of the BBC History Unit in the 1990s, who achieved BAFTA and critical recognition for his BBC series: *Nazis: A Warning from History* (1997), *War of the Century* (1999), *Horror in the East* (2001), *Auschwitz, the Nazis and the 'Final Solution'* (2005), and *World War Two: Behind Closed Doors* (2008).
3. The joke was based on the popular show *Walking with Dinosaurs* (BBC, 1999).
4. *Cheers* (1982–1993) is a very popular and enduring American sitcom.
5. Hadlow's books include *The Strangest Family* (London: William Collins, 2014), on the subject of George III's domestic life, revealed through his daughters' letters.

6 Jerome De Groot, 'Empathy and Enfranchisement: Popular Histories', *The Journal of History Practice*, 10:3 (2006), pp. 391–413.
7 John Corner, 'Backward Looks: Mediating the Past', *Media, Culture & Society*, 28:3 (2006), pp. 466–472 (p. 466).
8 Simon Schama cited by De Groot, 'Empathy and Enfranchisement: Popular Histories', p. 29.
9 *Ibid.*
10 Alan Rosenthal cited by Robert Rosenstone, *History on Film/Film on History*, 2nd ed. (Abingdon: Routledge, 2013), p. 98.
11 David Bordwell, *Poetics of Cinema* (New York: Routledge, 2007), p. 32.
12 David Bordwell cited in Jeremy Butler, *Television Style* (London: Routledge, 2010), p. 8.
13 Regia Anglorum is a re-enactment society that specialises in the Anglo-Saxon, Viking, and Norman periods.
14 Robert Rosenstone cited in Stephen Lipkin, *Docudrama Performs the Past: Arenas of Argument in Films Based on True Stories* (Newcastle: Cambridge Scholars Publishing, 2011), p. 15.
15 *Civilisation*, presented by Kenneth Clarke (BBC, 1969).
16 Pro-mist – covers the lens and helps make early digital look filmic.
17 Molinare is a successful post-production company based in Soho.
18 Justin Champion, 'Seeing the Past: Simon Schama's "A History of Britain" and Public History' *History Workshop Journal*, 56 (2003), p. 153.
19 *Ibid.*
20 *Ibid.*, p. 154.
21 *Ibid.*
22 *Ibid.*, p. 160.
23 O-Levels were public exams in the United Kingdom from 1951 until 1987, when they were replaced by GCSEs. Thomas Gradgrind was the teacher in Charles Dickens' *Hard Times* (1854).
24 Dr David Starkey was later discredited. According to the *Daily Mail* headline on 6 July 2020, 'Historian David Starkey apologises for saying slavery was not genocide because there are "so many damn blacks" around and says "bad mistake" cost him "every distinction and honour acquired in a long career"'.
25 The Pilgrimage of Grace (1536) was a popular uprising that began in Yorkshire in October 1536 before spreading to other parts of Northern England. It was, reputedly, the most serious rebellion during the reign of Henry VIII.
26 Angels is the primary costume house in Britain, based in London. Bristol Old Vic, like many provincial theatres, has a costume store, often more cost-effective than Angels.
27 A drama shoot requires a First AD to run the set, a Second AD to book the cast, and a Third AD to bring the cast to set.
28 *Seven Industrial Wonders of the World*, a BBC seven-part series celebrating phenomenal creations that changed the world forever. These stories of engineering achievement in the nineteenth and twentieth centuries reveal how the modern world was forged.

29 AB 1 is a socio-economic grade grouping people with higher and intermediate managerial, administrative and professional occupations.
30 John Willis, 'Past is Perfect', *Guardian* (29 October 2001).
31 *Ibid.*
32 *Longitude* (1995) was a book by Dava Sobel, published by Harper Collins, which told the story of the eighteenth-century Englishman who discovered how to accurately measure longitude. It received critical acclaim and was made into a television (docu)drama in 2000 by Channel 4.
33 Jerome De Groot, *Consuming History: Historians and Heritage in Contemporary Popular Culture*, 2nd ed. (London: Routledge, 2016), p. 151.
34 Steven Lipkin, *Real Emotional Logic: Film and Television Docudrama as Persuasive Practice* (Carbondale, IL: Southern Illinois University Press, 2002), p. 55.

2

2000–2002: From vignettes to fuller dramatisation

Introduction

That same year, 2000, Channel 4 transmitted another four-part series, *A Century of Troubles*, led by *The Great Plague* (Channel 4, 2000), in which I was fortunate enough to be involved with the executive producer Samir Shah and producer John Toba. It has no identifiable single presenter, but it took a post-watershed audience into the nightmarish world of infectious disease, societal breakdown, and enforced quarantines. All of this was achieved through the increasingly fulsome technique of dramatisation within a documentary. Within two years, the BBC responded with *The Great Pyramid* (BBC, 2002) – a truly fulsome dramatisation of the construction. It eschewed presenters and even the interviewees favoured by *Plague*, focusing on a personal drama spoken in the vernacular, made epic by computer-generated imagery; it was nominated for a prime-time EMMY. *Pyramid* transmitted on BBC One and garnered the largest viewing figures for a television documentary: the extraordinary number of eleven million. Hamish Mykura, then a junior commissioner at Channel 4, reflects: 'It was a virtuous circle. The more exotic the subject matter, the sexier the treatment of it, the greater the desire for it. But it all began with Schama versus Starkey' (Mykura, 2021).

These films should be studied not only as event-television 'hits' but also as early adopters of a new kind of history documentary that has not yet been drawn into a recognisable body of work. At the end of the chapter, I shall argue that a first stage in defining this corpus is determining what they have in common – which is that they bring drama *and* documentary modes together to bring to life the past on television. This common factor can be better described as the bringing together of what we shall call 'sense and sensuousness' to provide audience satisfaction that derives from appealing to both head and heart.

A Century of Troubles: Plague, Fire, War and Treason (Channel 4, 2000)

> Brief summary: *A four-part series about the seventeenth century, referred to as a 'century of troubles'. The series of feature-length films used what were called innovative forms of dramatisation to recreate the Great Plague and the Fire of London, as well as the Gunpowder Plot and Civil War.*

The series *A Century of Troubles* showed evidence of different aesthetic characteristics from *A History of Britain* and *Elizabeth*. It featured interviews with a number of different historians, rather than information imparted by a single narrator, and the dramatisation of the plague focused on the microcosm of a single alleyway. Another difference was the less iconic subject matter. Hadlow wanted to offer alternatives to the same-old representations of history: 'Henry, Hitler and Hieroglyphics' as they are known in history television, referring to the Tudors (ironic, since Hadlow had Starkey in her stable of history presenters), the Nazis, and Ancient Egypt. She believed there was a market for what she termed: 'O-Level subjects that people could vaguely recall, but actually knew precious little about … the 17th century has plenty of those, and as a series it stood a chance of making real noise in the wake of Starkey and Schama' (Hadlow, 2019). The subjects were not just the elite of society; the series offered a bottom-up view, which appealed to Hadlow, a rare television commissioner at that time in that she came from a non-Oxbridge university and a state-school background in North Kent. She also believed that women as well as men would be attracted to the plight of those who suffered through such turbulent societal times. The series made a strong contribution to the representation of less iconic history because it brought together four separate events and delivered a hitherto unique view of the century through that prism of horror. This was, again, an entertaining approach to take to a period for which it had always been hard for historians to shape a popular narrative. There had always been too many James's and Charles's, too many black hats, and an exhaustingly endemic state of civil unrest stirred by multitudinous differences in religion. Despite it being a series that did not have the automatic audience loyalty of the Tudors, Channel 4 commissioned a nationwide poster campaign, which was reserved for very few programmes, across every genre. They were committed to attracting a substantial viewership. Yet it is a risk, when selling the horror of an event, that it will repel rather than draw hither – and the consequences of that risk would be evidenced in the press criticism.

Hadlow commissioned a seasoned independent production company, Wall to Wall, to make two films, *Fire* and *Treason*, and one micro-company, Juniper, to make *The Great Plague*; I was able to observe the latter first-hand, working as the director but also on the production team alongside John Toba, the producer (and formerly a script editor on an ITV local soap opera).[1] Juniper was run by Samir Shah, previously Head of News and Current Affairs at the BBC under John Birt, and only recently set up as an independent specialising in political documentaries. It was yet another example of inter-disciplinary misfits being forced to work together.

Hadlow was impressed by the first pitch that Shah made, which was based on sources including Daniel Defoe's *Journal of a Plague Year* (1722), written admittedly almost sixty years after the year in question, but drawing from first-hand accounts of doctors such as William Boghurst. The language and idioms took one back in time to an epidemic that, in London alone, killed up to one hundred thousand people, or one third of the population within the city walls, according to the contemporaneous Bills of Mortality.[2] For the producers, the problem was how to realise such an event visually. To summon up the Great Plague of London was not televisually achievable, unless one returned to the presenter-led option, and the series was set up by Hadlow to avoid that. This was supposed to be a progressive new series, setting itself apart from Starkey and Schama. Hadlow's belief was that Channel 4 could not and should not compete with the BBC in terms of budget; hence the *Great Plague* episode was not to concentrate on the scale of the epidemic, but something more intimate. Shah and Hadlow just did not know what that might be, as Shah recalls: 'I kept offering suggestions, but Janice was not impressed. She told me in no uncertain terms, that we may have to forget it' (Shah, 2019). Shah spent the weekend agonising over the problem.

It is worth noting that Shah did not have a drama background at all, but he did have academic credentials, having gained his doctorate at St Catherine's College, Oxford, in Geography. The point here is that television, contrary to popular opinion, is not headed by executives with no concern for the veracity of ideas. 'Factual' was then, more often than not, helmed by an intellectual elite, many of whom had begun doctorates, if not completed them, in subjects they cared about *en route* to careers in departments that served those very subjects, such as science, history, and arts. It was not just a matter of luck, therefore, that Shah found a pamphlet in a bookshop in Marylebone that led him to Vanessa Harding, a scholar at Birkbeck College, London, and the author of *The Dead and the Living in Paris and London* (2002) – a study of the financial accounts of the churchwarden of St Dunstan's in the West, just off Fleet Street. These accounts were economic data saved from the Great Fire of 1666, and they told a narrative of moneys disbursed to blacksmiths to affix hasps and locks to doors in order to effect quarantine. It was a microcosm of sorts of the whole epidemic, although the parish itself was quite a large data set.

Interpreting a PhD monograph was one of Shah's skills, and that weekend, he found the solution Hadlow had been seeking: an intimate 'underdog-style' approach she could afford. For there in the disparate sets of data, was one set of information that was complete and ideally sized – the accounts of not just one street within the parish, but one alleyway off one street that housed twenty or so inhabitants right at the bottom of society, the ones most vulnerable to the plague, and subsequently most in need of the poor relief dispensed by the churchwarden. The alley lay behind the Cock and Key pub and was known simply as Cock and Key Alley. 'Hadlow got it immediately', says Shah, 'it was good commissioning from her, to keep pushing.' Davidson concurs, although admittedly he would go on to marry Hadlow: 'Janice was always pushing – and often against the grain. That's what makes her so special. She makes the weather' (Davidson, 2019).

As a representation of history, Shah's discovery of Harding's work, and that primary source, was a breakthrough moment. Schama and Starkey had occasionally quoted the lives of real men and women from the past in their television epics. Samuel Pepys's diary was the obvious choice as primary source for *The Great Plague*, but as Hadlow pointed out, the churchwarden's accounts were not, unlike Pepys's diary, intended to be read by peers or posterity. Shah recounts that the churchwarden, Henry Dorsett, 'was just doing his job, meticulously recording every penny spent on a candle for the widow, a lemon for the orphan child, or spades for the gravedigger'.

The producer, John Toba, utilised script-editing skills learned from five years working on soap operas to shape *The Great Plague* into a narrative that zoomed out to Pepys's macro view of London, showing the royal court fleeing to Oxford, the guards holding back anyone who could not prove they could read, and the Lord Mayor ingeniously conducting the business of the city from within a specially constructed box made of glass. He also had three waves of epidemic to draw on, enabling a three-act structure in the mode of a traditional drama. But what the reviewers and the peer group within the industry remembered was the story of Cock and Key Alley, and the community within: the essence of the dramatisation, the heart of the emotional story. It was this micro-narrative that was filmed as an impressionistic drama in Lord Leycester Hospital, a Tudor almshouse in Warwick town centre. The cast were amateurs, some taken from their final years at Arts Educational School in Chiswick, West London, and others cast locally; many were from working families, while some were in the local care system. They delivered what Jamie Muir on *A History of Britain* had proposed: 'a face from another time – a thousand-yard stare'.

The churchwarden was played by a retired local who had many years previously performed in some children's television as 'Shabby Tiger'. David Blight, the production designer and costume designer (a joint position that would never be contemplated on a drama production), built the alleyway off a courtyard in the old hospital and filled it with an earthen floor. But he did not believe it would stand up to scrutiny in daylight and suggested that the shooting should occur at night. Holistically, this was a good suggestion, since the film drew from the horror genre, and so a schedule of ten nights in succession was planned, ending with the digging of the plague pit. Director of Photography Simon Bray brought a go-pro camera lens and travelled down the narrow alley, passing the inhabitants on their doorsteps, a scene reminiscent of an alleyway in a developing-world shanty town to this day.[3] The inhabitants would be poor, but fiercely houseproud, always sweeping and cooking. The go-pro was most effective when pushing towards the plague buboes themselves, which had been constructed by the most experienced professional department on location: make-up. Veronica Brebner was an Oscar-nominated make-up designer for whom plague in the seventeenth century presented an interesting challenge between Hollywood jobs, and she was prepared to operate well below her usual rate of pay.[4] Her resolve was only tested when one of the care-home patients was revealed to be carrying fleas, an irony not lost on the crew. The film was edited by Charles Davies, a wildlife editor, and voiced by the Oscar-nominated actress Brenda Blethyn, with additional voices by a young Stephen Mangan, a college friend of Toba's.[5] The interviewees were authoritative: Lisa Jardine and Ronald Hutton were some of the foremost academics on the seventeenth century, while Carol Rawcliffe brought medical specialism. Vanessa Harding gave life to Cock and Key Alley, and Justin Champion weaved a thread through the whole complex tapestry.

The aesthetic afforded the interviews broke new ground as well, since they were filmed by Bray on track and dolly (i.e. moving shots as if they were part of a drama) so that they were not static bumps of information within the drama. The downside, according to Richard Bradley, a competing executive producer at Lion TV, was that the tracking shots then moved the interviewee off their eyeline, which he believed risked disconnecting the link with the viewer (Bradley, 2020).

The budget was around £300k, according to Shah, for a one-and-a-half-hour film. At £200k/hour, it was slightly above the budget level of a conventional Channel 4 documentary at £180k/hour (although this was dropping rapidly under Hadlow's regime to allow for money to move to drama reconstructions thereafter). The series followed the same non-presenter-led strategy. *Treason* dramatised the microcosm of the cabal behind Guy Fawkes, and their 'shoot out' in a manor house when capture became inevitable. *War* and *Fire* struggled with their hugely ambitious conceits. A fire that raged for four days and burned much of London was a difficult narrative to visualise without repetition of a flaming studio set – built by David Blight, again, on a limited budget.

The series began transmission on 15 October 2001 with *The Great Plague*. The previews (on which television executives depended, since reviews had no impact on viewing figures) were mixed. David Chater in *The Times* complained that 'the filmmakers should have relied much more on Samuel Pepys ... and Brenda Blethyn's voice lends unnecessary drama to the piece'. The other broadsheets responded to the unpleasantness on offer: 'don't let the vivid reconstructions of neck lesions put you off your supper' (*Express*); 'invisible, silent and deadly, no one was safe from the plague' (*Radio Times*); 'some wonderfully gruesome reconstructions, it paints a detailed picture of horror as the disease swept the capital' (*Evening Standard*); 'gruesomely over-graphic but a playground Ring-a-Roses won't sound the same again' (*Telegraph*); 'overly graphic, but otherwise excellent, piece of dramatic reconstruction reveals [the plague] in precise but harrowing detail' (*The Observer*).[6]

The aesthetic struck home with many of the reviewers, although Channel 4 may have misgauged the popular appetite for 'sensuousness' of a gruesome nature. It is also interesting to read Sally Kines' *Sunday Times* preview, which featured an interview with Hadlow and confirmed the importance of the film to the representation of history: 'it is fair to say that five years ago, this series wouldn't have got made, there was a time when it was hard to generate interest in any history that was pre-20th century'. Kines goes further, observing that 'now narrative-led, people centred history has come into its own, and it has never been more relevant. Since the attack on New York, historical parallels seem to be popping up everywhere.' She concludes: 'when the Gunpowder plot is described as the greatest terrorist conspiracy Britain has ever known, you want to get inside the heads of these 17th century terrorists and know what made them tick'.[7]

The response to *A Century of Troubles* at the rival public service broadcaster, the BBC, may have been coincidental. But it takes, on average, two years to develop a television project of any scale, so if one looks two years down the timeline, it is not surprising that one finds a BBC fuller dramatisation of a historical subject. Using a microcosm of two brothers in amongst the army of volunteers, it tells of the building of one of the man-made wonders of the world. It had BBC scale, increased amounts of non-speaking dramatisation, and considerable CGI, and it broke the records for documentary viewership.

The Great Pyramid (BBC, 2002)

Brief summary: *A single BBC film that tells the story of the building of the Great Pyramid. Using revolutionary CGI, and a host of extras, the film takes the viewer back to the banks of the Nile, seeing the grand royal project through the eyes of a man who spent a lifetime contributing to it.*

The Great Pyramid attracted the largest single UK audience for a history programme up to 2002 with over 10 million viewers, according to writer/director, Jonathan Stamp, commenting in the DVD extras. *Pyramid* followed the CGI techniques of *Walking with Dinosaurs* (BBC, 1999), which in turn was inspired by the theatrical release of *Jurassic Park* (Universal, 1993), in what J. T. Caldwell calls 'semiotic cluster bombs': the concept detonates in the cinema and sends shrapnel across the television landscape.[8] Although this was a science commission, Discovery was content to allow a history executive on the show because this was history that felt like science (it was at this time that the History Channel stopped showing history and started screening stories about men in beards who live and work in remote areas of the world, e.g. *Ice Road Truckers* [History, 2007–2017] and its predecessors). The executive producer of *Pyramid* was Laurence Rees, institutional power broker of BBC History, who was editor of *Timewatch* from 1992 to 2002 and had enjoyed great success with the 1990s BAFTA-winner *The Nazis: A Warning from History* (BBC, 1997). *The Nazis* was a series that contained compelling interviews with extant Nazis who had witnessed or participated in the horrors of the war. It had eschewed either CGI or dramatisation, but Rees could see that dramatisation could bring to life the building of a great man-made wonder of the world: a pyramid.[9] Rees described his ambitions in *Pyramid*'s press release:

> We wanted to explore people's timeless fascination with Ancient Egypt and the Great Pyramid. Crucially in the programme what viewers are able to see for the first time is the Great Pyramid actually being built. We're able to recreate this with stunning visuals which I believe will make compelling and immersive viewing, not only for those already fascinated by this period of history, but also those new to the genre. (BBC, 2002)

From the outset, the pre-title that is so often required by executives, working at the meso level, is an example of a Reithian enterprise: it delivers both information and education in abundance. The subject is worthy of epic, as the narration explains: 'the site is 13 acres in scale that would dwarf both the House of Commons and St Paul's Cathedral together; it contains 2.3 million blocks of stone, many 10 tonnes each, and some as much as 40' (BBC, 2002). The narrator then challenges the viewer's assumptions: 'These were not slaves building the pyramids, but free men, doing it for the greater good' (BBC, 2002). The human story is at the heart of the sell. In its press release, the BBC acknowledges its need to build the narrative around a single everyman:

> The history of the Great Pyramid's construction is told through the fictional story of a young Egyptian conscript called Nakht. His tale is told through drama reconstructions shot on location in Egypt and his voice is narrated by Omar Sharif. Nakht's world has been created by using the most up-to-date research into the era of the Pyramid builders and every detail of his life is based on the findings of archaeology. (BBC, 2002)

Stamp offers more detail: 'Nakht's story provides a powerful emotional focus enabling the viewer to engage directly with the past.' He continues, 'we learn of the hardships and the great dangers of the pyramid-builders' world, and also of its comradeship and fulfilment. By the time we have arrived at the end of Nakht's story we will understand the Pyramid as never before' (BBC, 2002).

The narrative choice is to centre the film on one man and his brother, plucked from obscurity down-river, to tell the lifetime's story of the Great Pyramid being built through this microcosmic and affective point of view. This was a Factual department stepping out of its BBC silo to operate somewhat like the Drama department, which worked in another BBC building. Science did not really mix with History and, as we have heard, Laurence Rees did not mix with other members of the History Department. 'It was a silo system, with departments separated by geography as well as culture' (Shah, 2019). Another innovation was the introductory sales pitch that would encourage an audience in 2002 Britain to sit down and watch something so alien to their quotidian experience. This is possibly explained by the 'greatest hits' sequence, a sales tool inherited from American television, which arrived on British screens at around the time of the millennium.

The pre-title sequence of *Pyramid* is exactly three minutes long and begins with a classically cinematic image: a helicopter shot flies the audience over the folding repetitions of sand dunes, reminiscent of the opening of the feature film *The English Patient* (1996). Added to the simple, eerie strain of pipes (which often denote generically ancient culture on film), there is the voice of the narrator, Michael Pennington. His voice, in documentary mode, is authoritative and does not rise in its tone to convince one that there is excessive drama afoot: 'it is 2481 years BC, and in this part of the Sahara Desert, there is nothing to see … but that's all about to change'. There follows a step change – the editor cuts to drama reconstructions of labourers in loin cloths working on huge square monoliths, and the music shifts into what has now become familiar as a Hollywood-style 'achievement/challenge' refrain, reminiscent of *Gladiator* (2000). This can often occur because editors were increasingly using the music from last year's Hollywood hit in the rough cut, and since the executive producers then cannot accept anything less stirring, the composer is then required to approximate the music used in that rough cut.

The narrator continues: 'labourers are brought here from all over Egypt, to quarry stone, to build a temple for Kufu their King, according to a secret code that will help them perform a miracle'. Step change once more to science-fiction imagery of stars in the night sky and a *Dr Who/Star Trek* hyperdrive journey through space: 'This is one of the only seven wonders of the Ancient World still in existence, hiding a mystery. Now we can unravel that mystery.' The music shifts again – to a more ethereal tone as CGI imagery, relatively unseen on British television up to that point, shows tiny humans, seen from above, drawing stones of impossible scale up previously inconceivable ramps. The narrator adopts a more dramatic tone: 'combining the latest up-to-date research with the latest technology we can travel back in time and see the great pyramid of Giza being built, through the eyes of the men who built it, and one man in particular'.

The camera pulls focus from a fire where labourers dance to an old man looking at the Great Pyramid, completed. The camera continues to track elegantly around his head, revealing the whole landscape behind him, as the narrator continues: 'he is not a real historical figure. But the events in his life are based on real evidence – from the journeys he travels, to the clothes he wears, to the enormity of the job assigned to him. His name is Nahkt. This is *his* story and of the monument to which he devoted his life.' As the sunset creates a silhouette of the pyramid in its Nile setting, the title card appears.

From a filmmaker's perspective, this is an opening sequence intended to evoke a sensation of anticipation at the cost of spoiling the reveal. It promises epic scale, scientific mystery, and, critically, the human touch of the story of one man, an everyman. It matters not that he is created solely for the purpose. This has been confessed; the combination of documentary and drama has been established, and the film is now authorised to tell its tale, primarily in dramatic microcosm.

It is a truism that drama is choice – and it is particularly true of dramatised documentary. Selecting Omar Sharif as the narrator is perhaps an obvious choice, given that he is the most famous actor to have emerged from Egypt, but it could have backfired. The younger members of the audience might have been alienated by an unknown voice; the older members might have been disappointed they were not going to actually *see* their iconic heartthrob; the critics could have felt themselves sold a Hollywood trick. But instead, the tenor of the legendary actor's voice mirrored the poetry of his faux-diarisation. This poetic approach was supported by the casting choices of ethnically appropriate actors portraying a world 2,500 years *before* Christ. The production design seeking to evoke this ancient society is plausible, if not entirely feasible. The effect is that of Paget's 'cultural tourism', taking the viewer to a contrived reality of ancient language and society. Ancient Egypt is to be observed – the crying of women for their taken men, confirmed by shots of a lost goat, the trip on a boat (cleverly constructed so as to multitask as all the boats in the film) where the workers break into spontaneous song and clap along (undirected, according to the DVD extras). Thus, the centuries appear to peel away.

What follows is part dramatisation, part science documentary, and it leads inexorably to the final stones being placed on the top of the pyramid by Nakht as an old man, whose career zenith is evidenced in a helicopter shot that pulls back to let the viewer see the completed Great Pyramid in its riverside setting. This is indeed a dramatic moment. But arguably it is reinforced by the programme's revelation of what the Great Pyramid was actually for. A combination of recent scientific discoveries, intersecting with intelligent guesswork, reveals that from the tomb of the pharaoh, in the heart of the giant structure, a tiny but direct passageway leads all the way up to the exterior wall, where an opening allows sight of stars known to the Ancient Egyptians as The Indestructibles, a constellation that gathers around an empty portion of the night sky. Thus it is revealed that this whole vast enterprise was built to house a single man and enable him to be transported to his version of heaven; and by means of their assistance in enabling the pharaoh's rebirth, all those who had built this heavenly transporter would be admitted to the afterlife as well.

As it is an early exemplar of the dramatised history documentary revolution, it is perhaps surprising that the film delivers intellectual and emotional resonances to such a high standard. Yet it explains why the UK audience numbers hit the unheard of (for a History programme) number of 11 million. In retrospect, however, the film is not without flaws. The CGI, as executed by The Mill in Soho, was an early-adopted, technical attempt at the representation of working men from above. The BBC Press Release quoted Dave Throssell, Head of The Mill, saying that the challenge for his team was to bring Ancient Egypt to life: 'our task is to create huge architectural and crowd scenes and to provide an immense but historically accurate environment. But my vision for the special effects is that the viewer doesn't even notice them. It will be as if they are there for real' (BBC, 2001). The present writer would argue, though, that the viewer *does* notice, as the CGI fails to convince with the shots that show the multiplication of workers. Even taking into account the technological rawness of 2002, the workers look like ants, drawn rather than screen-grabbed from physically accurate people shot on green screen from the correct angle. This is a regular failing of

CGI in the early stages of televisual development. The question is – does it distract the eye, especially twenty years on, when we are familiar with more detailed CGI crowd scenes? The answer is no, and this is thanks to the overwhelming power of the televisual feat, in terms of its harmony of education *and* entertainment.

Thus far, these first two chapters have covered the battle for the history audience between the BBC and Channel 4 between 1999 and 2002 from the point of view of the meso level of broadcasters (the commissioners of the channels) and the micro-level of the producers and their creative teams, who were the early adopters of innovation in the evolving aesthetic of the dramatisation of documentary. *A History of Britain* (BBC) versus *Elizabeth/ Henry VIII* (Channel 4) and *The Great Pyramid* (BBC) versus *The Great Plague* (Channel 4) have been selected as examples to represent the series of skirmishes occurring across a battlefield where lines were only beginning to be drawn. Across presenter-led and reality modes, the television subject of history was gaining popularity in parallel, but it was also becoming clear from popular ratings that a new type of filmmaking was emerging: that of the dramatisation of the past.

Television executives and producers had stumbled upon a combination of successful ingredients and did not feel the need better to understand the formula, only to capitalise upon it. They went into pitch meetings, declaring that they too had a story as epic as *Pyramid*, or a microcosm as immersive as the Cock and Key Alley of *The Great Plague*. But this book is predicated on the usefulness of theory to practice. Much of the theory on the combination of drama and documentary already existed in 2002. Paget had been writing on docudramas since 1990, and his seminal *No Other Way to Tell It* was published in 1998. Rosenthal's edited anthology *Why Docudrama?* came out in 1999 and Lipkin's *Real Emotional Logic* in 2002. While it is true that these works focused on dramas, commissioned by drama departments, that were based on true stories, a closer reading of them reveals principles that would have been useful to practising documentarians who used drama modes, and could certainly act as strong guidelines for such practitioners in the future.

None of the films thus far studied are fully scripted dramas, but there are clues within the theorists' work that hints at the non-speaking, impressionistic end of what we have referred to as 'dramatised' documentary. In *No Other Way to Tell It*, Paget quotes John Corner, who uses the term when he suggests that news and documentary departments use journalistic structures to enable the camera to go where it cannot go in actuality, producing a 'dramatised documentary'.[10] The term dramatised documentary might cover the spectrum of reconstructions from the prosaic *999* through to the epic *Pyramid*. The current writer would confirm this as a possible first phase in what Paget calls the 'current spectrum of "intergeneric hybridisation"'.[11]

By 2011, when he wrote an introduction to the second edition of his book, Paget observes that 'the variety of hybrids now available has benefitted the docudrama in ways I did not foresee previously'.[12] Since, by 2011, Paget had discussed *Smallpox 2002* (BBC, 2001) and *The Day Britain Stopped* (BBC, 2003), films that are part of the canon for this work, one may assume that history dramatisations are part of the 'hybrid' to which he refers. 'Hybrid' is no dirty word, and certainly by 2002, it is hard to describe the dramatisations that have emerged in this documentary mode in any other terms. Hybrid, like bastard or mongrel, is a literal mix of two distinct forms, in this case drama and documentary, with a spectrum of ratios. *A History of Britain* is at the form's inception, estimated by the current writer at 10 per cent dramatisation and 90 per cent documentary. By series three, it has moved closer to 25 per cent dramatisation and 75 per cent documentary. *Elizabeth* begins with 25 per cent dramatisation, and *Henry VIII and his Six Wives* edges towards 40 per cent dramatisation. *The Great Plague* offers 40 per cent dramatisation, *The Great Pyramid* 60 per cent. Setting out the ratios in this way makes clear the increasing reliance on dramatisation.

Paget reveals that, in 2003, docudramas (one imagines that he means the whole spectrum of films that combine documentary drama) made up 10 per cent of the top one hundred films screened in the United Kingdom, which is 'an awful lot for what I described in 1998 as an occasional genre'.[13] This is worth noting, as is the first tentative use of the term 'genre', although it is too early for anything like this term to be utilised. The history documentaries that included dramatisation had not been codified by the industry at this point; it was simply known that they were an opportunity to be grasped. Commissioners and producers had agreed that there was a duology that was popular with an audience, of documentary *and* drama combined. Drama, as commissioned by drama departments, had often based itself on documented facts, as Paget and Rosenthal had been exploring in *No Other Way to Tell it* and *Why Docudrama?* critical works that tackled films such as *Shoot to Kill* (ITV, 1990) and *Hostages* (ITV, 1992) starring established stars Colin Firth and Natasha Richardson. But there had been little or no dramatisation within the documentary mode. To this day, no theorist has undertaken an analysis of *this* combination. A new terminology is therefore appropriate, and it is proposed that this combination of drama within documentary can be framed, at least initially, and for the mutual comprehension of critics and practitioners, in terms of 'sense and sensuousness'.

'Sense and sensuousness': a proposed definition for history dramatisation

I would like to propose that the popular success of the four dramatised history texts analysed in these two chapters combined varying degrees of two distinct modes: sense and sensuousness. Sense is to be defined as the thing that *makes sense*. It is *not the use of the senses* – instead it sits at the far end of the logical spectrum, containing what are proposed here as the two Rs: research and reason. Research underpins everything in a history film that undertakes to draw from real life, or the raw material of the past. It sifts through the untidy raw material of 'facts', as Hayden White demonstrated in his article 'The Value of Narrativity in the Representation of Reality':

> Volume One of the Monumenta Germaniae Historica, series Scriptores, contains the text of the Annals of Saint Gall, a list of events that occurred in Gaul during the eighth, ninth and tenth centuries of our era.
>
> 709. Hard winter. Duke Gottfried died.
> 710. Hard year and deficient in crops.
> 711.
> 712. Flood everywhere.
> 713.
> 714. Pippin, Mayor of the Palace, died.[14]

White shows that annals, like this one, contain intriguing raw data but then asks what a historian is to do with it all. What does one make of the 'hard year and deficient in crops' of 710? Did nothing else happen in 714, other than 'Pippin, Mayor of the Palace, died'? Did nothing *at all* happen in 713? History, concludes White, is in dire need of a narrative. To achieve a narrative, one needs reason, and thus creates sense. It is research that finds such raw material, and it is reason that then arranges it into something coherent. Schama and Starkey did not set out on their respective TV histories without reasoning a narrative into the data lined up before them. Schama, the polymath art historian, had teams of researchers around him that supplied the sense he required to write and present a narrative of *his* history of Britain. Davidson, his executive producer, comes from an academic tradition and believes in the rigour of research and the application of reason, especially when attempting such a grand sweep of national self-reflection. (Davidson has an MPhil in History and climbed the ranks of television through the training of *The Late Show* (BBC, 1989–1995), which was well known for its intellectual strengths, and launched the careers of Roly Keating, now CEO of the British Library, and Janice Hadlow.) At the same time, on the other public service broadcaster, Channel 4, Starkey brought his theories on the

Henrician court to television after many years of close textual analysis of the Tudor court.

According to reviewer D. J. Taylor in *The Independent*, this history television successfully represented a duality of factors:

> *Elizabeth,* which accompanied last year's four-part Channel 4 series, attracted respectful reviews along with its thousands of purchasers. It is a safe bet that *The Six Wives of Henry VIII*, the forthcoming write-up of his new six-parter which starts this week, will do the same. Suddenly Tudor government, previously thought to be one of the duller nooks of early modern history, is not just fashionable, but sexy.[15]

'Sexy' is a television industry expression that implies the power to achieve popularity. Starkey's two shows for Channel 4 at the time of the millennium were stand-out hits. In analysing how he did this, with a previously underselling focus on the administrative detail of Tudor government, this book's notion of 'sense' comes into play. Both texts employed fresh and plausible storytelling that showed the gravitas of the presenter and the depth of his research. As Taylor notes, '*The Six Wives of Henry VIII* will, inevitably, be a huge success: provocative, intimate (actors are being used to dramatise certain scenes), suffused with bustling personalities and contending wills'.[16]

This aside, 'actors are being used to dramatise certain scenes' reveals how the device is being used to create intimacy. This is the other key component of the telling of history on television – and the one that was quite novel for the viewership: drama. Intimate drama evokes what this book will term 'sensuousness'. The non-speaking drama used in history documentaries was what the industry termed 'impressionistic', in that it attempted to create a non-speaking impression of the past. Whether speaking or not, intimate drama brought the court of Henry VIII to some semblance of life. It brought the horrors of the plague into a modern sitting room. It imagined the construction of a pyramid. This was the power of 'sensuousness'.

Sensuousness is to be defined as the thing that *packages sense*, which this book proposes is contained within the two Es: empathy and entertainment. The term 'empathy' has been inspired by Simon Schama, who insists we must have 'empathy, if you like, "alterity", immersion into the experience of others separated from us in time. Without the willingness to reach towards their world, their mental habits, history becomes, once again, an exercise in self-admiration'.[17] This is confirmed by Ann Gray and Erin Bell when defining the 'civilising gaze'. They claim that Schama's aims were 'immediacy, imaginative empathy, candid moral engagement, poetic connection'.[18] Entertainment might be more self-explanatory, but sensuousness is more substantial than just entertainment, especially in the newly termed definition of 'sense and sensuousness' as a package.

Translating the two terms baldly as 'information and entertainment' here is insufficient. If those Reithian terms were sufficient, then why not just use those terms rather than inventing an idiosyncratic terminology? There is a good answer to that (and it is not 'because it sounds good'!). It is proposed that the terms 'sense and sensuousness', in their similarity, suggest and reinforce the interdependence of the two qualities, and how each amplifies and feeds off the other. One cannot just use 'information' and 'entertainment' because one is talking about specific forms of those qualities that appear in particular ways within what we hope to show is a genre.

This definition of 'sense and sensuousness' is newly termed but is based on longstanding traditions. It is broadly Reithian. It is true that sense encompasses both information and education, while sensuousness reflects entertainment. But there is more to be elicited from these terms. 'Sensuousness' is a very rich term that should not be confused with 'sensual'. Both words share the same root, 'sense', but 'sensual' has different connotations, having long referred to carnal and especially sexual senses; the word 'sensuous' by contrast is believed to have been coined by John Milton in 1641 to mean 'relating to the senses instead of the intellect without the sexual connotation', according to the Collins dictionary. 'Sense', according to the same source, means the 'character of having good judgement, especially when it is based on practical ideas or understanding'.

Using the term 'sensuous' is not entirely new to the study of history on film. Lipkin, in a chapter titled 'A Feeling for History: Recovering the Past with Sensible Evidence' (2011), discusses Robert Burgoyne, who, in Lipkin's words, 'recognizes what he terms "sensuous" ways of understanding history, strategies for gaining access to the literal "sense" of social memory as the "cultural desire to reexperience the past in a sensuous form [that] has become an important, perhaps decisive, factor in the struggle to lay claim to what and how the nation remembers"'. Burgoyne claims, and Lipkin agrees, that there is a widespread cultural desire to re-experience the past sensuously, in all manner of public history. I welcome such an acknowledgement of the term 'sensuous', but am also aware that the term was used in passing, and frustratingly, it is not mentioned again in Lipkin's chapter, or elsewhere in scholarship in this field. The term 'sense' is also not used in the way that this book intends to employ it, as the rational alternative to the emotional quality of sensuousness. It is simply an access point to the words 'sensible' in the title of the chapter and 'sensuousness' in the text.

It will remain to be seen whether every film history text performed within this documentary drama mode truly contains both of these elements, or whether the elements are better categorised in terms of a sliding scale.

Pyramid and *The Great Plague* contain fine balances between the two modes. Schama and Starkey's series equally contained a balance, despite featuring less dramatisation, because their presenters were essentially what Stella Bruzzi calls 'performative'.[19]

The articulation of a conceptual duology of sense and sensuousness is hereby attempted for the first time, but it should be noted that a number of scholars have referred to related dualities. Corner in *The Art of Record* (1996) defines his own title as a duality of 'evidence and artifice' when describing documentaries as a discipline.[20] Documentary, as distinct from fiction, is founded upon evidence, although of course it needs artifice to package it. Corner refers to John Grierson, the 'father of documentary', as having followed another duality: 'creative and informative'.[21] He quotes Grierson as saying that documentary making 'requires not only taste but also inspiration, which is to say, a very laborious, deep-seeing, deep-sympathising, creative effort indeed'.[22] This goes somewhat further than the much-quoted Grierson remark on the 'creative treatment of actuality', and truly empathises with the nature of the creative effort, which is not always associated with documentary making. Corner continues:

> As a practice and a form, documentary is strongly informationalist (and therefore requires a level of 'accuracy') but is also an exercise in creativity, an art form drawing on interpretative imagination both in perceiving and using the sounds and images of 'the living scene' to communicate 'the real'.[23]

'The living scene'! Is this not suggestive of the sensuousness under consideration as articulated by a mise-en-scène that is emotionally alive?[24] Corner does not pursue this idea, but it is an intriguing concept for a practitioner. Corner knows there are critics of the dramatic treatment of documentary, such as Brian Winston, whose oft-quoted problem was 'that anything of the real would survive creative treatment?'[25] But Corner identifies a certain degree of exaggeration in Winston's question. Actuality and creative treatment can live side by side, and can even be enhanced by the presence of the other. Sense and sensuousness may follow this principle. In the 1950s, television critics for the national newspapers rejected the hybrid form of documentary and drama. Maurice Wiggin, of *The Sunday Times*, remarked: 'the whole point of a documentary is that it is literally true. If it is not literally true, it is not documentary but something else ... a kind of play writing ... we have had too much fact-based fiction cooked up in the studio and played by professional actors.'[26]

The binary notion of 'sense and sensuousness' is, of course, indebted to Jane Austen's *Sense and Sensibility* (1811), which dramatises the behavioural choices of two sisters. Of the two sisters in question, Austen characterises Elinor Dashwood, the reserved elder daughter, as representing 'sense': she always feels a keen sense of responsibility to her family and friends and places their welfare and interests above her own, suppressing her own (strong) emotions in a way that leads others to think she is indifferent or cold-hearted. Her sister Marianne's emotional excesses identify her as the sister exemplifying 'sensibility'. She undergoes the most character development within the book. Ultimately learning that her sensibilities have been selfish, she decides her conduct should be more like that of her elder sister. But here is the rub. Neither sense nor sensibility can live without the other. In order to obtain a happy resolution, both must be expressed and the other accommodated. Perhaps *Sense and Sensibility* has a lesson for history dramatisation? Just as both should be expressed to achieve a happy resolution, this book argues that a successful historical dramatisation should feature expressions of sense and sensuousness if it is to truly affect the viewer's heart and mind. Surely, therefore, the dramatised documentary, especially if well executed, is worthy of viewing and study?

And if so, then 'mongrel' or 'bastard' as a description of the mix is rendered less appropriate as we start to see the power that can be achieved by the sense and sensuousness combination. Of course, some films are poor examples of the hybrid, but that should not overshadow the fact that much of the time, the blurred edge between drama and documentary is a place of creativity and originality and a great deliverer of entertainment as well as information.

Conclusion

This chapter has considered a televisual phenomenon that captured the popular imagination in the first years of the millennium. Dramatised history also captured the ambition of television executives, for whom ratings success and critical approval in the national press were essential. The public service broadcasters, BBC and Channel 4, appear in retrospect to have been commissioning in direct opposition to each other, but the likelihood is that the competition on display in this chapter was at least partly coincidental. History dramatisation, however, was in the *zeitgeist*. *A History of Britain* and *Pyramid* were two high-budget BBC productions that delivered beyond the corporation's expectations, so too Channel 4's more modest Tudor series and *A Century of Troubles*. Among the reasons for the productions' popular success, I suggest, was their unification of what we might now call 'sense and sensuousness', and the terms will be used throughout this work, contributing to its core mission, which is to explore a growing corpus of films with a long-term prospect of determining whether there is a new genre to be defined.

Defining a new genre, mongrel or otherwise, will require an identification of its aesthetic characteristics, as the corpus evolves. Already we have seen that two historical dramatisations mix drama with star presenters, Schama and Starkey; one mixes the drama with interviews (*A Century of Troubles*); and one intersperses the dramatisation with science inserts (*Pyramid*). Yet all four critically combine sensuousness with sense, and the critics confirm that the drama is marked out as a very popular ingredient. This chapter has made a start in defining the shape of this corpus. If there is indeed a genre here, then it must have its originators. But to find these examples, one must go quite far back in time. There had been dramatisations in documentary-making since the origins of filmmaking, but in terms of documentaries commissioned by documentary departments that utilised drama to perform the past and the imagined future, there are two key examples, both produced in the 1960s: *Culloden* and *The War Game*.

Notes

1. I have selected one of my own films, not to self-aggrandise, but to offer yet more intimate perspectives on the developing potential genre, especially in its infant state. Since this is one of two films under consideration in this chapter, I trust that this choice shows sufficient balance.
2. Bills of Mortality were the lists of the dead and the causes of death posted in parishes on a weekly basis.
3. A go-pro lens is a hand-held lens that is very portable and can be taken from a wide shot right into an eyeball.
4. Buboes were the pustules on a plague wound.
5. Brenda Blethyn – Oscar-nominated for *Secrets and Lies* (1996). Stephen Mangan – starred in BAFTA-winning *Green Wing* (Channel 4, 2004–2005).
6. All previews/reviews date from 11 to 15 October 2001.
7. Sally Kines, *The Sunday Times* (11 October 2001).
8. J. T. Caldwell cited by Steven Lipkin, *Real Emotional Logic: Film and Television Docudrama as Persuasive Practice* (Carbondale, IL: Southern Illinois University Press, 2002, p. 70.
9. Rees later employed CGI and dramatisation with actors in his series *Auschwitz: The Nazis and the Final Solution* (BBC, 2005).
10. John Corner cited by Derek Paget, *No Other Way to Tell It: Dramadoc/Docu-drama on Television* (Manchester: Manchester University Press, 1998), p. 98.
11. Paget, *No Other Way to Tell It*, p. 3.
12. Paget, *No Other Way to Tell It: Dramadoc/Docu-drama on Television*, 2nd ed. (Manchester: Manchester University Press, 2011), p. 4.
13. *Ibid.*

14 Hayden White, 'The Value of Narrativity in the Representation of Reality', *Critical Inquiry*, 7:1 (1980), p. 8.
15 D. J. Taylor, 'David Starkey: The Apoplectic Academic', *Independent* (9 September 2001).
16 *Ibid.*
17 Simon Schama, 'Television and the Trouble with History' in David Cannadine (ed.), *History and the Media* (London: Palgrave Macmillan, 2006), p. 23.
18 Ann Gray and Erin Bell, *History on Television* (London: Routledge, 2013), p. 75.
19 Stella Bruzzi, *New Documentary: A Critical Introduction* (London: Routledge, 2000), p. 1.
20 John Corner, *The Art of Record: A Critical Introduction to Documentary* (Manchester: Manchester University Press, 1996), p. 2.
21 *Ibid.*, p. 13.
22 Grierson cited by Corner, *The Art of Record*, p. 13.
23 *Ibid.*, p. 15.
24 Mise-en-scène refers to what is placed on the stage or, in film terms, what is placed before the camera and then the editor.
25 Winston, 1995, cited in Corner, *The Art of Record*, p. 26.
26 Maurice Wiggin, *The Sunday Times* (1950).

3

1960s–1990s: Looking for progenitors

Introduction

In order better to understand the dramatised history documentary upswing of the early millennial era, one must look back to a select number of films from the previous forty years that could be considered to have acted as progenitors. It is no exaggeration to say that most of the millennial filmmakers interviewed in this book have acknowledged that two particular BBC documentaries of the 1960s were regarded as especially influential. Old copies, usually on VHS, were passed round commissioning tables at the BBC and Channel 4, and at both in-house and independent production offices in the 2000s. These films were *Culloden* (BBC, 1964) and *The War Game* (untransmitted, 1965). 'All of us in the production of *A History of Britain* watched *Culloden*', says Clare Beavan, one of its BBC in-house directors. 'A director showed *Culloden* to me, and frankly, we never looked back', agrees John Toba (2019), writer and producer of *Plague* (Channel 4, 2000). As for *The War Game*, which made the greater global impact – breaking the million-mark for BFI rentals and winning the Oscar for Best Documentary (1967) – 'we would not have made *Smallpox 2002*, or many other dramatised films at this time, without it' believes Alex Graham, former CEO of Wall to Wall, and arguably the driver behind the most audacious historical programming of the early twenty-first century.

This chapter will study these two films, *Culloden* and *The War Game*, and touch upon a couple of outliers from the 1990s, continuing to refer to the institutional context in which history was dramatised. It will specifically ask why, pre-2000, that context prevented these films from starting the boom earlier. The second approach is to explore the characteristics of these 1960s films to determine what it was about their – peer-acknowledged – originality of aesthetic that so influenced the millennial dramatised documentaries. Can one define this aesthetic, in its constituent parts, so that the programming of the first decade of the twenty-first century can be more clearly referenced? Finally, is it possible to fully and accurately estimate the extent to which these films contributed to televisual history?

Culloden (BBC, 1964)

> Brief summary: *The story of a battle in 1746 between British government troops and Jacobite forces, which defined the end of the Stuart claim to the throne, thereafter occupied by the Hanoverian dynasty and its offshoots. Shot in black and white, and wholly original in form, it is a dramatised account using amateur actors and faux interviews on the battlefield. On transmission, it was a considerable success.*

Culloden was a film that came out of the BBC Documentary department, commissioned by the then- Head of Documentaries, Huw Wheldon. The film's director, Peter Watkins, has been lionised for the making of this and *The War Game*, but it is argued here (as Watkins himself believes) that films are not made by a single individual and should not be credited as such, as is so often done in film literature. 'Film and TV are so powerful that they need to escape the single egotistical vision', Watkins told interviewer John Cook; 'they have a different degree of impact to the painting or the novel. The greater impact of the audio-visual form brings a greater responsibility with it. This is not often enough acknowledged.'[1]

Culloden was a documentary commission based on a book of the same title by John Prebble. More famously known for his war novel *Edge of Darkness* (1947), he was hailed by the *Spectator* as a writer whose work is 'marked by formidable research and passionate commitment to the cause of the poorest'.[2] In the opening, Prebble states that his book 'is not another history of the Forty-Five and it is not another story of Prince Charlie's wanderings after Culloden. It is an attempt to tell the story of the many ordinary men and women who were involved in the last Jacobite Rising, often against their will. For too long, I believe, the truth of this unhappy affair has been obscured by the over-romanticised figure of the prince'.[3] Prebble's book is full of the detail and angry polemic that subsequently infuses the counter-culture BBC film. Here is an example of his view of the ruling classes:

> The Duke of Cumberland's soldier 'wore a wide-skirted coat of heavy scarlet, well-buttoned and piped, and cuffed and faced with the regimental colour. It rarely fitted him. Colonels of regiments were supposed to have the material pre-shrunk, but most of them were too mean or too indifferent or claimed that it spoiled the hang of the cloth and the appearance of their men. Thus, the first shower of rain to which a battalion was subjected shrank the skirts, shortened the sleeves and added one more discomfort to soldiering'.[4]

The film script picks up the thread: 'A soldier in the government army will earn 6d a day', writes Prebble; 'two years' salary will not buy him the wig of the officer who leads him', continues the film script. Prebble used primary sources from the Regimental Order Books, contemporary newspapers, magazines, letters and memoirs of soldiers, and eye-witness accounts, and the BBC team conducted similar primary-source research.

The most influential element of the film, however, was the aesthetic of making a documentary as if it were conducted by a news team, transported back in time to the battlefield. This aesthetic is multi-faceted, and its context has been chronicled by John Cook, who interviewed Watkins and his team intermittently from 1973 to 2001. The overall aesthetic is attributed (against Watkins' avowed wishes) to Watkins himself. 'In many ways, Watkins can be seen as the father of modern docudrama', Cook states:

> His breakthrough professional debut film, *Culloden* ... was hugely influential in marrying dramatic performance (a meticulously researched historical reconstruction of the battle of Culloden in 1746 using actors) with a then-highly contemporary vérité shooting style to create an immediacy effect of gritty documentary authenticity; rendering the events of Culloden 1746 as suddenly as fresh and as relevant as a TV news report recently dispatched from the frontline of a modern war.[5]

Cook goes on to confirm that this is not just his opinion, but that of many of his even better-known peers:

> Shot in August 1964 and first premiered on BBC TV on 15 December of that year, it is important to realise that Watkins' experiments with a documentary vérité shooting style in *Culloden* predated the similar experiments of Ken Loach in his famous mid-sixties television plays *Up The Junction* (BBC TV 1965) and *Cathy Come Home* (BBC TV 1966).[6] Loach has acknowledged the enormous influence Watkins had both on himself and his generation of politically committed docudrama filmmakers.[7]

It is relevant here to confirm the distinction between the BBC documentary team that made *Culloden* from the drama team that made *Cathy Come Home*. *Culloden* draws from primary and secondary sources, and the team researched and created a script themselves. The small budget came from the documentary department (in *Culloden*'s case, around £3,000), and contained amateur actors. *Cathy Come Home* came from the much bigger drama department, where Tony Garnett, the legendary story producer (*Up the Junction*), was employed to drive dramas through their process. The script was written by Jeremy Sandford and adapted by Ken Loach (uncredited). It starred then-established actors Carol White and Ray Brooks. In the 1960s, as in the 2000s, drama and documentary departments did not coincide in any way at all. They operated from separate buildings at the BBC, known within the system as 'silos'. Hence, for the purposes of this book, it should not be imagined that a drama filmed in a documentary style is suddenly a 'drama documentary'. It is not. The drama will always be funded and set up according to drama rules that, certainly in the 1960s, were governed by a series of intractable unions representing actors, directors, electricians, camera operators, and so on. *Cathy Come Home* is a docudrama, a drama that is rooted in very real concerns, in this case, the housing problem of the 1960s. *Culloden*, on the other hand, is a drama documentary, commissioned from the documentary department and utilising many characters who are fully sourced and truly lived. Their footsoldiers are even named. *The War Game*, even though it is commissioned by the documentary department, involves the dramatic creation of characters and a situation to help elucidate a social concern, that of the threat of nuclear war. But the film holds drama and its documentary sources in equal esteem, which makes it a drama documentary. According to Hamish Mykura, a supporter of the drama documentary combination throughout his commissioning career at Channel 4 and Nat Geo, 'respecting the duality of both drama and documentary is the joy of these films, from *Culloden* and *War Game* to the films of the 2000s' (Mykura, 2021). This distinguishes these films from a docudrama like *Cathy Come Home*, which is based on good documentary-mode research, but allows the drama-mode to take over completely within the body of the film. But for now, this chapter shall examine *Culloden* and *The War Game*.

To return to the aesthetic of the 1960s films under review, one should look no further than the classification of both *Culloden* and the *War Game* as 'amateur'. This is meant in the most admiring sense. Cook explains:

> To understand Watkins, however, and his particular approach to actors, it is important to realise at the outset that he is, at heart, an amateur filmmaker. This is not meant in any derogatory, negative sense but rather that the roots of his practice lie in Britain's amateur cinema movement from which he first emerged in the late 1950s and early 1960s.[8]

Watkins worked not with professional actors but with an amateur theatre group in Canterbury, Kent, where he had been stationed during his National Service. They were called Playcraft, and not only did Watkins take this travelling troupe with him up to Scotland to play soldiers of the Government army in *Culloden*, he also chose to shoot his next film, *The War Game*, down in Kent so as to be nearer to the group.

Key to the experimentation of Watkins in the amateur movement of this period was his determination to react against what was believed to be the 'falseness' of Hollywood in the dramatic representation of reality, particularly in relation to conflict. In an interview with *Amateur Ciné-World* magazine on the eve of the first transmission of *Culloden*, Watkins referred to 'the typical star-ridden-film-set-cluttered thing which is always patently a piece of fiction'.[9] Instead, he said he now had a deliberate policy in his films of using amateur, or as he preferred to label them, 'non-professional', actors, because: 'I am trying to get into my films a style of realism … (using) ordinary people on location and (employing) a flat form of lighting – in fact often no lighting at all'. The result, he stated, was 'for my money something [closer] to real life'.[10]

Through his work with the amateur actors of Playcraft, Watkins and his team cast 142 non-professional actors from the Scottish Highlands and elsewhere to play the clansmen and the Redcoat soldiers who fought at Culloden, with members of the Playcraft group playing the speaking roles of the government forces. Here is the monologue of a young soldier, after the brutal massacre of a number of women and children, hiding out in the hills, in the aftermath of the battle: 'All these officers say the people up here are a load of savages, but I dunno, they look like ordinary women and children to me. I didn't like it, didn't like it at all.' This is clearly emotionally performative, and would not be entrusted to a local citizen who had not performed at all before, but would be within the range of a regular Playcraft amateur. As for the 142 locals from the Highlands brought into the performance, the BBC team presumably believed they had authenticity, for these were descendants from the very highlands and clans they were depicting, their faces confirming hardship, their accents revealing a legacy of Gaelic. To the viewer, the locals, playing the Highlanders, act as a portal into the past, as if they were confirming Lipkin's notion of 'a performance of memory'.[11]

In the 1964 interview, Tony Rose captures Watkins' reflections on casting ordinary members of the public, a practice often derided in professional film circles:

> A great deal of rubbish is talked about such people. When most professionals talk about amateur theatrical productions, they tend to groan and think of over-acting, but that is due only to bad handling. If you go up to a child of twelve or a woman of eighty and give them something to do which is within the bounds of their own characters and their own experience, then you can reduce them to tears, you can get a performance of pathos, you can get anything you like from them as long as you handle them carefully.[12]

This interview shows that there is much to be learned from the working process of the BBC documentary team on *Culloden* and supports the notion that one should study some of the theory behind films as well as watching the films themselves. This present writer wishes this illuminating interview had been researched before he himself was filming a series of drama documentaries in the 2000s. Watkins continues:

> Usually, it is better to get something fairly quickly. Untrained people tend to wear down much more quickly; they get tired and lose that little spark. Nearly everyone has a spark somewhere and it often comes out, if you have explained what you want, in the very first take.[13]

It was the initial 'spark' of the amateur that made the whole exercise worthwhile. For Watkins' team, the non-professional actor could bring something more spontaneous than the sometimes more theatrical style of the professional. After all, the BBC team was often looking simply for a stare or a glare, physicalised in a rain-sodden moor, and they were precisely asking for what filmmakers so often ask actors *not* to do: to look *into* the camera. This is a device that became much mimicked in the 2000s, as will be shown in later chapters.

The device of looking into the camera is clearly reproduced in *Elizabeth* and *Henry VIII*'s cinematic portraits, although the actors used were more professional. *Plague* also featured portraits of the poor, utilising exactly the kind of amateurs favoured by the 1960s team. *Culloden*'s employment of non-professionals developed into a full-blown political challenge to the so-called professionalism of drama, which appeared to exclude amateur members of the public from the creative process. By contrast, *Culloden*'s distinctive aesthetic followed a 'desire to add a dimension and a process to television … that of the public directly, seriously and in depth participating in the expressive use of the medium to examine history – past, present and future'.[14]

Watkins' ideas on the use of non-professional actors are now broadly agreed by TV industry professionals to be a clever and appropriate use of the public in representing historical events, and many films of the millennium could not have been made without the enormous contribution of re-enactors. After all, they are good value compared to actors or even supporting artists.[15] Directors such as Jamie Muir of *A History of Britain* (BBC, 2000–2003) and *Monarchy* (Channel 4, 2003–4/5) mimicked the process of representing historical events through what Muir calls 'faces upon which the audience could place their own emotional response' (Muir, 2019).

Watkins' 'democratic' form of filmmaking not only bypassed but deliberately flaunted longstanding professional media practices. After the first screening of *Culloden* in 1964, the British professional actors' union, Equity, complained to the BBC, and to the press, that professional actors should have been utilised. Gerald Croadsell, the union's General Secretary, pointed to an agreement that the BBC had struck with the union in 1947 that amateurs would not be used on television where professionals could do the job.[16] The unions at this time were a considerable force to be reckoned with, and the battle will be further discussed later in this chapter, in the wake of *The War Game*'s production.

The next facet of *Culloden*'s aesthetic is the use of drama script in a documentary. Almost all documentaries, unless they are strictly observational 'fly on the wall' articulations, have scripts that anticipate interviewees' contributions separately from drama inserts, with audio on the right on the page and visuals on the left, divided by a line – and boxed to indicate a change of mode. Many millennial dramatisations, attempting to bring dramatic life to their subjects, increasingly added to their drama boxes, but in the early days of 2000–2001 these were non-dialogue, referred to by those filmmakers as 'impressionistic' and – unkindly – by critics such as David Chater in *The Times* as 'dumb show'.[17] *Culloden* was far ahead of the 2000–2002 crop, in that the BBC team was mixing impressionistic observation with monologue quoted from detailed primary sources, and then some imagined but equally well-researched examples of what protagonists might have said if they were being interviewed. The conceits did not happen by chance. They must all have been put down on paper. Cook observes:

> In the early years of his career, with films like *Culloden* and *The War Game*, Watkins relied much more on scripts than with his later work. In early films, lines of dialogue for his actors would be carefully pre-planned and scripted in advance. As his career progressed and Watkins became more and more immersed in the notion of a form of 'community filmmaking' with the public as a direct challenge to the so-called professionalism of the mass media, he began to encourage a greater amount of on-set improvisation of actors' dialogue.[18]

The dramatisations in history documentary went in exactly the opposite direction, as will be articulated in later chapters. Impressionist drama led to improvisation and then to more pre-planned dialogue, and finally to award-winning scripts. Ratings success brought more investment from the broadcasters, which in turn raised the bar for increased production ambition, which included drama being fully delivered.

Above all, what Watkins left behind was a battle cry for a hybrid approach that does not abide by the strictures of drama or documentary but embraces the virtues of the intersection between the two, and even the creation of something altogether new. He never quite defined it as such, but he certainly created a term for the non-hybrid approach he derided, calling it 'monoform'; even Ken Loach became known for monoform, in Watkins' view. *Culloden* was an example of what Watkins called pluriform filmmaking.

There are other aspects of *Culloden*'s aesthetics that are not mentioned by academic sources and leave room for fresh observation. Captions (or intertitles as they are known in Media Studies) are heavily used at the beginning of *Culloden*. After a strong dramatic opening – establishing the two forces walking towards each other on that fateful day in 1746, across Culloden Moor – the title in a huge font that fills the screen is followed by opening captions that establish the intent of the film: 'An account of one of the most mishandled and brutal battles ever fought in Britain ... An account of the men, women and children who suffered for it.' The indefinite article is perhaps instructive. It is *an* account, not *the* account, reminding the reader of *A History of Britain*. This may seem obvious to any historian but is very much not obvious to an audience member sitting in front of the television set (and even less so with the next film under review, *The War Game*). There is an expectation of a certain amount of bias to be present in what is a personal view taken first by John Prebble and progressed by the BBC documentary team that produced *Culloden*. This is to be bottom-up history that would inspire *The Great Plague* – a story of 'men, women and children' and not of King Charles II or Bonnie Prince Charlie. The battle is categorically introduced to the public as 'mishandled', which does not suggest that the conduct of ruling classes is up for debate. Watkins and his team now had *carte blanche* to take a very personal view on a subject that is of national interest, being the last great battle fought on British soil. Viewers are presented with a choice: accept the captions or turn off. What is interesting is that the film does not use its captions to establish veracity. In millennial dramatisations such as *The Great Plague*, captions were invariably utilised to establish a key message: 'this is based on historical records'. It seems that Watkins and his editor, Michael Bradsell, did not feel it necessary to establish their sources. They only wanted to establish their dramatic intent.

Captions are subsequently not employed throughout the film, being replaced by voiceover and monologues that are a mouthpiece for historical information backed by detailed research. Captions are not missed as authentication of historical fact, because so many statistics offer support from within the narration. It will be argued that in the 2000s, every single variant and alternative to caption was attempted; many were disingenuous and unsuccessful, but those that were generally agreed by peers and critics alike to have worked well were statistical in nature, and that approach was pioneered in *Culloden*, albeit not in caption form.

Another device that *Culloden* experiments with is having an amateur actor play the role of a news reporter. In this case he is given an identity.

The 'Whig historian' Thomas Henderson, who is supposed to have attended the battle, recounts it minute by minute for the viewer. Henderson does not quote directly from primary sources, but instead conflates information compiled from eyewitness accounts. He stands behind a stone wall perpendicular to the two opposing armies, which was topographically correct and enables him to report on the damage received by the Jacobite army in the first minutes of conflict, their suicidal charge into the artillery of the Government army and the outflanking of the Jacobites by fusiliers, who literally muscle Henderson out of the way, as they fire beyond the wall beneath which he is forced to crouch. Henderson uses statistics efficiently: he tells us that '15 shots have been fired by government cannon to one of the rebels', but then seems to drop out of view, having been revealed as a device with limited uses.

The dramatic inclusion of an on-screen observer such as Henderson is not remarked upon by critics of the time, partly perhaps because there were other novelties to be admired. Millennial history dramatisations, however, have not copied this device, unless one includes the presence of Lucy Worsley in dramatisations, dressed as a domestic maid, making knowing asides to the camera. The success of this device with audiences has been mixed, and yet continues long after the dramatisation boom has cooled down.

Another device, also employing the unexpected power of mathematics in narrative, is the 'ticking clock'. The narrator, who in the industry is called 'the voice of God', gives a running commentary on the time elapsed through the battle. Its intention, one supposes, is to confirm the mounting horror of so many dead and wounded in the Jacobite army within such a short space of time. A monumental defeat, which arguably changed the relationship between Scotland and England forever, was concluded within one hour and eight minutes. Much of the decisiveness of the onslaught occurs in the first twenty minutes, when the Government army's cannon fire decimates the Jacobites. The clock is reported by the narrator: '1.17pm: Prince's artillery ... ceases fire ... 1.22pm: 200 of Clan Cameron shot to pieces, 180 of Clan Stuart shot to pieces'. This very dramatically creates a timeline that is plausible (if not known for sure), and which has been mimicked many times in films of the millennial era. *Trafalgar Battle Surgeon* (Channel 4, 2005), for instance, counts up the four desperate hours of a naval battle that hung in the balance until the last hour, and yet would decide the control of global trade routes from 1805 until 1914, and beyond. Other dramatisations have followed the opposing route of counting *down* to the known historical event, for instance *Seconds to Disaster* (Nat Geo, 2004–2018) and *1917: Countdown to Revolution* (BBC, 2017). Did *Culloden* lay down a marker for others to follow, historically as well as aesthetically? The answer, judging from peer review and with critical hindsight, is a resounding yes. As a representation of history, it is packed full of emotive and informative detail that is drawn from exemplary primary sources and employed with care and consideration. As a dramatic piece of documentary, it sustains a powerful and justifiable polemic: that the poor suffer when the rich go to war. It is a film of its times, the anti-authoritarian 1960s, and resounds still in contemporary times. Its aesthetic choices, radically new at the time, had a profound impact on dramatising the past in years to come. Nowhere was there better to look for inspiration within British television than *Culloden*, and *The War Game, which* followed it.

Culloden is by no means a film without fault. The downside of its amateurism is evident throughout the work. The battle of many thousands is reconstructed using just 142 men, and it often shows. This is pre-CGI, and therefore one never has the sense of the sheer volume of men at close quarters, let alone the appalling numbers of dead and dying. Derek Ware, the fight consultant, was no doubt under immense time pressure to educate many day visitors to the site as to how to plunge a bayonet into an opponent convincingly while at the same time addressing the camera appropriately. The cannons recoil often with great conviction but the firings are few and far between. The squibs – special-effects devices that explode a piece of ground in front of actors, are well employed but, again, not on any scale. Amateur actors too often clutch at a wounded knee where there is no wound and throw themselves backwards to indicate being hit by shrapnel, actions that are unconvincing to say the least. Later critics were not so forgiving. David Chater of *The Times* levelled criticism at *Trafalgar Battle Surgeon* (Channel 4, 2005) for its on-deck cannon 'recoil[ing] with all of the conviction of a shopping trolley'.[19] Yet *Trafalgar Battle Surgeon* was forgiven by its industry peers, who voted it the Royal Television Society Best History film 2005. So, too, *Culloden* is a piece of televisual theatre that elicits audience forgiveness. There is always a fine line between evident budgetary constraints carried with conviction, and the collapse of audience respect that leads to risibility. *Culloden* certainly had conviction in spades, ably supported by handheld camera, operated by Dick Bush, which covered a multitude of sins. This coverage was then also edited by Michael Bradsell in such a way that the eye never lingers on a technical weakness.

It would be useful in terms of the film's influence to make a checklist of the documentary drama aesthetics that were established by *Culloden*:

1. Narrative drawn from primary source records (as well as secondary source context).
2. Scripting derived from the production team (researcher/director/producer).
3. Performance of dramatic reconstruction by actors, whether amateur players, re-enactors, or subsequently professionals.

4. These actors looking into the camera, reaching across time.
5. Embracing the pluriform (in this case the hybrid of documentary, drama, and action film).
6. Constructing action sequences – theatrical conceits that are forgivable to the audience.
7. Captions establishing a contract with the audience including a countdown of time within the narrative.
8. Narrator as a 'voice of God', or a character within the drama (in this case, Henderson).
9. Constructing the image so it performs as possible archive (in this case, B/W footage).
10. Sound design that brings the reality of the image to life (in this case, diegetic music exists only as it would have been; marching drums is the only soundtrack).

These ten points capture the aesthetic of *Culloden*, which was to lay down many of the 'laws' of the dramatisations that were to follow so many years later.

The next film under consideration was made by the same documentary team from the BBC and involved the same Playcraft actors and many of the same aesthetic techniques. While it does not deal with history in the past, it is what could be described as history that has not yet occurred – a warning from future history.

The War Game (BBC, 1965 untransmitted)

> Brief summary: *An imagined nuclear attack on Britain in the 1960s is dramatised; the film follows the aftermath in a community in Kent, over weeks and months. The film was so realistic that the BBC pulled the transmission, causing the writer/director to withdraw his labour from the BBC and go into self-imposed exile on the continent for much of the rest of his career.*

When considering *The War Game*, the industrial and cultural conditions that surrounded the drama documentary are particularly relevant. *Culloden* had been an idiosyncratic film that emerged from the relationship between a patron, Huw Weldon, and his protégées in the documentary department at the BBC. *Culloden* came from an interest in a brutal battle that could have been avoided that was likely reminiscent of coverage emerging on television out of the Vietnam War. But culturally, *Culloden* was mostly relevant because John Prebble had published a book about the battle three years earlier. *The War Game*, by contrast, was steeped in its industrial and cultural context. Ironically, it was the film the production team intended to make first, but

Wheldon could see the political difficulties that surrounded it and commissioned *Culloden* first, no doubt buying himself some time. For where *Culloden* was a reflection on a piece of historical record, *The War Game* was always intended to be a conceptual 'what if' scenario, imagining a nuclear attack on Britain, utilising in-depth research into the state's lack of preparedness for such a war and its inevitable and literal fallout. The BBC's relation to the state, and its support for the state's fighting of the Cold War, meant that nuclear weapons were not much dealt with in the corporation's content. An article by Tony Shaw of the University of Hertfordshire explores this subject with the benefit of access to government papers that had recently been disclosed:

> In 1955, for instance, the BBC axed a program about nuclear fallout in the wake of Prime Minister Winston Churchill's complaints, made directly through the chairman, that it might foster defeatism ... while in 1957 the fire at the nuclear reactor at Windscale in Cumbria was portrayed by BBC news as a 'mishap'.[20]

In the context of the 2020s COVID-19 pandemic, it is not difficult to persuade today's audience that, over half a century ago, BBC officials, Whitehall, and politicians consulted each other on how issues such as the hydrogen bomb might be covered without frightening viewers and listeners. The Cuban Missile Crisis of 1962 must have brought thermonuclear war to the front of the Western world's imaginations. Meanwhile, the BBC was enjoying a liberal shake-up with the arrival of BBC Two in 1964; in Shaw's words: 'as the new Director-General, Hugh Carleton Greene, sought to shrug off the Corporation's stuffy image'.[21] *Culloden*'s radical hybrid approach had been a success for the new channel and the team behind it, and so it was agreed that the same team should proceed with research for a film employing a similar aesthetic of drama documentary techniques, which would tell the imagined story of what might occur in a nuclear war.

Watkins' team aimed to bring home to people the horrendous nature of nuclear war, and thereby, firstly, to 'make the man in the street stop to think about himself and the future'; secondly, to challenge conventional assumptions about the media's social function and, more particularly, the mechanisms for self-regulation adopted by the institutions governing television; and thirdly, to '*radicalise the documentary form*, primarily by taking advantage of the growing technological sophistication of television newsgathering' [my italics].[22] Herein lies a clear definition of the awareness in the BBC that Watkins and his team were 'radicalizing the documentary form' by creating a new kind of drama documentary. As if to drive this point home, the production team was allotted a budget of £9,000, the second largest ever for a BBC (documentary) film, and three times the usual allowance.

It is interesting to note the aesthetic choices Watkins and his team made in order to tell the unfolding narrative of a nuclear attack on Britain, imagined in the near future. Shaw, who interviewed Watkins throughout his career, reports that the team 'chose to focus on the plight suffered by those caught on the fringes of a nuclear strike, rather than at its epicentre. This was not only easier to depict on film but would also undermine official notions of survivability'.[23] This meant that the 'chamber piece' drama constructed for *Culloden* was to be repeated for *The War Game*. The first idea, according to Shaw:

> revolved around a television camera crew sent to Canterbury in the immediate aftermath of a nuclear strike on London, reporting over a span of ten days how the town's population physically and mentally collapsed. Elements of this made their way into the final print – the Kent location in particular – but the prominence of the camera crew theme was rejected, perhaps because it resembled Culloden too closely.[24]

Thus, *The War Game* presumably initially intended to have a faux camera crew, and possibly a faux reporter, present at the scene in the same way that Thomas Henderson, the Whig historian, was present at the battle of Culloden. But one imagines that *Culloden* had taught the team that telling the narrative through a contrivance such as a reporter was not necessary. The decision to use the same amateur actors from Playcraft in Canterbury became central to the concept, however. They then added to this actors' group with CND enthusiasts, who replaced the re-enactors used for *Culloden*, as Shaw confirms:

> [the] quest for authenticity dictated that the members of this community be utterly normal and thus entirely anonymous. Consequently, in March a cast of roughly 350 was assembled from several amateur dramatic societies in Kent, a handful of Culloden veterans and a few CND enthusiasts.[25]

The single-location filming was extended to a series of derelict sites in Chatham, Rochester, and Dover. This is an aesthetic choice that many of the millennial dramatisations subsequently followed. It is a budgetary choice in essence. Dramas often move locations regularly to achieve a variety of backdrops to keep the audience refreshed, and to confirm a sense of the epic. But *The War Game* team, despite having a high documentary budget, did not have a comparative drama budget.

Derek Ware continued as fight/action coordinator and had improved his ability to convince the audience with his stunts. The firestorm scene is very convincing to a director's eye. There is a great deal of fire, some of which would have been real, other parts being achieved through a gas pipe buried in the rubble, to be turned up to deliver more flame effect for the camera. Wind machines must have been utilised to aid the sense of the after-effects of Dresden or Hiroshima after their bombing. This is ambitious material to achieve on a limited budget, and suggests that the team had very cooperative 'stunt' players:

> [they] took pains in coaching the amateurs how to 'act' like dead bodies, making them lie convincingly askew amongst rubble, and checking their postures against photographs taken at Hiroshima. Students were chosen for the fight and riot scenes, on the assumption that they would less mind running the risk of getting in the way of an unpulled punch, and so make the violence more believable.[26]

Much of the documentary element of the film is derived from faux expert interviews; for instance, the bishop who recounts the position of the Church of England on nuclear arms is a Playcraft actor, but the words he speaks are taken from an ecclesiastical publication. His announcement that 'we must learn to love the bomb' is astonishing to an audience of any era, especially when placed directly in conjunction with images of the firestorm. This and the mock news narration keep an audience guessing as to whether they are watching a real event or not. As Shaw explains, 'unemotional narration, supplied by the well-known voices of documentary commentator Dick Graham and BBC news reporter Michael Aspel, lent the film an air of sobriety and respectability'.[27]

Again, as in *Culloden*, *The War Game*'s production team deliberately utilised 'cross bred' formats – the newsreel, street interview, current affairs programme, naturalist drama, and cinéma-vérité documentary – and consequently blurred established television-viewing 'codes'. The production team's script, use of actors, speaking to camera, use of narration, constructed experts, action sequences, and observational camera all contribute towards a hybrid that can best be described as uniquely pluriform, and was not to be seen until the second stage of the millennium's dramatisations, discussed in Chapter 5.

So, why did this radical form of hybrid filmmaking not prove to be a template for dramatised documentaries throughout the 1960s and beyond? The answer lies in the industrial context and *The War Game*'s post-production and distribution. First, Huw Wheldon received a promotion to BBC Two Channel Controller and vacated his job as Head of Documentaries for a new incumbent. While Wheldon was now potentially a more powerful supporter than previously, he was also acting as gamekeeper, not poacher.

In June 1965, the rough cut was shown by the editor (Michael Bradsell, as on *Culloden*) within the BBC for the first time, and there were a number of concerns, most notably that the film failed to set out the pros and cons of deterrence theory and thus 'smacked too much of a CND hand-out'.[28] The overall impression left by *The War Game* was that defence is a meaningless concept in the thermonuclear age, and that those who avoid the immediate effects of the bombs would be consigned to a fate worse than death. The BBC chose to shelve the film, and Watkins resigned from the BBC and moved to the continent. The BBC showed the film in 1984 to memorialise Hiroshima. By then, approximately six million people had seen the film in screenings and on video, according to Shaw.

But the critical question for this book is the following: whether the BBC's reaction to the film created an infertile culture in which other historical/imagined dramatised history documentaries might struggle to flourish in Britain. The answer, in part, is yes. Despite winning Best Documentary Oscar in 1967 for *The War Game*, Watkins attempted and failed to make other films through the BFI. Perhaps his subject matters were the issue. He did get to make a further magnus opus on the nuclear issue, in 1987, completing his fourteen-and-a-half-hour *Film for Peace: The Journey*. A pioneering documentary shot on five continents and in eight languages, *The Journey* explored the connections between the nuclear arms race, world hunger, gender politics, and the functioning of the mass media. This epic would reach only a tiny fraction of the mass audience that had seen *The War Game*.

A second reason that dramatised documentary did not take root at the BBC was the return to silos. Drama departments did not take kindly to competition, and so Loach and Garnett continued to make their political points within their own system while the BBC Documentary department returned to its intellectual heritage, making films presented by white males of a certain age. The third, and most important reason, however, was that those who had most benefitted from Watkins' approach, amateur actors, were considered to have been exploited. It is significant that after Watkins' dramatic resignation from the BBC in September 1965, following the television banning of *The War Game*, the experiment with amateur actors in BBC documentary productions ended. While director Ken Russell did continue to use actors in his celebrated music and arts documentaries of the 1960s, they were often Equity-registered professionals, not members of the public. Equity would tighten the rules on who could, and could not, appear on television. According to Cook, in his *Culloden* article:

> Instead, the radical documentary impulse shifted to BBC TV's drama department, with the documentary-style dramas of director Ken Loach and producer Tony Garnett's *Up The Junction* (BBC, 1965) and *Cathy Come Home* (BBC,

1966). Along with other TV plays of their kind, these continued the Watkins *vérité* style of dramatised productions that also seemed akin to current affairs broadcasts.[29]

As will become apparent later in this book, 'history rescues drama, then drama rescues history' (Davidson, 2019), in the words of Martin Davidson of the BBC. Loach and Garnett were very much of the drama department, and never came under the institutional pressure to achieve absolute documentary accuracy that Watkins had encountered in the BBC's Documentary Department. Nor did they have the same radical aesthetic commitment to working with amateurs as Watkins. While sharing with Watkins a commitment to eschew actors hired from central casting with no lived experience of the parts they were being asked to play, Loach and Garnett were easily persuaded to use professional actors for their central roles, even if they tended to be working-class, often unknown to the audience, or bringing improvisational experience and narrative timing from other corners of entertainment, such as stand-up comedy.

And so the original dramatised history documentaries, with their undeniably radical aesthetic – a product of the interdisciplinary blending of documentary and drama – came to a halt.

Or almost to a halt. There were documentaries in the intervening years that utilised drama aesthetics, but they are hard to find, and do not constitute admission to a solidified body of work, let alone a possible genre. A couple are worthy of mention, however. One is *The American Civil War* (PBS, 1990), which lies outside the scope of this book, being an American commission. It was, nevertheless, a very influential piece of work, and while it was full of archive images, it began the bid for reconstruction through its dramatic *audio tracks*. Actors played the observers of the time while powerfully constructed sounds of battle connected up the photographs that did not capture a single frame of action.

The other film that is worthy of mention in the stuttering slow march to dramatisation in history documentary is the very unusual *Wisconsin Death Trip* (BBC, 1999), made in rural America but for the BBC Arena arts strand.

Wisconsin Death Trip (BBC, 1999)

This film is a dramatised history documentary par excellence. The tale is drawn from the primary source of newspaper accounts at Black River Falls in Wisconsin. They tell of a mysterious Nordic-style depression that fell upon the population during a particularly harsh winter late in the nineteenth century and make for a truly memorable and eerie film on American social history. There are other primary sources too, for example, the black-and-white photographs of Charles Van Schaick, which are interspersed with dramatic reconstructions of the highest cinematic quality, filmed by Eigil Bryld. James Marsh, who would later direct *Man on Wire* (BBC/Discovery, 2008), was co-writer and director. The IMDb records make it clear that, like *Culloden*, the film was full of amateur actors, sourced locally, and there are other signs of hybridity. Each crew member has a number of jobs: the wardrobe designer, Ellen Kozak, is also the costume supervisor, and Marsh is also credited as the sound-effects designer.

The dramatisations are artfully shot. The soles of a pair of naked feet are seen, before it is revealed that the man is swinging from a vast, leafless tree. A crane shot rises above the virgin snow-filled landscape to reveal a single small boy running until he is shot in the back. A woman bound in an asylum's restrictive white suit is wheeled out into the bitter cold. The visuals are matched by newspaper reports of the haphazard events articulated on screen, but the voices are *whispered*. It is a truly gothic aesthetic for a documentary.

John Corner has written an article on this slice of American Gothic in *Screen Magazine*, in which he defines the journeys of historical dramatisations:

> History on film and television varies in the extent and manner to which it is organised as a kind of chair-based travel, a virtual journey in which alignments of past and present (for example, the bad past, the great past, the past as surprisingly like today, the past as surprisingly unlike it) are configured and made subject to assessment.[30]

The mention of 'chair-based travel' is reminiscent of Paget's 'cultural tourism'[31] and contributes to the list of terms that best evoke the enticing nature of historical dramatisation. It confirms that these films, at their best, are travels in time. They are sometimes accompanied by well-orchestrated narrative, sometimes less so. This film, according to Corner and most reviewers, lacks narrative structure and so, whilst it was considered impressive, and 'eerie', it outstayed its welcome as a '70-minute plus' entertainment. Corner does identify a seasonal structure, as the film moves from winter through the seasons to another, final winter – mostly to keep the concept of a death trip alive at the end, as at the beginning. He observes that the film focuses perhaps too much on 'the odd and the bizarre. This allows a rich depictive styling at the same time as it gives a degree of instability to the project and, as I shall suggest, finally raises some problems for interpretation.'[32]

The 'rich depictive styling' is impressive in the extreme, and it is notable that at the very moment dramatised history documentary was evolving, a DVD copy circulated in the various documentary offices of the BBC, well beyond the silo of the Arena strand. Martin Davidson, as he was preparing *A History of Britain*, spoke highly of its 'exquisite use of 19th-century still photography, from which it derived its dramatic reconstructions, in that very image'. Here was an example of pre-moving archive history being brought to life. Both the Science and the History departments took keen notice of that leap in style – more than the subject matter itself, which was regarded as obscure even for an Arena film. 'The broad aesthetic design (music controlling mood and pace, slowed motion, tracking shots, an expansive pictorialism)' was admired and Corner went further to define the film as depicting 'a pathology of place'[33] that was also admired but would not be adopted in the BBC's millennial history of the British Isles. Neither did *Plague* or *Pyramid* borrow from its aesthetic. They were busy telling narrative-driven stories that did not have time for art-inspired slow imagery. Yet that style remains intriguing for future films beyond this book, into the 2020s. As Corner continues: 'I am suggesting that *Wisconsin Death Trip* works with a distinctive approach to conveying viewers into history. This depends on the fashioning of a strong 'archival aesthetics' around the records of the past.'[34] This author concurs and would go further. The visual team on *Wisconsin Death Trip* expanded the aesthetic style beyond the archive and into every facet of the production. Even the observational documentary footage of old folk in the present day is filmed with a matter-of-fact macabre sensibility.

There is much to admire about this production, but this is not the place for expansive discussion as it has no more narrative than the annals of St Gall. Historians need a narrative, and so do audiences. Corner wonders to what extent 'the film is to be regarded as an historical documentary and the extent to which it is to be seen primarily as an "art project"',[35] and it is clear to this author/director that the answer is the latter. Corner notes that 'many critics registered the "unrelenting strangeness" of the portrayal'.[36] The term 'unrelenting' is well considered here. It matters little that *Wisconsin Death Trip* is an art film that challenges the norms of Hollywood narrative. What matters to this book is that *Wisconsin Death Trip* did not 'move the dial', to use a term from industry. It was not a major influence because it did not grip the collective viewers' and critics' imagination, as Starkey and Schama, *Plague* and *Pyramid* were to do over the next years.

Conclusion

The history filmmakers of the millennium were not originating from scratch a problem-solving dramatising aesthetic but instead were able, if they chose, to seek out a tool kit to help television explore history in an era before the existence of moving-picture archives. There were examples of sensuousness accompanying sense to be found, if only filmmakers were aware of them. *Culloden, The War Game or Wisconsin Death Trip* did not need to be direct precursors of the dramatisations to come, since they contained inspirational ingredients: in vision, in sound, in performance, in narrative structure. Drama in its various guises; amateur actors for Watkins' team; professional voices and a dramatically emotive soundtrack for *Death Trip*: such innovations could provide some solutions and inspire others.

Culloden and *War Game* are clearly the central case studies of this chapter on progenitors. In terms of their sophistication, a director in the early 2000s coming across them would be like a Dark Ages Briton discovering traces of a Roman bath system, underfloor heating, or an arrow-straight road. Although reaching the same heights as *Culloden* was still some way off, in the early 2000s to achieve work of a similar calibre was a known ambition among documentary filmmakers.

But as we return to the 2000s, it is appropriate to contextualise the new dramatisations within the macro level of broadcasting: in terms of the evolution of the independent production company, the technological advances that aided the aesthetic revolution, and the explosion of choices available for the representation of history. The corpus of films covered in this chapter continues to offer an extraordinarily diverse mix of dramatisation techniques. The next chapter focuses on four films made between 2000 and 2004 that might appear to have very little in common. Some are for Channel 4, some for BBC; some are ancient history, others are almost contemporary; some are heavy with dialogue, others less so. But they all have two things in common that distinguish them: first, they are all dramatised history documentaries; and second, they are all produced by a single independent production company. This raises a question that will be answered in the next chapter: was the growing canon of work being driven by one or more auteurs?

Notes

1 Watkins, 2001, cited by John R. Cook, '"Don't Forget to Look into the Camera!": Peter Watkins' Approach to Acting with Facts', *Studies in Documentary Film*, 4:3 (2010), p. 240.
2 Andro Linklater, 'Fade Far Away, Dissolve, and Quite Forget', *Spectator* (10 April 1993), p. 40.
3 John Prebble, *Culloden* (London: Secker & Warburg, 1961), p. 10.
4 *Ibid.*, p. 24.
5 Cook, '"Don't Forget to Look into the Camera!"', p. 227.
6 A 1998 Radio Times readers' poll voted *Cathy Come Home* the 'best single television drama', and a 2000 industry poll rated it as the second-best British television programme ever made, after *Fawlty Towers*.

7 Cook, '"Don't Forget to Look into the Camera!"',, p. 228.
8 *Ibid.*
9 Tony Rose, 'Faces of the "45"', *Amateur Cine World*, 8:25 (1964), p. 834.
10 Watkins cited by Rose, *ibid.*
11 Stephen Lipkin, *Docudrama Performs the Past: Arenas of Argument in Films Based on True Stories* (Newcastle: Cambridge Scholars Publishing, 2011), p. 1.
12 Watkins, cited by Rose, 'Faces of the "45"', p. 837.
13 *Ibid.*
14 Watkins, cited by Cook, 'Archive Aesthetics and the Historical Imaginary', p. 230.
15 SAs (Supporting Artists), as they are known in the industry, used to be called 'extras', before it was considered a belittling term.
16 D. Marlborough, 'To Arms Brothers, They Were Blacklegs at Culloden', *Daily Mail* (22 December 1964).
17 David Chater, TV Review, *The Times* (January 2001).
18 Cook, '"Don't Forget to Look into the Camera!"', p. 239.
19 David Chater, TV Review, *The Times* (August 2005).
20 Tony Shaw, 'The BBC, the State and Cold War Culture: The Case of Television's The War Game (1965)', *The English Historical Review*, 121:494 (2006), pp. 1351–1384 (p. 1356).
21 *Ibid.*, p. 1357.
22 *Ibid.*, p. 1361.
23 *Ibid.*, p. 1370.
24 *Ibid.*
25 *Ibid.*
26 *Ibid.*, p. 1371.
27 *Ibid.*, p. 1388.
28 *Ibid.*, p. 1403.
29 Cook, p. 231.
30 John Corner, 'Archive Aesthetics and the Historical Imaginary: *Wisconsin Death Trip*', *Screen*, 47:3 (2006), pp. 291–306 (p. 291).
31 Derek Paget, *True Stories: Documentary Drama on Radio, Screen and State* (Manchester: Manchester University Press, 1990), p. 26.
32 Corner, 'Archive Aesthetics and the Historical Imaginary', p. 292.
33 *Ibid.*, p. 293.
34 *Ibid.*
35 *Ibid.*, p. 303.
36 *Ibid.*, p. 304.

4

2001–2003: Was the flowering of dramatised history documentary led by auteurs?

Introduction

> There are many different ways to tell stories of the past.
> (Alex Graham, 2020)

This chapter charts the expansion of dramatised history documentary through a series of different aesthetic choices made in the industry that led to an increasingly successful genre. I shall explore the field of historical programming in the formative years of 2001 to 2003 through the prism of one particularly ambitious independent production company, Wall to Wall TV. This was a period of innovation, according to Alex Graham, CEO of Wall to Wall, who does not attribute the ambition just to his own company, but also to the commissioners and controllers of channels: '2001 to 2003 was a golden age in the innovative powers of both the independent production sector but also the brave commissioning of broadcasters', he recalls. Both Graham and Wall to Wall are the focus of this chapter because they offer a unique context within which the growth in popularity of history drama documentary can be best studied.

Analysis of Wall to Wall's work might also begin to bring a shape to an amorphous and disparate body of films that has previously defied definition. Furthermore, if Alex Graham was to be regarded as an *auteur* in the same way that François Truffaut argued for Alfred Hitchcock to be considered an *auteur*, then perhaps the rest of the films made in this period could be seen as following in his creative wake.[1] It should be noted that this *auteur* approach appears to conflict with some of the current writer's beliefs that films should not be credited to a superstar director. This work has gone to some lengths to credit instead the production companies that surround them, for filmmaking is a collective enterprise. It is therefore consistent to look at the potential auteurism of a collective of individuals within successful production companies from this period. Perhaps we might discover an auteur production company, and through its prism, a whole series of other *auteur* production companies emerging.

As a useful context, Wall to Wall TV was, and remains at the time of writing, arguably the dominant force in all modes of offering history on British television. It was the creator of the very successful Living History franchise, building upon the enormous success of its own *1900 House* (Channel 4, 2000), and was also behind the single most successful celebrity-focused history franchise, *Who Do You Think You Are* (BBC, 2004–present), which continues to this day. Alongside these pathways, Wall to Wall also made some of the most innovative films of the early history dramatisation corpus, which will be the focus of this chapter. The drama documentaries, while very successful at the time of their transmission, have not consolidated their reputations to date and are now largely forgotten. Yet it is the continued purpose of this book to reclaim them as a canon of work that will contribute to a growing notion of a new genre.

Through the study of these films, it will be argued that Graham and Wall to Wall radically influenced the evolutionary curve of history programming by means of their innovations within the drama documentary mode. This was achieved by Graham's commitment to the challenge of, in his own words, 'filming the unfilmable'. This brings to mind Lipkin's belief, in his book *Docudrama Performs the Past*, that 'a basic function of docudrama is to make visible the known but unseen, to bring to light the hidden, the otherwise inaccessible'.[2] Graham was always interested in making visible 'the unseen' and bringing to light 'the hidden ... the otherwise inaccessible' throughout his television career, but this was especially evident in his historical drama documentaries. He believed that the drama documentary mode was appropriate for a number of the problems set by the inaccessibility of history specifically – confirming Lipkin's view, set out in an earlier book, *Real Emotional Logic* (2002), where he suggests that 'docudrama, as a form of historical film, can have historical value to the extent that it offers motivated, truthful invention, close proximations and analogies, and contributes constructively to the debate surrounding efforts to visualise or understand the past'.[3]

The four films that Graham himself regards as truly innovative, in the context of 'filming the unfilmable', will be analysed in this chapter. *Smallpox 2002* (BBC, 2001) realised the thing that hadn't yet happened; *George Orwell: A Life in Pictures* (BBC, 2003) realised an archive where none existed; and both *Neanderthal* (Channel 4, 2001) and *Ancient Egyptians* (Channel 4, 2003) realised the sights and sounds of personal drama within deep history. These films also offer a link to one of the final parts of this book, in Chapter 6, where an analysis is made of Wall to Wall's return to drama documentary to produce one of the greatest drama documentaries of the modern era: the Oscar-winning *Man on Wire* (BBC, 2008).

A single theme focusing on Graham and Wall to Wall provides this book with more than a chronological shape, covering the period from 2000 to 2010. This chapter also offers a unique route through the institutional context of history on television, alongside television's aesthetic evolutions and its representations of history, thus bringing research material to bear on three of the book's research questions. On reflection, it has been a privilege to have gained sufficient access to Graham; he has agreed to be interviewed many times, between 2019 and 2022, in various locations around London and, latterly during the pandemic, on Zoom. Where possible, his narrative has been cross-referenced with the producer/directors who worked with him and the executives at the broadcasters who worked alongside him.

Wall to Wall TV: emergence from institutional and technological innovation

As in previous chapters, I take a granular approach to the structure of the television industry, considering the macro to micro levels, which is especially necessary since the primary focus of the chapter is better to understand the role of Wall to Wall TV as an indie (as the independent production company will henceforth be termed), and better to determine its muscularity – its ability to both make and sell exciting new products in a burgeoning international television marketplace.

Indies had emerged in the 1990s, with the opening up of the BBC to indies, due to the imposition of the 25 per cent quota, being a slow and painful process. The quota was introduced in the Broadcasting Act of 1990, but it took almost a decade for the BBC to come to terms with that reality. Arguably the appointment of Wall to Wall's founding partner, Jane Root, to run the Independent Commissioning Group at the BBC marked the BBC's final acceptance that the world had changed.[4] Graham remembers this period well in terms of 'competitive forces driving innovation':

> What I think was interesting about this period was Channel 4 deciding to take on the BBC at its own game of high-end specialist factual programming. The likes of Tim Gardam, Janice Hadlow, Sara Ramsden et al felt they had for the first time – in Juniper, Darlow Smithson, Windfall, Lion, Wall to Wall etc. – the creative resources to take on the BBC, which had until then had it all its own way. The result was a perfect example of competitive forces driving innovation. As has been pointed out the genius of the system was that the broadcasters were not competing for cash; they were competing for talent. (Graham, 2022)

New companies rose quickly on the backs of a single commission and soon became hubs of employment in competition with in-house jobs at the BBC. Juniper TV was one such, responsible for *The Great Plague* (Channel 4, 2001) and *Bareknuckle Boxer* (Channel 4, 2003). Lion TV was another, specialising in glossy international co-productions such as *Lawrence of Arabia* (PBS, 2002) and *Medici: Godfathers of the Renaissance* (PBS, 2003). Oxford TV, Windfall Films, RDF, Darlow Smithson, and Tiger Aspect are among the dozen or so early independent makers of multiple documentaries that incorporated some drama.

Wall to Wall, however, is unparalleled among its drama documentary peers, having won BAFTAs, Emmys, Griersons, RTSs, and, in 2009, an Academy Award for its drama documentaries. Graham, as CEO, would be considered by any neutral observer as the pre-eminent driving force behind the success of the indies in this period, and he has been the chairman of the Producers Alliance for Cinema and Television (PACT), the trade association for the UK film and television industry.

The institutional context of Wall to Wall's arrival into the drama documentary mode of historical programme making will be examined first. It is a story that is representative of many of the indies that enjoyed the same opportunities at the turn of the millennium, and Graham is a uniquely informed narrator for such a narrative. Graham had helped found Wall to Wall in 1987 to run *The Media Show* (C4, 1987–1991) with Jane Root and Michael Jackson.[5] The company had been a provider mostly of arts and science shows until 1997, when Jane Root left for the BBC. There had been 'a small spat over her shares', admits Graham, and he did not receive work from her for a number of years. He turned to Channel 4 and was commissioned to produce the lion's share of Janice Hadlow's seventeeth-century season, *A Century of Troubles* (the episodes *Treason* and *War*). But, according to Graham, his most productive relationship at Channel 4 was with Sara Ramsden, Commissioner of Science, for whom, the year before, he had conceived the hit *1900 House*, transmitted in 2000. This did not employ dramatic reconstruction but was nevertheless an extremely innovative 'living history/science' format, sending a family to live in a late-Victorian house in late-Victorian conditions. It proved a considerable ratings success.[6] It was through Ramsden that Graham had *Neanderthal* commissioned, 'but to understand how *Neanderthal* and its ilk worked', says Graham, 'you have to understand the growth of the independent sector under Channel 4'.

The growth of the indie sector strongly influenced the culture of innovation that followed, and the indies in turn grew out of the emergence of Channel 4. According to Graham, who lived through these changes, Channel 4 had emerged from the 1975 Annan commission on the future of television, in which the idea of a fourth channel was proposed. The early years of Channel 4 were troubled, as Graham confirms. It was labelled by the press 'Channel Bore, Channel Snore', until Michael Grade arrived in 1988 and raised its market share to a very competitive 10 per cent. Margaret Thatcher, who now favoured the competitive new channel as a Conservative creation, set up the Peacock Committee in the mid-1980s to discuss the increase in the number of independent production companies that aimed to compete with the broadcasters for the production of their programmes. This contributed to the breakup of the monopoly of the BBC and ITV – the latter of which, Roy Thomson had notoriously claimed, 'was a licence to print money'.[7] Peacock recommended a 40 per cent quota for independents at all of the channels; as Graham has previously indicated, in the 1990 Communications Act, only 25 per cent was passed, but it 'was enough to keep Wall to Wall and other indies afloat', according to Graham. This quota ensured that independent production companies were flourishing in the 1990s, with a guarantee that at least 25 per cent of all programming would pass through their newly established company books.

Meanwhile, Jackson and then Root were given lucrative posts at the BBC. Graham never wanted to join the bureaucracy: 'it was a terrible business to be in, with a thousand producers and two or three commissioners, but I avoided having to work at the BBC. I was interested in television as a creative medium, what you could do with it.' Graham had taken a considerable risk, resisting the lure of a well-paid, well-pensioned job at the BBC in favour of the independent life of a production-company supremo. It was a decision that reflects his sense of independence and, above all, his refusal to follow an established route – aspects of his approach that will be discussed throughout this chapter. Ultimately, this decision would prove timely, creatively rewarding, and very profitable.

After the growth of the indie sector, the next important industrial change that led to drama documentary innovation, Graham says, was technology: '*Neanderthal* to a lesser extent, but *Ancient Egyptians* to a greater, could not have been made without the development of computer-generated imagery (CGI).' At some point in the 1990s, perhaps even across the whole decade, technology changed. Rather as medicine and industry benefits from military developments, television is a hand-me-down of the movies, and science programming as a discipline was the beneficiary at first, before history. The theatrical blockbuster *Jurassic Park* (1993) didn't just take creature animation to a new level; the art of compositing those wire frames into plausible *surroundings* made substantial leaps as well.[8] The Science department at the BBC borrowed the idea and launched *Walking with Dinosaurs* (BBC, 1999), utilising a new creature-animation television department at a visual-effects house, Framestore, based in central London. The BBC could afford to use the wire-frame and compositing effects thanks to an economy of scale over six episodes. Wire frames are an expensive way of creating a single dinosaur movement: raising its head to eat, lowering it to nuzzle, and moving its legs can be three individual movements. But when repeated in a variety of different locations, or between an adult or a baby, or multiplied in a herd, the extra expense is negligible. Similarly, the composite of a volcanic landscape peppered with ferns and monkey puzzle trees reduces in cost the more times a dinosaur is placed within it. Close ups are achieved by using a puppet dinosaur head, teeth, eyes, claw, foot – to constantly reassure the audience that the wide shot they just saw has real physical presence: steam came from nostrils, the eyeball rolled and reflected light, and feet stamped on volcanic soil, shifting dirt and causing powder to rise. All these effects seem obvious to us now, but in the mid-1990s they were revolutionary.

It is also crucial to note that the BBC could afford all these new technologies because of the emergence of BBC Worldwide, which increased factual budgets by pre-selling big BBC productions around the world.[9] The Natural History department led the way, but History and Science followed quickly with films such as *Pyramid* (BBC, 2001). If one can rebuild a pyramid, why not rebuild a whole Egyptian city, or a Neanderthal camp? I argue that 'sensuousness' was now available to all at a price, though admittedly a far higher price than factual departments were used to. What the BBC brought to the equation was to contribute the 'sense' of great research – into both life on earth 35,000 years ago, and life on the Nile 6,500 years ago. The ability to discover the 'traces of the past', as described by the history film scholar Robert Rosenstone, had been afforded by technological advances intersecting with historical research. Rosenstone uses this key phrase in *History on Film/Film on History*: 'Like the work of written history, the documentary "constitutes" facts by selecting traces of the past and enfolding them into a narrative' (2006, p. 79).[10]

The next technological change was the shift from television's traditional and expensive 16 mm film to video tape and then to digital, and a simultaneous shift to more flexible lenses, as was seen in *The Great Plague* (Channel 4, 2001) – although the new technology was not yet being fully exploited. At this time, however, cultural and institutional developments encouraged the loosening of another blockage in a long-atrophied filming system: the actors' union, Equity, began to relax their strict rules that had put a block on filming with amateurs after *The War Game* in the mid 1960s. If documentaries were to start invading the world of drama, a deal would need to be struck. The negotiation with Equity was slow and hard-fought and took place between 1995 and 2005. By the end of that period, little-known actors were performing all over historical films on TV, and big stars were joining in the fray if they had some down-time in their schedules. It was the agents who relented, in the long run. Too many actors, too few TV dramas, and a native film industry in decline, mixed with a Blairite acceptance of the new market economy, brought actors to the place they sought – a place of work.

Now the scene was set for Wall to Wall and Alex Graham to take advantage of these confluences and bring them to bear variously in *Neanderthal* and *Ancient Egyptians*, *Smallpox 2002* and *Orwell: A Life in Pictures*, at both Channel 4 and the BBC, between the years 2001 and 2003. This period is described by Graham as 'the years of innovation'.

Neanderthal and *Ancient Egyptians* are the first films to be studied here, as they were comprehensively witnessed by director Tony Mitchell and his wife-to-be producer, Ailsa Orr. They were involved in the inner workings of Wall to Wall as an indie team working with Alex Graham as the driver of historical drama documentary, and they offer some clues as to the culture that surrounded him as they attempted to 'film the unfilmable'.

Neanderthal (Channel 4, 2001)

Brief summary: *A dramatic reconstruction of the last imagined Neanderthal family troop on Earth as they come face-to-face with their nemesis, Cro-Magnon man. Using CGI, prosthetics, and a created language, this film was considered the height of originality.*

Despite improving technologies and cultures, some concepts for bringing the past back to life were considered too outlandish to attempt, and this would especially have applied to a film set in a period best described as deep, dark prehistory. In the late 1990s, the rational observation of animals within *Walking with Dinosaurs* was in development, but the notion of telling the story of one of our ancestors in a way that involved emotion was a considerable stretch. Lipkin has best defined how the mix of drama and documentary aids the recovery of emotions from the past: 'the docudramatic mode of representation becomes a logical means of recovering the physical sensation and emotions that are arguably important keys to understanding our past'.[11] Like many others, Graham could see that natural history was a leader in the field, to be followed by history, but where he was distinctive was in his intuition that this opportunity could be successfully exploited through emotional narrative. Graham's second skill was in his ability to navigate the opportunities available.

In commercial terms, Graham noted that in order better to follow the success of natural history, and to pre-sell internationally, a history idea should have science at its heart.

Graham was looking for ideas that intersected history and science with his international distributor Paul Sowerbutts, who worked for the ITV distributor ITEL (1993–2005), bankrolled by ITV's natural history strand *Survival* (1961–2001).[12] ITEL had been working closely with Graham for a decade, and it had been a blow to discover that the BBC was planning *Walking with Dinosaurs*, but they still had buyers lined up for something similar. 'Then someone suggests *Neanderthal*', recalls Graham. Wall to Wall had some experience in prehistory, producing around a hundred episodes of *Paleoworld* (1994–1997) for TLC.[13] There had been a small amount of impressionistic drama reconstruction in those programmes, but no CGI.

Graham's distinctive approach is evident in his preparation for a film, his devotion to research, his fearlessness in the face of radicalism, and his commitment to what he terms 'authenticity', the definition of which will be further explored in this chapter. Before the decision was taken as to what aesthetic to employ, Graham assembled his young team: Tony Mitchell (known as Mitch) and his assistant producer, Ailsa Orr, both of whom agreed to be interviewed for this book. Orr recalls Graham shutting them into a meeting room with a tape assembly of good and bad prehistory, including *Quest for Fire* (1981) and *2001: A Space Odyssey* (1968). 'Every time we pitched an idea [of] more than one sentence, Graham would shake his head, and leave the room. This went on for days. Then we realised it was mostly because the conceit was too drama, too movie', says Orr.

It is ironic that drama was the new buzzword in documentary-making, and yet Graham continued to eschew its employment for some time. He felt that the audience needed to believe what they were seeing in the way that they believed they were seeing 'found footage' in the hit movie *The Blair Witch Project* (1999). This was a radical departure from other horror films, and it was defined by its sense of creepy 'authenticity'. But Graham admits he was not able to determine the appropriate new style for *Neanderthal* himself. As a producer, he claims he can more often see what he does *not* want, more than what he does. Hence, he knew he needed to rebuff Mitch's and Orr's suggestions until he was convinced. In terms of a leadership style, according to Mitch and Orr, Graham *looked* presidential – that is, that he would lead from the front with an authorial idea, imposed from his great height at 6'5". But Mitch and Orr believe that, in actuality, he was more of a chairman than a president, in that he would court opinion from those around him and would not relent until he had received the best proposal. The observational documentary style of *Blair Witch* provided the clue that unlocked the conundrum. The team decided to return to their roots as documentary filmmakers, as Mitch explains: 'we were going to send a natural-history film crew back 35,000 years to observe Neanderthals in their natural habitat'. It was a found-footage concept, created to feel as if it had been bleached by time and ice, giving a rawness to its aesthetic. Graham instinctively enjoyed the radical nature of the idea, and also rejoiced in what Paget has called 'mischief making'. In his article on Stephen Frears' and Peter Kosminsky's documentary dramas about Tony Blair, Paget suggested that 'there is also a heightened awareness in difficult times of the ability of docudrama (especially in the hands of a Frears or a Kosminsky) to be playful, provocative, questioning and critical in its representation of events and issues that the powerful would rather conceal'.[14] This specifically refers to an anti-authoritarian, political 'playfulness', but it also describes Graham's approach to any authority, across the spectrum of his dramatised documentaries. Later, in *Smallpox 2002*, for example, Graham takes a more specifically political view. In *Neanderthal*'s case, the playfulness was in his irreverent approach, to tempt an audience into thinking they are watching 'found footage' from 35,000 years ago. The intention was never literal, but a wry 'come-hither': come and see what was found buried in the ice.

Regarding *Neanderthal*, Channel 4's Sara Ramsden could see the potential immediately, and she believed the messiness of the observational-style documentary suited the youthful brand of Channel 4. Graham, the businessman, then 'pulled the budget together from Discovery/ NDR(Germany), with ITEL selling other territories', showing that he needed an idea that was commercially modish, backed up by a filmmaking concept that was striking in its simplicity and based on what Mitch describes as 'a dedication to what Alex calls authenticity'.

The pursuit of Graham's 'authenticity' required everybody working at Wall to Wall to familiarise themselves with the latest in current thinking on a subject. Lipkin argues that 'docudrama offers an appealing representation of actuality because of its coherence. Its representation of history does not pretend to be documentary in nature ... its validity stems from its proximity to its subject.'[15] 'Proximity to its subject' is what Mitch would understand as authenticity derived from considerable research. Lipkin further describes how this quality of 'proximity' is fundamental throughout the filmmaking process, described below in comprehensible shorthand:

Proximity is a key word for historical dedication: Proximity to pre-existing texts
Proximity to living sources
Proximity to public knowledge
Pictorial proximity – to production design of the time
Proximity to temporal order – a decent chronology/plot that messes with it?
The closer a work's proximity to its referents, the greater will be its effectiveness as discourse, as persuasive argument.[16]

London is, fortunately, a hub for museums and libraries, and a place of intersection for academic discourse, and the location enabled Mitch and Orr to achieve a high degree of proximity, considering the immense age of the subject matter. They discovered that the foremost expert on Neanderthals was Chris Stringer at the Natural History Museum, who told them that 'the existing Neanderthal bones could fit into a single suitcase', recalls Orr. But this restriction forced the two filmmakers to make a lot out of a little and led them away from attempting to cover clans of Neanderthals through the ages – in Gibraltar, France, and Eastern Europe, for instance. Instead, they chose the 'Cock and Key Alley' approach, constructing a narrative around the last clan of Neanderthals to share the planet with Cro-Magnons (the term used at the time for early modern humans in Europe). This microcosmic approach would make the narrative simpler to follow and enable the viewer to make an emotional investment in one extended family bravely resisting their tragic ending. From each of the bones inside the imaginative 'suitcase', they derived characters. One bone in particular showed an older male, Mitch explains, whose injuries were those of a 'modern-day rodeo rider, full of wear and tear'. This 'rodeo' male was perhaps too old to have survived without aid, and that indicated compassion within the clan, 'so we built the clan around this older male', continues Mitch. Hayden White would have approved of such narrativity being imposed on such a slender primary source.

That set of Neanderthal bones lands one in a culture long past. As White notes, 'the text summons up a "substance," operates in the domain of memory rather than of dream or fantasy and unfolds under the sign of "the real" rather than that of the "imaginary"'. Now that the list has become real, it needs a narrative: 'it is because real events do not offer themselves as stories that their narrativisation is so difficult. What is involved, then, in that finding of the "true story," that discovery of the "real story" within or behind the events that come to us in the chaotic form of "historical records"?'[17] With this argument, White suggests that humans need to turn whatever fragments of evidence they can find into a story that makes sense of their own world. None of this theory was a conscious part of Mitch and Orr's quest, but they knew, in practical terms, that they needed to turn the suitcase of bones into a narrative that might well be a construct but would enable a television audience to come to a subject matter about which it knew very little, if anything. To attract such an audience would be an achievement, and so Mitch and Orr adopted a narrativisation that would enable the documentary to feel more like a drama.

Some of the bones in the hypothetical suitcase suggested that females were involved in hunting, their teeth adapted for skinning animal pelts, their jaws expanded for holding the pelts while they employed sharpened flints. The ninety-minute film was a series of extrapolations from such thin evidence, with composite characters drawn from imaginative leaps. Yet it should be remembered that *Walking with Dinosaurs* was also drawn from similar leaps of the imagination. If the filmmakers had not taken these risks, modern television audiences would have been denied access to these prehistorical inhabitants altogether; the representation of prehistory in *Neanderthal* must be said to have been bravely attempted, given the paucity of evidence available. The filmmakers took a risk, for instance, when they suggested that Cro-magnons and Neanderthals may well have interbred, and the Natural History Museum was deeply concerned by such an assertion, yet this is now an accepted fact. The 'sense' of the film was extraordinary considering the amount of evidence available.

The tone and content of the film may be understood by looking at the pre-title sequence. The opening shots are of a bleached-out windswept landscape with snow falling. Woolly mammoth roam, as the first intertitle appears: '35,000 years ago. Southwest France.' The font is broken and jagged as if confirming the 'found-footage' nature of the film. Down in the valley, two Neanderthal men hunt a deer with spears. The narrator, actor Kenneth Cranham, intones: 'They were one of the most successful human species ever. For over 250,000 years they dominated Europe, a continent ravaged by ice ages, and stalked by wild animals.' Images appear of a baby being born in a cave. 'Then 35,000 years ago, they faced the ultimate challenge: another human species. Only one would survive.' The hunters come face to face with a taller human figure. 'This is the story of the last time that two species of human shared this planet.'

It is an epic narrative crystallised into less than one and a half minutes, showing that the inherited Hollywood skill of the pre-title was truly mastered at this time. The rest of the film is evocative of a time before memory, a compelling vision of the last clan of seven Neanderthals, driven to the point of extinction by the harsh winters of the Ice Age ('where France is 25 degrees below zero, the equivalent of modern Canada') and competition from Homo sapiens and other predators. Building a narrative from one microcosm, this conceit of a family driven from their home in search of refuge is television 'sense' meeting 'sensuousness'. The 'found-footage' drama fills 80 per cent of the screen time, with scientific inserts that remind the audience of the evidence – a series of bones filmed by motion control in a dark, cave-like environment, for instance, always 'warranting the dramatic choices', as Lipkin refers to such an approach. 'Docudrama represents past events, warranted moral structures, moral perspectives with clear links to actuality', Lipkin notes, approaches that 'ultimately provide the presence as well as the coherence of history'.[18] Lipkin explains what he means by 'warrants': 'the viewer is invited to accept the argument that re-creation warrants, that what we might see might have "really" happened in much this way'.[19] Furthermore, he refers to 'warrants' as a noun as well as a verb in the following sentence: 'warrants forward the claims the film will make'.[20] Thus, *Neanderthal* is offering proof, of some kind, that this branch of our ancestry existed, was intelligent and compassionate, and died out in the face of competition with a rival that hunted better in packs. Lipkin concludes the 'warranting' notion by defining two rules: the first is that this story deserves to be told, and secondly that it must be told in this way. *Neanderthal* answers both: the Neanderthals' reputation as brutish and ugly needed to be corrected, and what better way to tell their story than through a close observation, as if in the found footage of a natural history programme?

From the filmmakers' perspective, the structure is an emotional contrivance by Mitch and Orr to hold their audience through to the end of a ninety-minute film, which, when played on Channel 4 with all its adverts, fills two hours of viewing time. The story is structured to take the viewer on the arc of a family's journey, from a female joining the family group and then giving birth, to an ending which shows the old 'rodeo' male struggling to keep up with the hunt for food. It is a bitter-sweet structure that offers not just ninety minutes spent in the company of the past but engagement with a tale that is essentially tragic. The narrator confirms that the end of the species was not inevitable: 'if their birth rate had been 2% higher or their mortality rate 2% lower, they would have survived'. As the rodeo male dies, the narrative concludes; there is a mournful 'sensuousness' that accompanies the passing, which confirms the 'found footage' dramatic mode as an ideal story-telling cache.

The attempted aesthetic of the series has attracted criticism. Davidson calls it 'ape mask prosthetics', and Mitch accepts that the technology surrounding prosthetics has moved on since 2000. 'It does feel quite dated in that respect. We used latex foam that has been surpassed by recent developments in silicon, which allows the skin to radiate through' (Mitchell, 2020). According to Mitch, the make-up was so time-intensive, it determined the entire schedule. Each character took five hours to be made up, so 'contrary to usual practice, we shot the close ups first, then the mid shots and finally the wide shots when the prosthetics were hanging in rags. It didn't help that we were filming in Ireland, where it never stopped raining', says Mitch. Jez Harris of Crawly Creatures, who worked on *Walking with Dinosaurs*, supervised the prosthetics, and increased the speed of production once it was clear that the factual budget of £600k/hour (for a two-hour Channel 4 film) was placing ever-increasing pressure on the schedule.

Graham's practice of requiring the most up-to-date research to be carried out for any of his productions at Wall to Wall was evident throughout the rehearsal and shooting process of *Neanderthal*. Orr and Mitch found an actress from the prehistoric adventure film *Quest for Fire* to teach the amateur actors how to speak. The language, licensed from the film, was based on an Indonesian language that repeated words. It had been devised by Anthony Burgess and Desmond Morris and was a sincere attempt at imagining the sounds of the past.[21] The actress, Ailsa Burke, developed the supposed gait of the Neanderthals with help from the Natural History Museum, and she passed this physicality onto a cast of non-professional film actors. 'We mixed some theatre actors with a couple of Irish rugby players', explains Mitch, 'so we got around Equity, and in retrospect we felt that we just about got away with it with the whole film actually.'

From a technical perspective, Mitch eschewed the use of video cameras, agreeing with Schama that he abhorred the plasticity of video. Instead, Mitch sought the textural nature of film, which he believed made the image seem painterly and obscure, evocative of a distant past. Graham supported this artistic requirement, always backing up his creatives, and supplied two Aaton 16 mm cameras. As if the image was not obscured enough, every time the camera operator Ed Kadysewski set his position, Mitch would drag an uprooted tree in front of it so the film would look determinedly observational. Occasionally, the camera would move in for contrivedly close shots to explain certain key details, such as the craft of jewellery-making, that potentially seem at odds with the key conceit. But overall, the film courageously maintained its 'found footage' rawness and this strategy was backed to the hilt by Graham. The 16 mm film was processed from negative to print with a bleach bypass that was irreversible. Graham knew this was his director's aesthetic choice and authorised it without sharing the information with the executives at Channel 4. This kind of maverick production choice is unthinkable in today's highly pressurised global television culture. Mitch remains buoyed by Graham's loyalty in this regard: 'it couldn't happen today, with all of the interference one gets from execs now. I wanted to show that this was found footage from Ice Age Europe, and just couldn't risk missing the opportunity to print it that way from the outset.'

Graham, who is credited as the producer, told Mitch and Orr that he had re-mortgaged his house to make *Neanderthal*, and he kept the commissioners Sara Ramsden and Charles Furneaux at arm's length.[22] According to Mitch and Orr, Graham 'was loyal, and stuck to his guns. We did not know how the narration would work, whose perspective it was, and Alex would not let them lean on us till we had cut and recut and got the match on screen for our original mission statement.' This defence of a creative team by the head of a production company whose investment is very personal is a very rare event. In most experiences, the production company usually sides with the channel, which is paying the bills. The legendary skill of Richard Bradley at Lion TV or John Smithson at Darlow Smithson is their ability to negotiate successfully between broadcaster and creative filmmaker through diplomacy that is often wrongly seen as a submission to the broadcaster. In

Graham's case, there is more often a belligerence that pushes back against the broadcaster until the creatives have fully determined their visionary process. Despite this book's rejection of the practice of short-handing films by the names of their authors, be it director, producer, or writer (in the case of Watkins, for example), Graham's professional behaviour begs the question as to whether Graham and his indie company should be credited in this way. He was certainly distinctive in his approach both to commerce and to creativity – in his determination to 'film the unfilmable'.

Neanderthal received mixed reviews but was applauded within Channel 4 for its innovative conceit and its ambitious aesthetic, resulting in Wall to Wall being commissioned to make more feature-length science/history films for Channel 4, the height of success for a hand-to-mouth production company. There was to be no repeat of prehistorical subject matter for Wall to Wall, but instead an approach to redefine a particular type of ancient history that had been consistently successful on television: Egyptology. Some of the same factors remained in play, however. The concept of making a series of personal dramas in the antiquarian past was another decision to 'film the unfilmable'. Graham remained the driver, his loyalty keeping Mitch at the helm, to help secure Ramsden as the commissioner. They were now a 'battle-hardened team', according to Graham, as the scale of the enterprise increased exponentially.

Ancient Egyptians (Channel 4, 2003)

> Brief summary: *A four-part, glossy, epic series of tales from the entire two-thousand-year stretch of Ancient Egypt's civilisation. The stories are taken from court records deciphered from ancient papyri and are presented as a compelling collection of ancient mysteries. They are performed in* the original language *by huge casts and set within a CGI replication of how Ancient Egypt may have once looked.*

Ancient Egyptians is what Graham calls 'the apotheosis' of the dramatised documentaries that Wall to Wall made, and while I do not infer that he means an 'apotheosis' in terms of every aspect of aesthetic creativity, it was no doubt a financial apotheosis, from the perspective of a producer travelling the world and drumming up a vast co-production package. This was the series that best displays Graham's ability to build relationships world-wide, to intuit a subject matter that was of the moment, and to create a persuasive package that indicated a striking and radical approach – one that would excite both large viewerships and critical praise in each of the territories that were pre-sold.

Graham, ever the pragmatist, had a product to sell that has always had international appeal: Ancient Egypt. The subject has always crossed the boundary between science and history and, as Graham notes, 'usually involves the solving of a mystery', no matter how spurious. One could add it to the list of history top sellers: Henry, Hitler and Hieroglyphics. But unsurprisingly, Graham's pitch included a radical innovation that was unlike anything his rivals possessed. He offered a four-part series derived from papyrus records in the British Museum and from stone carvings at the Temple of Karnak in the Valley of the Kings, constituting an appealing slice of what Paget calls 'cultural tourism'.

But Graham was, and is not, a 'cultural tourist', and so he added his radical twist. Each one of these primary source records, transcribed from papyri, had been chosen so as to offer narratives not of Ancient Egypt but of *Ancient Egyptians*, the title of the series. The stories would not just be those of pharaohs but of everyday Egyptians from the past – the trial of a tomb robber, for example, and the records of a war correspondent. As an added selling point, *Ancient Egyptians* was to deliver what Lipkin calls the 'physical sensation and emotions' through the use of the actual words recorded.[23] It would be like reciting the Odyssey in Ancient Greek.

This was an immensely bold step for Graham and shows his confidence, *1900 House* and *Neanderthal* having been considerable successes for Wall to Wall and their broadcasters. To the battle-hardened team of Graham, Mitch, and Ramsden, this spoken dialogue in ancient language was another confirmation of what they referred to as 'an authenticity of sound and visual immersion'. Their belief was that only Wall to Wall would take such a radical new step: to ask the viewer to watch a foreign-language film on terrestrial television in the United Kingdom (and beyond). This was a step beyond Paget's 'cultural tourism' where the story is translated into 'easy-to-understand' modern vernacular for the tourists. Graham's intention was to offer the opposite. He was convinced that the Reithian imperative was to challenge unsuspecting viewers with the vernacular of Ancient Egypt, thus immersing them in an imagined journey back in time and space. Viewers would hear a court case revealing the corruption of Thebes' society; they would be present as generals discuss tactics. While there would be a narrator to act as hand-holder and interpreter, the primary sources offered such a unique opportunity, it was felt, that it would be wrong not to attempt such a feat. As Graham had said when he chose not to take the commissioning path at the BBC, he was truly interested 'in what television could do', and this had extended into what history on television could do. Graham hoped that the excitement of battles and tomb robberies would enable the audience to take that step away from their tourist guide who translated everything – in what Hayden White called a 'presentist' presentation of the past. Instead, they were following what White called an 'antiquarian' stance in evoking the language of the time ('antiquarians' are those who rejoice in the foreignness of the past). It was a bold step, especially for such an early moment in the drama documentary evolution.

The ambitious drama concept would prove to be expensive at over £1 million/hour and so needed international partners. It is testament to Graham's persuasiveness that the eventual co-production was built upon money from C4, Discovery, NDR (Germany), Canal Plus (France), and Asahi (Japan). For factual television, this was one of the biggest budgets ever pulled together: £4.5 million for four hours and, according to Graham, it felt like 'a Hollywood movie that threatened to get out of hand'. The team assembled, with Ben Goold as producer, replacing Ailsa Orr, who had been co-opted to the BBC to help liaise between the CGI team and the scientists on *Walking with Dinosaurs*.

The documentary-mode parts were filmed all over Egypt – in Luxor, Aswan, Cairo – while the drama-mode part was filmed in Morocco, which has an established support system for film crews making all manner of 'swords and sandals' films. One of the problems on set in Morocco was the language, and not just because Morocco is francophone. As Mitch recalls, the key to filming the series was finding a 'Danish guy who studied the ancient script, and who taught the actors to speak in an ancient Egyptian language, literally verbatim'. But it meant that either ancient Egyptian or Moroccan French was being spoken on set, with almost no English at all, leaving Mitch and Continuity having to guess when a sentence had been completed.[24] 'It was like making a foreign-language film', recalls Mitch. There were over 150 actors and supporting actors over a number of months, and the scheduling of the series meant that in the course of a day, Mitch was shooting episode 4, scene 20 then episode 2, scene 01 with a completely different cast – but always speaking ancient Egyptian, with different dialects selected from different periods over a thousand years. There was also, surprisingly, no economy of scale, as is usual in a series, because Ben Goold, the producer, was so fastidious over the representation of history that with every change of episode, so too changed the doorways, hairstyles, costumes – and none of these were off the shelf; they were hand-made by Janti, the costume designer, who had worked with Ridley Scott on *Gladiator* (2000). 'Authenticity was paramount', confirms Mitch, who had mixed feelings about the decision to pursue quite such rigorous authenticity. He suggests, in retrospect, that the desired 'sense' could have been appropriately achieved without having such a negative impact on the opportunities to deliver maximum 'sensuousness'. Filmmaking requires short-cuts, whether it is *Gladiator* or a glamour shoot. *Gladiator*, apocryphally, ran out of gladiator helmets for the supporting artists and so resorted to spray painting motorcycle helmets. In a world of smoke and mirrors, authenticity in every detail can be over-rated.

The documentary element, as with *Neanderthal*, was key to suspending disbelief in the veracity of the spectacle. It was essential to the authenticity that the texts be filmed with the original ancient Egyptian words legible, and they were filmed, as before, in a studio setting with a motion-control rig. To enhance the 'sensuousness', even of the 'sense' sections, 'snakes and scorpions ran across the texts, as if they had been found in a tomb', recounts Mitch. The series aired in 2003 on Channel 4 and all the other partner territories, and it was nominated for four BAFTAs, one of which it won – the award for best cinematography, by Peter Greenhalgh, whose agent Sarah Putt had, less than presciently, told him to stop 'messing around with drama documentaries, when he had proper dramas on offer', according to Mitch. Having worked on *Poirot*, *Marple*, *Upstairs Downstairs*, and other period dramas, it is instructive to note that this was to be Greenhalgh's only BAFTA win. The series was also nominated for best visual effects and represented a considerable step forward for CGI technology on television. There was seamless multiplication of supporting artists in crowd scenes, a ground-breaking reconstruction of the interior of the Temple of Karnak, and the creation of epic battle scenes that summon Stella Bruzzi's 'jouissance of recognition' in a manner reminiscent of *Gladiator* or *Braveheart* (1995).[25]

At the heart of the series was the bold concept purposefully devised by Graham's team – of opening a portal into another time and place. Natalie Zemon Davis, historical adviser to one of the definitive portals into the past, *The Return of Martin Guerre* (1982), has defined successful history films as those that have passed three tests: genesis, synopsis, and judgement. This approach is summarised by Robert Rosenstone in *History on Film/Film on History* (2006):

> First, the genesis – who got the idea for the film, what were its sources, how did various producers ... bring it to the screen and what were his/her/their intentions. Second, a synopsis, one that highlights the characters and events, and also points out the major deviations from the historical record. Third, the judgements – why should we care about the film, what does it contain that makes us think seriously about the past, and how might it be changed to make it more valuable as a historical work?[26]

The 'genesis' of the idea, the conceit, should be strong, and identifying primary sources that tell previously untold stories underpins the strength of the concept of *Ancient Egyptians*. 'Synopsis' refers to a lack of deviation from that original concept, and Goold's devotion to the original language and the production design is testament to that approach. 'Judgement' asks whether the audience *believes* it has been transported into the past, and hearing an ancient language voiced for the first time in thousands of years, with its society's customs and traditions and even its law system resurrected, must be considered a privilege for a modern television audience, whether it enjoys that privilege or not. The film certainly passed the test set by Lipkin mentioned above, in that it brings 'to light the hidden, the otherwise inaccessible'.[27] Thus, it was truly a radical representation of history, and one that previously had been unseen and unheard.

Graham reflects upon the series with mixed emotions. The viewing figures were not as anticipated, and Ramsden did not look to repeat the commission. Mitch and Goold had fought over cost versus 'on set authenticity' in the debrief traditionally held after transmission, and Goold soon found work elsewhere, while Mitch reteamed with Orr to make science drama documentary *Supervolcano* (BBC, 2005) for BBC One, regarded critically and in terms of viewing figures and awards as the greatest hit of his career to date.[28] *Ancient Egyptians* was undoubtedly radical, and Graham remains sanguine about it to this day, albeit conscious that some bold choices succeeded and some did not. It is notable that he does not lay blame or seek an easy post-mortem. Instead, he is reminded that on the transmission of the French version, he was invited to Paris, where there was a special screening at the Louvre for dignitaries and academics under the glass pyramid. 'The head of Egyptology wanted to thank us for having made such an authentic representation of a past she cared so much about', remembers Graham. Note that term 'authentic' is used once more; it will need further definition at a later point in the book and is best tackled alongside discussion of other programme-makers' slants on the term. But for now, the compliment pleased Graham: 'it doesn't get much better than that. But bloody hell, it wasn't cheap.'

While the filmmakers at Wall to Wall were progressing dramatic reconstruction in history and science documentaries, it would be remiss not to mention the other strand of operations, which in many ways advanced the representation of history further and faster: The '*House*' series. *1900 House* had been a huge hit for Channel 4, and was soon to be repeated in *1940s House*, *Edwardian Country House*, and more.

Meanwhile, Jane Root at the BBC had been promoted from commissioning independents to Controller of BBC Two. She took Graham to lunch. According to him, she said: 'I love *1900 House*, why didn't you bring it to me?' To which he answered, 'because you wouldn't answer my phone calls for three fucking years'. Root then enquired what else Graham might have for her. His answer was smallpox.

Smallpox 2002 (BBC, 2001)

> Brief summary: *A single film that follows a high concept 'what if' scenario of a terrorist who discharges a payload of smallpox in a travel hub, in this case New York City, and causes a global pandemic. The interviews with scientists, police officials, and victims' relatives are all filmed as documentary but performed by actors.*

A revelatory glimpse into the institutional and industrial context of the drama documentary mode can be found in a first-hand account of the production of *Smallpox 2002*. Alex Graham recounts that his number two at Wall to Wall, Jonathan Hewes, had read an article that debated whether or not the World Health Organisation should destroy the samples of smallpox virus it held in secure locations. This then begged the question: are there more samples held in the former Soviet Union? Reminded of the nuclear threat still posed by Russia, Graham and Hewes looked back at the most memorable television programme on nuclear war: *The War Game*, defined in Chapter 3 as one of the progenitor history drama documentaries. This sparked the notion that a narrative set in the future but told in the present tense could work. Graham proposed to the producer, Simon Chinn, and the director, Dan Percival, that they go one step further and tell the story in the past tense. The conceit they arrived at was that this film was imagined to be looking back from 2008 to a global pandemic that had taken place in 2002, although the film was actually to be made in 2001.

Graham insisted that it did not matter how convoluted was the conceit so long as it was based on verifiable research. As previously mentioned, this is one of the key attributes of his approach, which he explains thus: 'ultimately, the form depends on content, and content depends on research. You need to know your world like God knows this one.'[29] This approach, he believes, is the source of his 'authenticity'. He required his creative team to apply themselves to research at a scale reminiscent of Peter Watkins and his team before shooting *The War Game*, when they went so far as to interrogate scientists on what nuclear material actually tastes like. Rival companies also spent time and money on research. Sometimes a broadcaster would invest £5,000 or £10,000 in a promising idea, but more often than not, the production company would have to spend a proportion of their own profit margin on in-depth development. This explains why some historical productions are scantily drawn, a reasonable criticism from academics who perceive television treatment of history as cursory. But Wall to Wall had a reputation for conducting research more deeply than was usual, and that decision came from the top, from Graham himself.

Root pitched the *Smallpox* idea at MIPCOM and brought in Jana Bennett at TLC (previously Head of BBC Two), and so development began in earnest.[30] Now that the funds were being paid by broadcasters, Chinn and Percival were dispatched to the United States for two months of research and scripting, which is a long time in a segment of the industry characterised by its low profit margins. They conceptualised the film increasingly in the drama mode, imagining interviews with doctors and civic personnel played by actors, which 'did start to frighten Jane (Root), and she tried to pull it back', according to Graham. But Graham told them to keep going; after all, he firmly believed that the device of actors playing official personnel, quoting their jobsworth guidelines, had worked in *The War Game*. In their research, Chinn and Percival talked to the Office of Emergency Management in the most ironic of locations: Number One, World Trade Centre. 'Remember, this was before September 2001, just', says Graham, aware that history and the present can intersect in strange and unpredictable ways. (This intersection was to occur once more at Wall to Wall, with the unspoken 9/11 spectre that haunted their 2008 film *Man on Wire*.)

Chinn and Percival could see their narrative unfolding: a discovery of cases in New York; a businessman carries the disease on a flight to London. They could not agree on the start, however, and here, on reflection, Graham suspects that the conceit foundered. The genesis (to follow Natalie Zemon Davis's tripartite framework) was strong, but the synopsis, in the hands of Chinn and Percival, did not always sustain. Research showed that a laboratory accident could most likely be contained, while the modelling suggested that a deliberate terrorist attack was eminently feasible. 'Remember, again, that there was a terrorist history at the Trade Centre, when in the 1990s there was a failed attempt', recalls Graham. The terrorist element of the film was not fully crystallised, in that it was not clear in Graham's head who the terrorists were and what was their cause. *The War Game* had been very clear as to who was launching the missiles, with the first five minutes of the film outlining the international crisis that provokes the Russian state into a nuclear response. But in 2001, shortly after filming ended, the Twin Towers were attacked, and the whole question of formally naming a specific terrorist organisation affiliated to a specific nation or belief system as being mass murderers became a somewhat fraught and contested enterprise. However, Graham and Hewes had ensured that the film had momentum. The BBC and TLC liked the script very much, except what they referred to as the rather 'melodramatic start', with its suggestion that the outbreak had terrorist origins, but Graham prevailed with his 'trust me, I've done this before' salesmanship, backed up by his mantra of 'trust the form depending on content and on research'. The film received the green light.

Smallpox 2002 filmed in spring 2001, involving 'possibly some of the last ever helicopter shots of the Twin Towers', says Graham. They finished filming in summer, with editing taking place in London in September with two edit suites, side by side: one was *Smallpox*, the other *Treason* (part of Channel 4's quartet alongside *Plague*, *Fire*, and *War*, as discussed in Chapter 2). 'Then 9/11 happens, with echoes of the 17th century', recalls Graham. For *Smallpox 2002* it was a determining moment, where the hypothetical future intersected directly with the very real present. It is also ironic that the film began to suffer a loss of confidence similar to that suffered by *The War Game* at the hands of the BBC in 1965. The broadcasters who had wanted relevance in the terrifying subject matter they had commissioned became alarmed by *too much* relevance. Bennett from TLC, now owned by Discovery (yet more shades of *The War Game*), felt they could no longer show the film. Not all broadcasters reacted the same way. Root at the BBC wanted to know how quickly the film could be ready to air. Graham recalls searching for another US champion and found one in Nancy Abraham at HBO, who offered to buy it and return some investment to TLC,[31] whereupon John Landgraf, from a new upstart channel, FX, made a very serious counteroffer.[32] He wanted to reshoot some footage to strengthen the American angle, but he also wanted to develop a strand – that holy grail of television business (as exemplified by *1900/1940 House*). Graham had to make a decision about which way to go. 'This was a key moment', says Graham, 'when an independent asks itself: can you fuck a channel?'

This may well be a critical juncture in Graham's development, as he realised that with the success of a single film comes the possibility of a franchise, and a well-funded franchise can give an artist parity with the broadcaster. Two or more franchises delivers immense strength at any negotiating table. This is an immensely rare position to reach for any indie, and at this point, remained in the future for Graham and Wall to Wall. Graham was risking the continuation of longstanding relationships to land more dependable business models. But Graham is a risk-taker, and 2001–2003 was a particular challenge: 'We realised we were taking risks, collectively, at Wall to Wall, but you have to go for the franchise', confirms Graham.

Graham sold *Smallpox 2002* to the FX Channel and was rewarded in 2003 with another commission: *Oil Storm*, about a hurricane dismantling America's oil supplies, which received many more airings after Hurricane Katrina hit Louisiana within weeks of first transmission. *Smallpox 2002* also created a franchise in the United Kingdom: 'it was a huge hit for the BBC. The relationship with Jane (Root) re-blossomed, and we remembered why we had always liked each other.' The BBC then commissioned two more modern-history drama docs, *The Day Britain Stopped* (BBC, 2002) and *The Man who Broke Britain* (BBC, 2004). To this extent, *Smallpox*

2002 can be said to have significantly contributed to establishing the popularity of what must have seemed (but had not yet been defined as) another variant of the dramatised history documentary; it stands in close relation to other successful franchises such as *A History of Britain* and *Elizabeth/ Henry VIII and his Six Wives*, as well as to smaller variants represented by individual series such as *Plague, Fire, War, and Treason* and single films such as *Pyramid*.

The film itself merits analysis from several industrially reflexive and scholarly perspectives. Aesthetically, what relation does it bear to its progenitor, *The War Game*? Can a documentary based on rigorous research be sustained by a hypothetical premise that borders on falsehood? The work of Hayden White can be brought to bear on the latter question. In *Content of the Form* (1989), he observes that 'One can produce an imaginary discourse about real events that may not less "true" for being imaginary.'[33] White notes, however, that such a discourse must be based on reality: 'the authority of the historical narrative is the authority of reality itself: the historical account endows this reality with form'. In this way, narrative achieves what White terms 'a truth value'.[34,35]

Smallpox 2002 has authority that lends itself to a plausible 'truth value'. This is exhibited in the film's opening, which features three documentary-style interviews, including with Jack Hill, Director of the 'NYC Office of Emergency Management, 2001–3':

> We knew that smallpox existed, that it could be used as a bioterrorist weapon, and I had been trying for a long time to get people to be more proactive in this, to be creating more vaccine, to be creating a war book of exactly what we should be doing, should something like this happen. It wasn't until this attack that people took me seriously.

The images that accompany 'interview' statements such as this are in the documentary mode: headstones of mass graves, bodies in bags being bulldozed into pits. A narrator, consistent with a documentary voice of God, resumes the audio: '2002 saw the biggest mass murder in history, using a disease that nobody had seen for over 20 years. It killed 60 million people worldwide.'[36] Just like *The War Game*, the film's opening was a hypothesis dressed up as a statement of fact.

The interviewees were all actors performing as plausible health and safety professionals or victims such as 'Mary Cooper', a member of the public with a harrowing tale to tell. The images were adapted from archive: the headstones were graves from the Second World War, the body bags being ploughed into the ground from a developing-world health calamity. But the whole conceit was derived from the dramatic mode: 'It was a normal day, with the usual winter problems and a mild flu epidemic, so when Cynthia Sheldon came into the ER complaining of a fever, it was nothing out of the ordinary'. recounts one 'Dr Carl Jocelyn, Long Island College Hospital ER 2001–3' – and thus the narrative is set on its ninety-minute journey. The drama follows an arc that tells the story across all societal levels with the most emotionally compelling micro-narrative centring on the family of Mary Cooper, for whom the endgame comes late in the global experience, with the rush for vaccination. The genre evoked is that of the science thriller, which develops quickly into a plausible version of horror, as when Mary Cooper's son is woken in his internment bay by shuffling in the dark and, on turning on his torch, discovers a fellow quarantined patient vomiting blood onto the floor; or, in a more emotion-laden version of the horror genre, when a young married couple is separated and the husband dies alone three thousand miles away, having turned black and bled to death from the inside. Very little of this distressing detail is shown, however, since the predominant mode in which the film is made is that of the responsible documentary. The victims are often glimpsed opaquely on recordings by CCTV cameras that detect their last known movements, thus amplifying the feeling of intrigue. Home video is offered, as if from family archives, to intensify emotional engagement with a character at a moment of joy in their lives – video, for instance, of a wedding in the back garden, a kind of emotional shorthand that audiences are likely to share. The combination of drama and documentary is purposefully intertwined and wholly plausible. Like *The War Game*, it is debatable as to whether the structure and form is more docudrama than drama documentary, but for the purposes of this book, it shall be included in the data set of drama documentary.

There is also no intertitle at the start, preparing the viewer for the contrivance at hand. In the drama documentary corpus, it is very unusual for the contract with the audience not to be spelled out with words such as 'this is based on a true story' or 'this is drawn from real research'. It is striking that the same absence of a contract is found in *The War Game* and in the *War of the Worlds* radio broadcast.[37] All three are a particular variant of the drama documentary mode, one that relies on the audience's credulity – their belief that the smallpox outbreak, nuclear attack, or alien invasion is actually occurring. It is borderline irresponsible broadcasting, hence the fear of broadcasters to show such programming, but when they do take the risk, it lends this variant of drama documentary an unforgettable power.

Yet it is necessary that the audience plays its part in the game of watching a drama documentary. As Robert Rosenstone argues in *Visions of the Past* (1995), 'it is necessary for us to learn to judge the ways in which, through invention, film summarises vast amounts of data or symbolises complexities that otherwise could not be shown'.[38] It is up to the audience to learn to watch drama documentaries with a tutored and critical eye, especially the variants that purport to be showing the real in a deliberate manipulation.

What justifies such manipulation is the now-familiar depth of research employed by a Wall to Wall TV production. Take, for instance, this one brief but compelling statement from *Smallpox 2002*: 'in the 20th century, smallpox killed more people than all of the century's wars combined'. This is a truth ignored by many in the developed world, in the same way that nuclear weapons' potential capacity for mass mortality was ignored by a sleepwalking British public in the 1960s. But the main thrust of the research followed the mitigations put in place for a pandemic disaster of this kind, and this is where the film adapts itself to the horror genre. In Mary Cooper's council estate, families are locked into their flats by faceless authorities in hazmat suits, the doors then hammered shut with blocks of wood and iron bars by confused and ignorant neighbours. Throughout, the aesthetic is created by handheld-camerawork reminiscent of an observational documentary. At each stage of the film, a different documentary truth style is applied: home video, rostrum camera on photographs, speeded-up commuters, the earth seen from space as it slowly turns, archive footage of traffic jams, hospitals overwhelmed, panic buying at supermarkets, mass rioting. Captions are used liberally, confirming the number of days since first instance of infection. Music is kept to a minimum, to support the 'responsible documentary' ethos. All these documentary-mode practices are utilised to achieve the greatest 'sensuous' impact on a viewer drawn into the mounting horror of what could be a ghastly reality unfolding right before them. Again, this very much echoes the effect of *The War Game*. At numerous points, the (real) BBC newsreader Gavin Esler appears on the screen, apparently in his official capacity, calling for people who are worried to call a Free NHS helpline on 0808 157 0980.

The arc of the pandemic builds to a peak before falling away, offering a simple but effective chronological structure, but throughout the arc, a detective story plays out involving the faux FBI and the programme's faux journalists, searching for a perpetrator. The detective story is inserted at ten-minute intervals, heralded by a short caption drawing from the tropes of drama documentary: 'the suspect', 'the body', 'the weapon', 'the message'. The detective trail is, in general, convincingly expressed, cutting from CCTV footage of a man with a backpack getting on the subway to a Steadicam shot following the suspect.

Some shots are unworthy of Wall to Wall's vigilance, however. The aforementioned Steadicam shot of the killer that follows his hand reaching out to touch various passers-by on their way to work, or school, is evidently staged. The following shot is a device used in many programmes in which a suspect's movements are reconstructed, yet this was an implausible addition to the film, given that the camera was not actually present as the killer went about that day. It is a Steadicam shot taken from the drama mode and misplaced in the observational-documentary style.[39] The clues lead first to a dead body in the subway tunnel, thence to a rented apartment where a King James Bible sits on a tabletop, open at the Book of Ezekiel with its warnings to those who bring about the vengeance of God. There is no name for the killer, no conclusion at all to the 'sense' of this strand of the film. Perhaps 9/11 put paid to this approach, but *The War Game* had established its credentials in a much more satisfactory way. If one is going to apply immense amounts of research into a whodunnit conceit, then it is a disappointment to deny the audience one has primed in every other respect. Then again, perhaps the film is an example of what Paget terms 'mischief-making', and perhaps mischief makes its own rules.

It is certainly mischievous to end the film – after the credit roll of cast, costume, makeup, and all the associated confirmation of the drama mode – with a caption that announces: 'the following contributors are not actors'. One is titled 'Dr A. Henderson, Director, US Office of Public Health Preparedness', who speaks earnestly about the real dangers of bioterrorism at large. The second is 'Dr Ken Alibeck, Biodefence Scientist', a Russian-sounding laboratory doctor who confirms that such toxins did indeed mysteriously vanish from the USSR. The problem is that Dr Alibeck was used in the main body of the film, as convincingly as the actors who played the authorities. Suddenly, the drama/documentary divide is a mischievous blur of convenience.

In conclusion, *Smallpox 2002* progressed the range of aesthetics available to documentary, newly informed by drama. The documentary mode's ability to tell a fictional story with a characteristic relentlessness opened the doors to other 'what if' films, which captured the imagination of the British viewership in particular. *The Day Britain Stopped* (BBC, 2003), for instance, is variously referred to as a dramatic pseudo-documentary and a mock-doc drama. Its mischievous assumption is that if the train network and M25 orbital road were to become gridlocked, then air traffic control would not be able to reach Heathrow and disaster would ensue. Balancing the domestic scale with a portrait of a society on a knife-edge, it holds the authorities to account effectively – perhaps the ultimate purpose of a drama documentary, whether historical or not. Paget, in *War on Terror* (2015), observes that these films, *Smallpox* and *The Day Britain Stopped*, 'included the hyper-naturalistic element of acted reconstruction, but even this was different from "classic" docudrama. Using unknown actors who could plausibly pass for social actors (police, emergency, medical staff – even politicians), these docudramas masked their fictionality and pointed towards the real witness of documentary.'[40] Paget quotes the director, Gabriel Range, on the difficulty, for actors, of performing documentary-style scenes: 'the witness/expert interview, a staple of documentary and news filming is not easy to act – as Range has noted, it is unforgiving of an actor's performance. In their training, actors may well use "hot seating" improvisations to explore character as part of their preparation, but they are rarely asked in normal performance.'[41] What is clear, from Paget's review of these 'what if' films, created by Wall to Wall, is that they were a considerable success: 'a spectrum of creative possibility was thus exploited, and associated ethical questions inevitably raised. So lively is the whole arena of factual television that docudrama itself has become almost respectable (especially when compared, say, to Reality TV)'.[42]

The next film under consideration conferred considerable respectability on the dramatised history documentary. *George Orwell: A Life in Pictures* (BBC, 2003) is a study of a man of letters, and as such would ordinarily have been siloed by the broadcasting industry as an Arts programme. Graham and his collaborative commissioners, however, had now adopted an increasingly 'porous' approach to true stories. The dramatised history documentary was morphing in many directions in Wall to Wall's hands, and the company was considered eminently capable of telling history through the arts and biography through fiction. Alex Graham's notion that 'there are many different ways to tell stories of the past' was coming to fruition.

George Orwell: A Life in Pictures (BBC, 2003)

> Brief summary: *A study of the twentieth-century battle against rule by the privileged few, as seen through a biography of George Orwell, author of* Animal Farm *(1945) and* 1984 *(1949). Every word spoken is derived from his documented writing; every moving image has been fabricated by drama.*

While *Ancient Egyptians* was in post-production, Wall to Wall turned its collective mind to an anniversary that was considered important to the commissioning literati of public service television, if not to the viewing population in general. The year 2003 was the centenary of the birth of George Orwell, an old Etonian who changed his name, joined the Spanish Civil War, lived among the down and outs of Paris and London, went down mines, and wrote the dystopian tracts on Marxism *Animal Farm* and *1984*. For the lifelong Trotskyite Graham, Orwell was his hero, and he knew that Root at the BBC, as a middle-class left-wing intellectual, shared his admiration – and that BBC Two was partly intended to bring literary figures like this to the screen for the edification of the British public. It should be noted here that BBC Four did not come into being until 2004 but was soon to draw heavily from such literate programming.

Dan Percival (of *Smallpox*) and Ben Goold (of *Ancient Egyptians*) were to take charge of developing the project, but Graham was not convinced by any of the directions on offer, and certainly not Percival and Goold's idea of a life looked back upon from Orwell's deathbed. Graham recalls: 'Dan Percival was really cross. I think I used the word cliché. He said I hadn't understood it. But I just knew that Jane wouldn't buy it.' One of the major problems for the project's representation of history was that Orwell had enjoyed a privileged youth and had lived through so many significant moments of the twentieth century – the Spanish Civil War, the Blitz, the dosshouses of post-war Britain – but there was not a single frame of footage of him, added to which, the BBC had mislaid or destroyed every piece of his audio from his various propaganda radio recordings, so there was no sense even of his voice. (When *A History of Britain* had made their programme *The Two Winstons*, counterpointing Churchill with the protagonist of *1984*, the producer/director Clare Beavan had employed Charles Dance to voice Orwell's imagined upper-class tones.)

Graham had almost given up when, as he recalls, 'early one morning, Emma Willis came in from a dinner party the night before, with an idea'. Willis was a relatively new producer at Wall to Wall who had produced *Treats from the Edwardian Country House*, a food-oriented spin off from the celebrated re-enactment series. 'She said that the dinner party had discussed the dilemma and come up with the suggestion: use Orwell's *words only* to show your veracity and then *fake all the visuals* – archive his life as if he had been filmed fulsomely and make a virtue of it' (my italics). Graham could immediately see the 'form'. It was part *War Game/Smallpox*, but always derived from, and validated by, terrific research. Ideas like this may seem obvious in retrospect, but retrospect is a poor viewpoint for judgement; there is always a conceptual leap to be made, and each time, with each subject, the leap is subtly different.

In dramatic terms, there simply was 'no other way to tell it', to echo Paget's 1998 book title, and the film offered considerable 'historical value', to echo Rosenstone's remarks in *Revisioning History* (1995): 'docudrama can have historical value if it offers motivated, truthful invention, close proximations and analogies and contributes constructively to the debate surrounding efforts to visualise and understand the past'.[43]

Orwell offered to contribute constructively to the debate about how to visualise the past and, as such, was entering unchartered territory. The single idea later spawned a franchise of biopics, including *Ian Fleming: Bondmaker* (BBC, 2005), *H.G. Wells: War with the World* (BBC, 2006), and *Elizabeth David: A Life in Recipes* (BBC, 2006), all made by Wall to Wall in the years to come for BBC Four. The microcosmic setting and attraction to star actors and writers made for very good-value drama based upon truth and became a staple – a highlight – for BBC Four for many years thereafter. Graham reflects on *Ian Fleming*, *H.G. Wells*, and *Elizabeth David* as copies of the original film: 'they are fine, but if I had to take only a select few shows to a desert island, this [*George Orwell*] would be one of them, it was so madly inventive'.

The film opens in a television studio. Orwell is being interviewed, in black and white. He is asked what he likes. He replies:

> I like ... English cookery, English beer, French red wine, Spanish white wine, Indian tea, strong tobacco, coalfire, candlelight and comfortable chairs. I dislike big towns, noise, the motorcar, the radio, tinned food, central heating and modern furniture.[44]

The narrator, actress, Barbara Flynn, then sets out the rules of engagement, which were so clearly missing from *Smallpox 2002*:

> Famous for writing 1984 and inventing Big Brother, George Orwell witnessed and reported on some of the defining moments of the 20th century. But there are no moving pictures of Orwell nor are there any recordings of his voice. He did leave a vast written legacy, penning insights into everything from diet to revolution. It is this we used to create his life in pictures.

The conceit is presented here, but it is a big conceptual leap, even for the sophisticated Wall to Wall film researcher, and so the point was repeated:

> The pictures are invented but every statement Orwell utters is his own. In an early documentary, Orwell is an imperial policeman, in a film essay he is a kitchen hand, in newsreel he is glimpsed as a freedom fighter and war reporter.

The narration is accompanied by extracts from these various filmic devices – made by a drama team in order to appear to be of the documentary mode. The film returns to the studio interview where the actor – future BAFTA winner Chris Langham, who bears an uncanny resemblance to Orwell – smokes heavily, contributing both strangulated tones and a sense of shyness. The next answer is taken from Orwell's confessional essay *Why I Write*: 'all writers are selfish and vain and at the bottom of their motives lies a mystery ... I do not think one can assess a writer's motives without knowing something of their development.'[45] Thus, the film launches into ninety minutes of biography. In an opening scene, Langham approaches an iron bed isolated in a spotlight, and proceeds to remake it, with hospital corners. Meanwhile, he recounts his formative early experience – as a child at prep school, where he wet the bed, and then on to Eton and a rejection of the entitled privilege that would define his work. He then wistfully takes the teddy bear away with him into the darkness. This prelude gives a sense of playful performance that recurs throughout the film.

Playfulness and mischief-making are two characteristics that make Graham and his company, Wall to Wall, so distinctive. Other indies that originated drama documentaries at this formative stage were not so engaging. Lion TV's films on the Medici and Martin Luther are straight-faced renditions of the heroic past, while *The Man Who Saved Children* (Channel 4, 2003) made by RDF TV is emotionally led without possessing wit. Graham as a person is a hard taskmaster but an avuncular presence in any room, and his playfulness draws an audience towards him. This puckish sense of fun, arguably, is exactly the tone that brought viewers to drier subject matter. *Orwell* could have felt like a literature or a history lesson, without the playfulness that the drama mode can bring to a documentary. Beginning the film with Orwell's long list of likes and dislikes draws an audience towards the subject, and this engaging quality is reinforced by the casting of a tragicomic genius like Chris Langham.[46]

The following analysis aims to give an overview of the playfulness displayed by *George Orwell: A Life in Pictures* and the degree to which the film is laced throughout with invention. It was this joyful approach to the past that would help to build an entire sub-genre of charm-laced dramas about tortured writers and comedians on BBC Four, and the success of those dramas can be traced back to this enterprising film. After its engaging opening, the film relocates to Burma, where Orwell opposes British rule – revealed through the specific case of the hanging of a Burmese man by his colonial overseers. This is playfully reconstructed in an English back street, with production-designed bamboo sheets covering the shape of an industrial factory beyond, but the point is not to re-enact 'authentic' locations; the film aims for a Brechtian minimalism that invites its viewers to suspend disbelief.[47] The scene is further lifted by Orwell's reflection that the condemned man walked around a puddle as he went to his death, as if it mattered whether his feet were wet or not. Orwell maintains this was a sign of the condemned man clinging to life, and it moved him extraordinarily. A scene like this, simply visualised by the journey of the condemned man seen in the puddle, intensifies the visual and aural experience and contributes to the sensuousness that might be missing from a straight documentary. For this, Graham credits Durlacher, yet it is no coincidence that Graham is so amused when he recounts the making of the film, since it was made much in Graham's image. So too is the next moment, when Orwell is then placed – by a post-production trick – into a scene with other colonial officers, in a manner reminiscent of Woody Allen in *Zelig* (1993).[48] Minutes later, as Orwell describes the tragedy of his tuberculosis, the filmmakers insert him into a government health-warning film. The effect is altogether engagingly immersive, and it is possible to see, solely from this first ten minutes of black-and-white reconstructed footage, how other potential subjects – writers, actors, and comedy icons – could all be tackled with just such a delightful and, equally important, budget-conscious style.

Fifteen minutes into the film and Orwell has moved to his parents' house in Southwold, a smart beach community in Suffolk, where the film reverts to traditional documentary style, with colour footage of the town in contemporary times. It is an odd transition, seemingly unworthy of the aesthetic of the piece, but it helps the viewer to transition to a series of real-life interviews with two old ladies who knew Orwell's parents: 'he was a disappointment to his parents and not at all good looking', they proclaim. Narratively, it helps to turn the corner into the question of why he changed his name. He was born Eric Blair and changed his name to George Orwell on the publication of his first book, *Down and Out in Paris and London* (1933), in order to avoid bringing any more shame upon his parents.[49] Perhaps this shift of mode was intended to give the viewer respite from the contrived black-and-white faux drama; it certainly enables the film to return to the drama mode refreshed. The effect is somewhat reminiscent of *Das Boot's* (1981) moments of respite above the water line, which enable the film to continue to pursue an atmosphere of relentless claustrophobia down below on the submarine. Or perhaps the shift of mode was chosen because this interview with old family friends exists in colour and as such was considered too good to miss. Graham and his team often display pragmatic choices by using what is available; the secret lies in how you use it.

The film progresses with its predominant mode of mockumentary in what is ostensibly an arts film (it went on to win the Grierson Award for Best Arts Film and an International EMMY), although it also acts as a vehicle for telling a worm's eye view of the history of the period, taking in the 1926 General Strike, the Wall Street Crash, the rise of fascism in Spain, and the war against the Nazis. This is history in disguise, a device that Wall to Wall went on to use to good effect with their greatest franchise: *Who Do You Think You Are?* Graham, in his independence from broadcasters, was keen to avoid silos, to avoid compartmentalising arts, science and history, let alone factual and drama. For him, and for indies like his company, texts were to speak to other texts, and an arts approach was a good way to offer a history narrative, just as natural history was a good way to tell the story of human prehistory. This open-mindedness is another of Graham's distinctions, and a multitextual approach spread quickly around the independent sector. If a popular drama actor like Chris Langham could bring an audience to the documentary study of an intellectual novelist, then television could open itself to subjects that were supposedly reserved for the literati. Graham's aspiration is to break down class barriers and introduce an increasingly university-educated audience to further education by means of entertainment. Graham believes that Orwell is 'the greatest writer and thinker of the 20th century' and is intent that his work and thought should reach as large an audience as possible.

Through the film, Graham and his team are able to express much of Orwell's manifesto in terms that a middle-brow audience can grasp, and that might encourage viewers to reach for Orwell's books themselves, or to read around them, thus discovering an often-overshadowed strand of European history. Avoiding a complex explanation of Spanish Civil War politics, Orwell (through Langham) is heard to say that he was fighting merely 'for common decency', and he explains how the Communists also became his enemy, since they were fundamentally anti-democratic. The seeds of Orwell's anti-authoritarianism are shown; as he admits in the film, 'every book written since 1936 has been written directly or indirectly against totalitarianism'.

Above all, this BBC commission intended to hold a mirror to the British audience of 2003, and so the Wall to Wall team selected quotes that chime with its enduring patriotism:

> We are a nation of flower lovers, pigeon fanciers, stamp collectors, amateur carpenters, coupon snippers, darts players, crossword puzzle fans, all the culture that is most native centres upon things that are not official – the liberty of the individual is still believed in. The totalitarian idea that there is no such thing as law, only power, has not taken root.

Orwell, sometimes regarded as a contrarian, nevertheless continues his individualistic yet patriotic stance, in the filmmakers' hands, when he joins the Home Guard. Langham is inserted into footage of the real Dad's Army, and he is found standing by rubble being inspected during a royal visit to the East End – all of which convinces him that there will never be a revolution in Britain while such 'inarticulate patriotism exists – the fact that a million men have rifles in their bedrooms, which does not trouble the authorities, marks out Britain as the most stable society in the world'. The phrase 'inarticulate patriotism' reminds this author of Schama's epithet 'patriotically insecure', two similar, clever descriptions of the United Kingdom's uneasy yet enduring relationship with the monarchy.[50] Yet the contrarian side of Orwell continues to emerge as the film traces the chronology of his life and times. An hour into the film – a critical moment, when an audience's interest tends to waver – the edit cleverly reaches the iconic touchstones of Orwell's continuing fame. Over an image of a corridor, with no interruption from Langham, the viewer is told that Orwell goes to work for the 'ministry of information propaganda unit' at the BBC, and works in an office, named and numbered Room 101.

In its last twenty minutes, the film concerns itself with the two works that made Orwell's reputation. He is seen typing *Animal Farm* (published 1945) in the context of what he perceives as an unholy alliance with Russia in the latter years of the war. 'I wanted to turn political writing into an art', Orwell explains, as a cigarette hangs from his lip – underlining the performative approach to his biography, thus engaging an audience that might not have watched a straight, presenter-led documentary, nor read Orwell's works in print. Drama documentaries such as this were intended to increase the tiny high-brow television viewership on BBC Two and reach a larger audience that might follow up on a writer it had heard about but not actively embraced. It would be interesting to chart the change in the socio-political nature and education of the viewership at this time, but it is beyond the scope of this work.

In the last ten minutes, Orwell retreats to a croft in the Hebrides to write *1984*. Langham is interviewed *en route* to the cottage, sitting in the back of a car, by one of many young ladies to whom he proposed in his dotage. It is a curious personal note that a man with such intellectual acumen should have been so foolish in his approach to the opposite sex, and this aspect of his life is handled without sensationalism, again confirming Graham's intuitions when it comes to propriety. The drama helps to humanise the man obsessed with the fight against totalitarianism, but it does not turn his life into soap opera (that was to come with the advent of other biographical dramas on BBC Four). Orwell's personal story is offered in service to his writing, and thus the death of his wife, under anaesthesia, is obliquely referenced through a home-made film on the joys of milking a goat and of raising an adopted child. It is subtle nuances like this that run through Wall to Wall's films: an instinct for good taste.

At the end, Orwell is in a race to finish *1984* before his fragile health fails entirely. Faux archive shows his last days at UCL Hospital, and in a faux documentary interview he is seen in his bed, Langham having been made up convincingly to indicate Orwell's approaching death: 'this is the direction the world is going in ... imagine the picture of a boot stamping on a human face forever. The moral is a simple one. Don't let it happen. It depends on you.' Langham turns to face the camera, breaking the fourth wall as he has done throughout the film – because this is a conversation between an imagined George Orwell and his imagined audience, fulfilling the promise of the writer's impact when he speaks to his reader through the arrangement of words into a compelling argument. In the documentary mode, captions reveal the author's lifespan: 'George Orwell 1903–1950'. Then the credits roll, shifting into the drama mode – and confirming that George Orwell was, in truth, performed by Chris Langham, and he was supported by other actors of certain note (Rebecca Front, Tom Goodman-Hill, and so on) and made up by a Make-Up Artist, Caitlyn Tanner, and the sets were designed by Production Designer Patrick Bill, and so forth.

Perhaps the combination of sense and sensuousness is the reason why Graham would choose this film to take to that desert island.

Wall to Wall/Alex Graham as an auteur?

Having explored Alex Graham's distinctive contribution to the dramatised history documentary in the early years of its development, 2001–2003, it is useful to reflect on whether scholarship can help capture quite why that contribution was so significant. From analysis of the texts, and through interviews with Graham, one can conclude that he displays a rigour towards research, a courage in the face of commissioners, a playfulness with form and a commercial ruthlessness – building a production company on modes that generate repeatable profit. He is also a radical thinker who catalyses creativity among his employees and the commissioners, whom he sees as partners rather than superiors. His philosophies of life are so deeply represented by the work of Wall to Wall that he and the company might well attract an epithet usually reserved in scholarly work for directors: that of 'auteur'. Wall to Wall is, after all, the only production entity in this book for whom a whole chapter is reserved.

The question of whether or not films (or in this case television films) can be regarded as being authored prompted much vigorous scholarly debate from the late 1940s to the 1960s and beyond. Alexandre Astruc created the term 'la camera-stylo' (the camera pen) in which he suggests that the filmmaker/author writes with 'his' camera as a writer writes with 'his' pen.[51] Graham was neither a writer nor director, yet he was invariably the conceiver of the idea, reminding one of what Davis refers to as the creator of the 'genesis' of the idea. Astruc argues that the auteur attempts:

> by means of a certain form and a certain story ... to evolve a philosophy of life, how can one possibly distinguish between the man who conceives the work and the man who writes it?[52]

Graham certainly evolved a philosophy of life, founded in deep research, and a drive for what he termed 'authentic' proximities in all modes of his filmmaking. It was this, a cornerstone of his approach, that he sold to every broadcaster-partner, and which he required from every creative individual that worked for him. It is possible that Ben Goold misread Graham's determination for every detail of authenticity in *Ancient Egyptians* – a determination that cost Mitch so dearly in trying to balance shooting ratios with attention to detail. But the French Egyptologist at the Louvre certainly appreciated the devotion to the search for authenticity at the heart of Graham's philosophy of life, as expressed in his company's filmmaking.

In 1954, François Truffaut offered his own thoughts on auteurs: 'Their films enact their vision of life: each frame carries their signature. To understand their vision fully we need to know their body of work.'[53] In this chapter, a sufficient amount of Graham's work has been discussed – four drama documentaries, one re-enactment series, and one celebrity series – to know that there are certain consistencies in the work, but there are also pragmatic commercial choices. One can say that each of Wall to Wall's films enact Graham's 'vision of life' but not that 'each frame carries his signature'. Surely, the micro-analysis of 'each frame' is for a writer or a director to own, not an executive producer.

Andrew Sarris in 1963 accepted that auteurism was not always useful in that it risked pigeon-holing certain filmmakers. Yet 'the auteur habit of collecting random films in directorial bundles will serve posterity with at least a tentative classification'.[54] I agree with this notion, although in Graham's case this chapter has been collecting random films in *producorial* bundles. This process of making a tentative classification is at least attempting to make a contribution to knowledge, especially in the case of drama documentaries. Peter Wollen follows Jean Renoir's thought that 'a director spends his whole life making one film', adding his own consideration, that 'it is only in the study of the whole corpus which permits the moment of synthesis when the critic returns to the individual film'.[55,56] A moment of synthesis – in one film? This is reminiscent of Graham's reflection that he would take one drama documentary onto a desert island: *George Orwell: A Life in Pictures*. Perhaps Graham is right that *Orwell* could be justifiably considered a synthesis of his philosophy of life: it is a film that exemplifies the best of all four of the drama documentaries under discussion here (*Neanderthal, Ancient Egyptians, Smallpox 2002, George Orwell: A Life in Pictures*). It contains deep research and an uncompromising playfulness within a radical conceit that best shapes its narrative for the viewership, and viewers responded to its combination of education and entertainment. To use Wollen's words, the film 'provides catalysts, scenes which fuse with his own preoccupations to produce a radically new work. Thus, the manifest process of performance, the treatment of a subject, conceals the latent production of a new text'.[57] Just as this film provides catalysts, it is arguable that Graham himself was a catalyst for so much of the creativity at Wall to Wall in the formative years of drama documentary. He did not write the scripts, but he oversaw the writing of scripts and wrote many of the pitch documents that crystallised the aesthetic ideas. He did not direct the actors on set, but he watched the rushes and every stage of the edit, ensuring that the project continued to realise the pitch he had made to the broadcasters. As an executive producer, he did not necessarily actively, on set every day, *produce* each of the films (he did produce *Neanderthal*), but he oversaw the producing of each film from his vantage point as executive producer.

But Graham, who eschews such academic labelling, would recognise himself better in the anti-auteur voices, most notably Roland Barthes and Michel Foucault. Barthes, in 'The Death of the Author' (1967), rejected the notion that authors 'owned' their texts like capitalists, and likened 'authorship as authority'.[58] However, this analysis does not apply to television makers in the sense that Alex Graham never claimed authority over a subject matter. Because of the volume of material achievable by television, Graham would assert that *Neanderthal* is *a* version of early hominin, not *the* last word on early hominins. Commissioners and their producers are encouraged to make their case partly to provoke an alternate point of view on another channel in another year. *Smallpox 2002* is mischievous, as described above, in order to provoke a response. *Dirty Bomb* (BBC, 2004) was made in-house by the BBC, but once again utilised Dan Percival as the director, taking a different approach to a similar situation. *A History of Britain* purposely employed the indefinite article to allow room for an alternate vision of these islands' past.

Michel Foucault rejected the idea of single authors in 'What is an Author?' (1969), instead creating 'monstrous families' by combining a series of authors or idealists into loose groups, who, critically, 'brought about change'.[59] Graham would mischievously enjoy the idea of creating a 'monstrous family' of drama documentarians, especially if they bought about debate and ultimately 'change' in a society. *Smallpox 2002* was intended, as was *The War Game*, and the subsequent *Dirty Bomb* and *The Day Britain Stopped*, to make the public think about the underlying flaws and dangers in the system. Graham was one of a number of television creators who aimed to bring about educative change through the prism of very well-informed entertainment. He wished for change in the context of an early twenty-first-century Western society that had become complacent about bio terrorism, nuclear threat, underfunded railway systems, overreliance on a single orbital road around a growing metropolis. Graham was one of several drama documentarians – including the makers of *Surviving Disaster/Chernobyl* (BBC, 2006) and *Spanish Flu, The Forgotten Fallen* (BBC, 2009) – who can be considered to make up a part of Foucault's 'monstrous family' of socially responsible journalists. He also anchors other 'families', many of whom are looking to 'film the unfilmable', and oftentimes, they look to Graham for encouragement that it can be achieved. As Nick Murphy, writer and director of *Surviving Disaster/Chernobyl* comments, 'Alex Graham produced some of the most experimental drama documentaries in the early 2000s, that encouraged the rest of us to dramatise a variety of stories: biopics, what-ifs, epics, disasters and so on' (Murphy, 2020).

It is evident, therefore, that both the auteur and the counter-auteur theorists offer prisms through which to see Wall to Wall and other indies who made similar if not equal contributions to the dramatised history documentaries of the first decade of the twenty-first century. But these theories have been challenged and expanded in recent years, and a recent theorist has suggested a completely radical approach, which Graham would find mischievous in the extreme. This theorist is Erik Knudsen, part-practitioner, part-academic, and he has devised the idea of the 'Total Filmmaker', the idea of which 'allows us to move away from the quagmire of debates around the notion of the auteur' proposed by Truffaut as he 'wrestled with where authorship sits in a collaborative art form firmly rooted in industrial processes and institutions'.[60] Knudsen would support Graham's own view of himself that, as well as having firm guiding principles, he was immensely adaptable to the changing environment around him, not only culturally but institutionally. Graham knew how to sell broadcasters what they needed, and hence he cornered the history market (in all areas except the less profitable, less franchisable drama documentary area, which he chose not to heavily target). His adaptability was his greatest strength, bringing to mind Knudsen's analogy with Dutch football in the 1960s and 1970s, 'where the football manager, Rinus Michels, developed a highly successful theory and strategy ... of flexible and interchangeable outfield players able to reshape, reinvent and respond to ever changing game circumstances'.[61]

While Graham is not a writer/director/producer, able to play in all areas of the field with consistent expertise, he is a creative executive producer, who can write from pitch to poster, and synthesise complex ideas into a roadmap for other creatives to follow. He is not a director, but he understands the grammar of directing and could step in, if needed, to supervise a shoot with his authority over the bigger vision. He chooses not to perform these roles regularly because he is most valuable as a commander-in-chief, deciding the critical balance of making art that makes money. Wall to Wall has been 'able to reshape, reinvent and respond', maintaining its position of what is known industrially as a super-indie for thirty-five years. It continues to thrive, to the time of the writing of this book, and in the world of domestic television, such longevity is remarkable. It must be concluded that Wall to Wall has been worthy of its own chapter, for its chronological relevance to the subject matter at hand, and, above all, for its solid foundations, which were built on research that led to content that led to form – and dramatised documentary was a variant of that form.

Graham and Wall to Wall were, until recently, one and the same, and they operated with a significant degree of creative power, which could be considered authorial. But this work avers that not even Peter Watkins operated alone, and that debating the applicability of the moniker of auteur is at best a useful exercise; creative collaboration remains the more appropriate model, beyond the central driver, beyond even the production company but including the patrons at broadcasting channels. Graham is a collaborator in creativity, and forms 'monstrous families' around him as one of the driving forces of history programming and drama documentary in the early years of the twenty-first century. As he says (and as quoted above), he began working 'with a battle-hardened team of himself, Mitch, Orr and Ramsden' and would not present an idea 'because Jane Root would not buy it'; both statements reflect his practice of teamwork and collaboration beyond the production company. Graham was supported by Hewes, Chinn, and numerous others in the Wall to Wall family, just as Watkins had the critical support of Huw Wheldon for his two formative films. Ultimately, Graham's role brings to mind Samuel Goldwyn's remark: 'I made Wuthering Heights, Wyler only directed it'.[62]

Conclusion

To define the growing corpus under consideration as a body of work driven by the auteurism of Graham, or Wall to Wall TV, has not been a fruitless exercise. Graham was an important catalyst for anybody looking to film the unfilmable. *Smallpox* realised the thing that hadn't yet happened, *Orwell* realised archive when none existed, and both *Neanderthal* and *Ancient Egyptians* realised the sights and sounds of deep history. And at this point, Wall to Wall was yet to produce one of the greatest drama documentaries of the modern era, *Man on Wire* (BBC, 2008). This film was made for BBC Documentaries, Discovery, and the UK Film Council, and produced by the man who cut his teeth on *Smallpox 2002*, Simon Chinn, for whom the film earned the Oscar for Best Documentary in 2009. But, as Graham notes, 'drama documentaries at Wall to Wall were mostly quite conventional after 2004. The innovations lay in other, often smaller indies, many of whom made drama documentaries for love, with great writing and recognised stars that competed with dramas themselves.' It is to this outpouring that *A New Genre?* turns in Chapter 5.

Notes

1. François Truffaut was a self-styled auteur writer/director and leader of the French New Wave movement in the 1960s and 1970s. Truffaut wrote about himself and Alfred Hitchcock as fellow auteurs. Hitchcock was an English filmmaker who was one of the most influential figures in the history of cinema. His dominance over a genre caused him to be known as 'the Master of Suspense'.
2. Steven Lipkin, *Docudrama Performs the Past: Arenas of Argument in Films Based on True Stories* (Newcastle-upon-Tyne: Cambridge Scholars, 2011), p. 47.
3. Steven Lipkin, *Real Emotional Logic: Film and Television Docudrama as Persuasive Practice* (Carbondale, IL: Southern Illinois University Press, 2002), p. 41.
4. The Independent Commissioning Group at the BBC was tasked with commissioning programming from independents to compete with BBC's in-house providers.
5. Michael Jackson and Jane Root were the original partners in a company set up expressly to run *The Media Show*. When Jackson brought Graham in as a partner, it was Graham's idea that the company should have a life beyond *The Media Show* and hence renamed it Wall to Wall Television – a name that could cover all commissioning eventualities.
6. *1900 House*: One family gets to have the ultimate adventure, traveling back in time from the Information Age to the Victorian era.
7. At an AGM in 1957, a reporter asked how his TV station in Scotland was doing, and Lord Roy Thomson replied: 'It's a license to print money.' The words were, apparently, never used at the AGM, but the reporter had his introduction, and the insensitive remark became folklore.
8. A wire frame is a digital sketch of the image one wishes to finally bring to life.
9. BBC Worldwide (BBCWW) emerged in 1995 from BBC Enterprises.
10. Robert Rosenstone, *History on Film/Film on History*, 2nd ed. (Abingdon: Routledge, 2013), p. 79.
11. Lipkin, *Docudrama Performs the Past*, p. 104.
12. ITEL was the alternative distribution entity to BBCWW and essential to indies at ITV and Channel 4.
13. TLC – The Learning Channel, a member of the Discovery Channel family.
14. Derek Paget, 'Making Mischief: Peter Kosminsky, Stephen Frears and British Television Docudrama', *Journal of British Cinema and Television*, 10:1 (2013), pp. 171–186 (p. 174).
15. Lipkin, *Real Emotional Logic*, p. 45.
16. *Ibid.*, p. 54.
17. Hayden White, 'The Value of Narrativity in the Representation of Reality', *Critical Inquiry*, 7:1 (1980), pp. 5–27 (p. 5).
18. Lipkin, *Real Emotional Logic*, p. 45.
19. *Ibid.*, p. 4.
20. *Ibid.*, p. 5.

21 Anthony Burgess, author of *A Clockwork Orange* (1962); and Desmond Morris, zoologist and television presenter of *The Human Animal* (BBC, 1994).
22 Graham does not recall re-mortgaging his house for a production. As he says, 'I may be a maverick, but I'm not stupid!' (Graham, 2022).
23 Lipkin, *Docudrama Performs the Past*, p. 104.
24 Continuity – the often-unheralded person who follows the script to aid the Director, the Director of Photography, the Art Department, and ultimately the Editor.
25 'Approximation is the "jouissance of recognition" of knowing a work's point of reference' (Stella Bruzzi, *Approximation: Documentary, History and the Staging of Reality* (London: Routledge, 2020), p. 9.).
26 Rosenstone, *History on Film/Film on History*, p. 30.
27 Lipkin, *Docudrama Performs the Past*, p. 47.
28 *Supervolcano* (BBC, 2005) won an EMMY and a BAFTA for special effects and was nominated for an EMMY for best television film.
29 Graham credits the story guru Robert McKee for this line (Graham, 2022).
30 MIPCOM is an international television marketplace, usually based in Cannes.
31 HBO: Home Box Office, founded in the early 1970s as an American pay-television network, also producer of outstanding history drama documentaries – *Conspiracy* (2001), *Band of Brothers* (2001), and *John Adams* (2008) among them.
32 FX Channel is owned by Fox and produces shows such as the TV series *Fargo*.
33 Hayden White, *The Content of the Form: Narrative Discourse and Historical Representation* (Baltimore, MD: Johns Hopkins University Press, 1989), p. 57.
34 White, cited by Rosenstone, in Lipkin, *Real Emotional Logic*, p. 38.
35 Graham confirms: 'We actually came up with a pitch line for *Smallpox* which I think FX used in a poster campaign: "Everything in this film is true. It just hasn't happened yet"' (Graham, 2022).
36 The industry terms a narrator as the Voice of God if that voice is as all-knowing as current knowledge extends. This separates the omniscient narrator from the personal narrator, who will have a more subjective, and therefore restrictive, view of the world.
37 *The War of the Worlds* was an episode of the CBS Radio series *The Mercury Theatre on the Air*, broadcast on 30 October 1938. It is based on an H. G. Wells novel that tells the story of a Martian invasion of Earth.
38 Robert Rosenstone, *Visions of the Past: The Challenge of Film to Our Idea of History* (Boston, MA: Harvard University Press, 1995), p. 71.
39 A Steadicam shot is a variant on the handheld shot, employing a kind of special hydraulic harness that smooths out the bumps and jerkiness associated with the typical handheld style.
40 Derek Paget and Stephen Lacey (eds), *The 'War on Terror': Post-9/11 Television Drama, Docudrama and Documentary* (Cardiff: University of Wales Press, 2015), p. 18.
41 Ibid.
42 Ibid.

43 Rosenstone, *Visions of the Past*, p. 7.
44 The quotation is from the BBC/Wall to Wall film under consideration. All of the following quotations follow suit.
45 *Why I Write* (1946) was Orwell's autobiographical approach to his craft, published four years before his death.
46 Langham was soon to be immortalised in the first two series of *The Thick of It* (BBC, 2005), for which he won a BAFTA for best comedy performance in 2006.
47 'Brechtian' refers, among other theatrical devices, to minimal sets and actors speaking directly to the audience, breaking the fourth wall.
48 *Zelig* (1983) is a 'documentary' film about a man who can look and act like whoever is around him.
49 *Down and Out in Paris and London* (1933) is a memoir in two parts on the theme of poverty in the two cities; it was written deliberately in a non-academic register. The name George came from George V, and Orwell from a local Suffolk river.
50 Simon Schama, cited in David Cannadine (ed.), *History and the Media* (London: Palgrave Macmillan, 2006), pp. 20–33.
51 Alexandre Astruc, originally printed in *L'Écran française* (30 March 1948) – my quotation marks to raise the out-of-date gender references.
52 Astruc, p. 2.
53 Truffaut, cited by Sam Solecki, *A Truffaut Notebook* (Montreal: McGill-Queen's University Press, 2015), p. 38.
54 Andrew Sarris, 'The Auteur Theory and the Perils of Pauline', *Film Quarterly*, 16:4 (1963), pp. 26–33 (p. 29).
55 Jean Renoir was a French film director, screenwriter, actor, producer, and author.
56 Peter Wollen, *Signs and Meaning in the Cinema* (London: British Film Institute, 1969), p. 85.
57 *Ibid.*, p. 95.
58 Roland Barthes (1967), cited by Laura Seymour, *An Analysis of Roland Barthes's The Death of the Author* (London: Macat Library, 2017), p. 16.
59 Michel Foucault (1969) cited by Steven Smith, *Modernity and its Discontents* (New Haven, CT: Yale University Press, 2016), p. 299.
60 Erik Knudsen, 'The Total Filmmaker: Thinking of Screenwriting, Directing and Editing as One Role', *New Writing: The International Journal for the Practice and Theory of Creative Writing*, 13:1 (2016), pp. 109–129 (p. 110).
61 *Ibid.*
62 Samuel Goldwyn, cited by Sam Solecki, *A Truffaut Notebook* (Montreal: McGill-Queen's University Press, 2015), p. 36.

5

2003–2005: Working towards fuller dramatisation and a new genre?

Introduction

Within two years of Wall to Wall's successes, there was an explosion in dramatised history documentary, the numbers of programmes commissioned rising from six in 1999 to twenty in 2000 and soaring up to ninety-eight in 2005.[1] Other channels joined the BBC's and Channel 4's lead: National Geographic, History, Discovery, and soon BBC Four and Channel 5. This outpouring of dramatised documentaries was clearly part of what Sir David Cannadine had referred to in his 2006 statement, quoted in the introduction to this work: 'in Britain, the late 1990s and early 2000s witnessed what was widely regarded as an unprecedented interest in history: among publishers, in the newspapers, on radio and on film, and (especially) on television; and from the general public, who it seemed, could not get enough of it'.[2]

Money was increasingly being found by broadcasters for films made in the drama documentary mode, even if it was not profitable for production companies. As Alex Graham recalls, 'the innovations lay in other, often smaller indies, many of whom made drama documentaries for love'. In general, he was right about this – the innovations in most dramatisations lay in more singular productions, but perhaps he underestimated how many of these productions there would be.

This chapter will study those experimental films, made by smaller indies, that take dramatised documentary forward through the boom period of 2003–2005. Broadly, two variants of drama documentary were evolving. The first employed impressionistic dramatisation. This chapter uses *Bareknuckle Boxer* (Channel 4, 2003) as a case study of this variant, where the drama was non-speaking, and impressionistic images were offered to support the presenter or interviewees in the documentary mode. These films elected to keep the documentary mode foregrounded, entrusting experts to provide sense. The second variant followed Wall to Wall's example of venturing into scripted drama, which will be the subject of another case study, *The Trial of The King Killers* (Channel 4, 2005). These fuller dramas were tentative steps, retaining documentary devices like voice-of-God narration, but they required the primary sources to be adapted into scripted dialogue as well as narration.

Usually, this adaptation was performed by the documentary director or producer, but increasingly, a new hybrid writer was introduced to the mode. While the writers concerned would not have regarded themselves as being hybrid, let alone 'mongrel', they would have accepted a term like 'adaptable'. Tim Kirby, who wrote *King Killers*, remains a very skilled writer who also directs and produces. But the drama silo does not, on the whole, recognise these skills to be incorporated into one person. Hence, the diminution of a 'mongrel' part dramatist, part documentarian begins to arise, whereas I believe that Kirby and others should be recognised for their adaptability and phenomenal breadth, elucidated later in this chapter.

Meanwhile, we return to the variants, impressionistic and scripted, which reveal the *ad-hoc* nature of growth within the whole dramatised history documentary arena. The term 'variant' is deliberately used here, for the films of this boom period were immensely varied in their form, funding structures, and subject matter. The word 'boom' is appropriate, since these films were the result of a surge of public interest and broadcaster appetite, two factors that account for the variants that emanated.

The primary purpose of this chapter is to attempt to bring structure to this explosion of material, including both variants, devising a canon that can make sense of the energy and historiography that underpinned it all. In television theory, this would be achieved by defining the data set as a genre, with rules that define what lies within the generic walls and what lies without. The previous chapter, on Wall to Wall's contributions, helps to define the edges of the possible genre, which contains those films that employs a drama mode, partially, if not wholly, to render the documentary message. *Neanderthal*, *Ancient Egyptians*, *Smallpox 2002*, and *George Orwell: A Life in Pictures* all lie within the new genre of historical drama documentary. Wall to Wall's other products, *1900 House* and *Who Do You Think You Are*, although excellent exponents of history, lie outside the genre: *Who Do You Think You Are* is a history documentary but does not employ dramatisation at all; *1900 House* uses re-enactments by modern contestants placing themselves into old clothes, and does not use reconstructions, the building bricks of dramatisation.

Thus, we begin to edge towards a definition of a genre that draws together films that combine the three conceptual approaches I have been using throughout the book, which can be articulated as three key words: (1) *dramatised*; (2) *history*; (3) *documentary*. Every film that has been the subject of a case study has combined all three core approaches. In terms of next steps, I shall first attempt to draw together a data set covering the first half of the period under examination (2000–2005) so that an informed approximation of the extent of the set can be given in the form of a list, with relevant analysis. Secondly, I shall measure this data set against scholars' rules of genre, testing it against one of the hardest questions: how does one define a genre in the first place? Thirdly, I shall address the question of how (if it is accepted that there is a genre to be considered) can any particular film, from within such a varied genre, be placed on the broadly accepted arc of a genre's rise and fall?

To begin to answer these questions is the challenge facing this chapter, and the first means of answering is to assess the data set, which has been compiled for the first time for this book. The data set has been drawn from, and limited to, the extensive databases of the independent UK production companies under consideration and confirmed by the many interviewees, including those who commissioned a great number of these programmes at Channel 4 and the BBC, including most recently the respective heads of History, Hamish Mykura and Martin Davidson. It should also be noted that this list focuses on what Paget defined as drama documentaries and *not* docudramas. Therefore, dramas based on fact but commissioned by the drama departments, such as *The Deal* or *Band of Brothers* are not included. Documentaries that involve drama and are commissioned by documentary departments are very much included. Sometimes, the films selected might be questioned in terms of their historical integrity. The slew of films such as the '*If …*' (BBC, 2004–2005) series are considered by both Davidson and Mykura, somewhat ironically, as 'future history and are commissioned by documentary departments' (Davidson, 2019). Just as future histories, *The War Game* and *Smallpox 2002* are acceptable, so too must the *If* series. It is clear that the edges of the list are 'entangled', as Paget and Ebbrecht so rightly termed the difficulty in 2016. Furthermore, the list, outlined below, contains the dramatised history documentaries of both core variants (impressionistic and full scripted), and indicates the presence of a 'boom' by means of a clear volume increase in programming between 2000 and 2005. (The year 1999 has been included to show the very low numbers of drama documentary before the millennium.) Finally, Mykura notes that the list focuses most readily on the BBC/Channel 4 battle. As a commissioner who left for the National Geographic Channel in 2012, he maintains that 'the minnows in drama documentary were Nat Geo, History Channel and Channel 5. But none of their films in this period exhibited changes of any great magnitude. At that point, they were followers' (Mykura, 2020).

The data set (2000–2005) according to numbers of historical drama documentary programmes: **the total of programmes in bold.**

1999 – *The People's Duchess*/C4
1999 – *Station X*/C4 (x4)
1999 – *Wisconsin Death Trip*/BBC
1999 – 6 drama docs

2000 – *A History of Britain*/BBC (x6)
2000 – *Holocaust on Trial*/C4/PBS
2000 – *Escape from Colditz*/C4
2000 – *Elizabeth*/C4 (x4)
2000 – *Joan of Arc*/C4
2000 – *When Money Went Mad*/C4
2000 – *The Day the World Took Off*/C4 (x6)
2000 – 20 drama docs

2001 – *Smallpox* 2002/BBC
2001 – *Egypt's Golden Empire*/BBC (x3)
2001 – *History of Britain 2*/BBC (x6)
2001 – *Six Wives of Henry VIII*/C4 (x4)
2001 – *Plague, Fire, War and Treason*/C4 (x4)
2001 – *Neanderthal*/C4
2001 – *The Crusades*/History (x2)
2001 – 21 drama docs

2002 – *Pyramid*/BBC
2002 – *A History of Britain*/BBC (x3)
2002 – *The Battle of the Atlantic*/BBC (x3)
2002 – *Christmas under Fire*/BBC
2002 – *Cleopatra*/C4
2002 – *Spartans* C4/PBS (x3)
2002 – *Luther*/C4/PBS (x2)
2002 – *Dambusters*/C4
2002 – *Charge of the Light Brigade*/C4
2002 – *Hitler's Britain*/C5/History/PBS
2002 – 17 drama docs

2003 – *Leonardo*/BBC (x3)
2003/5 – *Days that Shook the World*/BBC (x16)
2003 – *Colosseum, Rome's Arena of Death*/BBC Discovery
2003 – *Seven Wonders of the Industrial World*/BBC (x7)
2003 – *George Orwell: A Life in Pictures*/BBC
2003 – *The Day Britain Stopped*/BBC

2003 – *Walking with Cavemen*/BBC (x4)
2003 – *Pepys*/BBC
2003 – *Redcoats and Rebels*/BBC (x4)
2003 – *Ancient Egyptians*/C4 (x4)
2003 – *Georgian Underworld: Invitation to a Hanging, Peterloo Massacre, Coram's Children, Bare Knuckle Boxer*/C4 (x4)
2003 – *Royal Deaths and Diseases*/C4 (x5)
2003 – *Lawrence of Arabia*/PBS/C4 (x2)
2003 – *Witchcraze*/C4
2003 – *Lionheart*/C4
2003 – *Touching the Void*/Film Four
2003 – 56 drama docs

2004 – *Dunkirk*/BBC (x3)
2004 – *Agatha Christie, A Life in Pictures*/BBC
2004 – *The Man Who Broke Britain*/BBC
2004 – *Wren, the Man Who Built Britain*/BBC (x3)
2004 – *D Day 6.6.1944*/BBC
2004 – *Terry Jones' Medieval Lives*/BBC (x4 TBC)
2004 – *Seconds from Disaster*/BBC/Nat Geo (x19)
2004 – *Days that Shook the World*/BBC (x20)
2004 – *If ...*/BBC (x5)
2004–6 – *Monarchy*/C4 (x10)
2004 – *Medici, Godfathers of Renaissance*/C4/PBS (x4)
2004 – *Princes in the Tower*/C4
2004 – *Dragons*/C4/Animal Planet (x2)
2004 – *Agincourt*/C4
2004 – *D-Day (ultimate conflict)*/C5/Nat Geo
2004 – 76 drama docs

2005 – *Blood on Our Hands: English Civil War*/BBC
2005 – *D Day to Berlin*/BBC (x3)
2005 – *Ian Fleming: Bondmaker*/BBC
2005 – *Days that Shook the World*/BBC (x20)
2005 – *Seconds from Disaster*/BBC (x25)
2005 – *Hiroshima*/BBC
2005 – *Auschwitz: The Final Solution*/BBC (x6)
2005 – *If ...*/BBC (x7)
2005 – *Trafalgar Battle Surgeon; Rum, Sodomy and the Lash*/C4 (x2)
2005 – *Trial of the King Killers*/C4
2005 – *Helen of Troy*/C4

2005 – *Guns Germs and Steel*/C4/Nat Geo (x3)
2005 – *The Year London Blew Up 1974*/C4
2005 – *E=MC2*/C4
2005 – *Great San Francisco Earthquake*/C4
2005 – *Blitz, London's Firestorm*/C4
2005 – *The Somme*/C4
2005 – *Monarchy*/C4 (x10)
2005 – *The Flight That Fought Back*/C4
2005 – *Ape to Man*/History
2005 – *Vic Reeves Rogues Gallery*/Discovery (x9)
2005 – *Oil Storm*/FX
2005 – 98 drama docs

As can be seen, the year before the millennium, 1999, features only six history drama documentaries across two broadcasters, the BBC and Channel 4. In 2000, the number of drama documentary hours leaps to twenty; in 2001 it rises to twenty-one, in 2002 dips to seventeen; in 2003 rises once more to fifty-six; in 2004 to seventy-six; and in 2005 to ninety-eight. The numbers reveal an increasing commitment by broadcasters to delivering history programming in the drama documentary mode to the extent that they indicate the evolution of an identifiable genre. Viewers still enjoyed receiving their history through presenters and 'living history', but the drama documentary mode was increasingly popular.

One of the reasons for this significant rise is the ease of sale to co-producers abroad. The dramatised documentary did not have a British presenter that needed excising, nor British present-day contributors that would be irrelevant to another country. A drama documentary had a narrator's track that could be dubbed and interviewees that could be subtitled, and, above all, this mode contained a degree of sensuous drama that was not available to many broadcasters outside the United Kingdom. France, Germany, Spain, Italy, and Japan, for example, were increasingly willing to collaborate with Anglo/American-financed histories.

The domestic and international interest in history was stretching considerably, going beyond the traditional fare of 'Henry, Hitler, and Hieroglyphics'. Interest was now evident across the fullest extent of history, from prehistory through to the latter half of the twentieth century. If the list is reorganised by historical period, it looks like this:

Prehistory:
Neanderthal
Ape to Man
Walking with Cavemen

Ancient History:
Pyramid
Ancient Egyptians
Egypt's Golden Period
Helen of Troy
Colosseum
Spartans
Cleopatra

Middle Ages:
A History of Britain (covers all the sections)
Medieval Lives
Crusades
Lionheart
Joan of Arc
Agincourt
Medici, Godfathers of the Renaissance
Princes in the Tower
Leonardo

Sixteenth and seventeenth centuries:
Henry VIII and his Six Wives
Elizabeth
Witchcraze
Trial of the King Killers
Plague
Fire
Pepys
Wren

Eighteenth and nineteenth centuries:
Redcoats and Rebels
Trafalgar Battle Surgeon
Rum, Sodomy and the Lash
Peterloo Massacre
Charge of the Light Brigade
Seven Wonders of the Industrial Revolution

Twentieth century:
Somme
Lawrence of Arabia
Dunkirk

Dambusters
D-Day 6.6.1944
E=MC2
George Orwell
The Day London Blew Up 1974
Days that Shook the World
Seconds from Disaster

Organised in this way, the list takes on a newly informative shape, indicating that British history, as it was then understood, was being broadly well represented (albeit, to the viewer of 2025, in a rather old-fashioned framework). It is also clear that over a five-year period, history as a subject matter was being dramatised, in part or wholly, for a willing audience. This would continue for another three to five years, where the missing global elements of America, China, Japan, and the Middle East were added to the list just as British history was further mined in microscopic detail. It is true that South America and Africa were woefully overlooked, and history was ignoring stories of gender and race – a shocking absence that this chapter will attempt to address. But otherwise, there was a great deal of variety in the growing corpus, another confirmation that this was a boom period, the study of which might benefit from a new, definable genre.

I therefore propose that the prevalence of this putative genre on television caused an identifiable programme type to emerge, the nature of which critics and viewers could quickly glean from how it was presented in the advanced television listings. The audience and critics did not think to refer to the corpus by a single heading, hence the desire of the present writer to reclaim it as a genre in retrospect. The definition of a genre will be useful in helping to ask some key questions of the data set. Is it always part drama, part documentary, both respected throughout? How many variants are there? How did they evolve? How many resembled progenitors such as *Culloden* or *The War Game*, which I argue could be regarded as the original history drama documentaries? The more one can understand the genre, the better one can see connections within this data set and links from the originators through to their inheritors today.

Additionally, why was the genre so often derided – as being neither one thing nor another, and hence a 'mongrel/bastard'? I shall hope to prove that while the evolving genre was often poorly constructed, it was also often a brilliant mash-up of information and entertainment, of sense and sensuousness, and should be appreciated as such.

Finally, by employing a generic set of rules to the list of films, above, it should be possible to approach this list in a more informed manner. The next step is to examine genre theory and investigate which elements of it can cast light on this intriguing list of history television films.

Genre theory and the corpus

According to Steve Neale, a scholar of film genre, 'genres do not consist only of films: they consist also, and equally, of specific systems of expectation and hypothesis that spectators bring with them to the cinema and that interact with films themselves during the course of the viewing process'. He argues that 'these systems provide spectators with a means of recognition and understanding'.[3] Such systems also help to construct the bodies of text that can be seen to form part of a genre. Rick Altman suggests, in this context, that it is important to 'subject the corpus to analysis, to locate a method for defining and describing the structures, functions, and systems specific to a large number of the films within it'.[4] Having described these systems, Altman asks the viewer or the critics to seek out 'texts which correspond to a particular understanding of the genre, that is, which provide ample material for a given method of analysis', and which 'will be retained within the generic corpus'.[5] As Tzvetan Todorov points out, 'each era has its own system of genres'.[6] This brief insight is especially helpful considering the minutest arguments which emerge in some attempts to define genres. As a scholar for whom television studies intersects with history, this makes sense in the same way that historiography shows that each era tells its history according to its unique perspective. Ultimately, it confirms that the definition of a genre is an ongoing process. As Neale confirms, 'genres are best understood as processes. These processes may, for sure, be dominated by repetition, but they are also marked fundamentally by difference, variation, and change.'[7] The term 'variation' is also applicable to the corpus of work under consideration here, since it has already been established that there are a number of variants in the data set. At its core, the primary variation is whether the drama is impressionistic or a fuller scripted version, yet both variants are part of the greater corpus of drama documentary.

So where does hybridity fit into all of this? Is the drama documentary simply a hybrid of the two forms that constitute its name, rather than a genre of its own? Neale asserts that 'hybrids are not genres ... even hybrids are recognised as hybrids – combinations of specific and distinct generic components – not as genres in their own right'.[8] There is, then, the issue of whether a genre that contains hybridity, or is considered half a genre, should be termed a sub-genre. Alan Williams accepts that this is 'mainly a question of terminology' but wonders if 'we ought to consider the principal genres as being narrative film, experimental/avant-garde film, and documentary [...] What we presently call film genres would then be *sub-genres*'.⁹

Sub-genre is another diminution! It will not surprise that I disagree with Neale and Williams in this. Drama documentary may well be a hybrid of drama and documentary but – as this book has already shown and will subsequently reveal more fully – the corpus of these films is large and varied, and is not just a hybrid of the two modes. The corpus creates its own rules, and while it is true that at their worst, as contemporary critics pointed out, the films within are neither one thing nor another, at their best, they can achieve a distinctive offering of 'sense and sensuousness' combined. As will be seen, drama and documentary have an equal footing in this genre, just as sense and sensuousness implies, whereas docudrama is more heavily weighted towards drama. Drama documentary in relative harmony can, in short, be an ideal mode for storytelling, and not one to be belittled as simply a 'hybrid', 'a sub-genre' or 'a mode of presentation'.

A genre is a corpus of work defined by scholars or practitioners as sharing certain common features. Stella Bruzzi, in an article on 'the current documentary obsession' with true crime documentaries (a genre much favoured in the Netflix era), argues that 'ultimately this heterogeneous series of individual texts loosely constitute a genre'.¹⁰ The obsession that she rightly identifies is one of commissioners and viewers alike and is reminiscent of the popularity of history drama docs in the 2000s. Bruzzi describes the texts as 'heterogeneous', which is also true of the variants within the history arena. But the key point here is her assertion that these texts 'loosely constitute a genre'. Critics, commissioners, producers, and viewers alike would concur; when contemporary viewers see true crime stories on Netflix, or copied by the terrestrial UK channels, they know that similar rules are at play. Bruzzi adds:

> Bookended by *The Staircase* from 2004 (the genre's touchstone or foundational text) and *Making a Murderer* from 2015 (the genre's most notorious example to date), this discussion will look at a diverse range of examples (series, podcasts, one-off documentaries) that nevertheless share common concerns around the law and how it can be represented, the truth, evidence and miscarriages of justice.¹¹

To apply Bruzzi's terms to the New History Drama-Documentary, the genre's touchstone would be *A History of Britain*, from 2000, and the most noted example would be *Man on Wire*, from 2008. This book will look at 'a diverse range of examples (series, podcasts, one-off documentaries)' of the history 'boom' (although the podcasts came later). It will seek out the films that share 'common concerns' about the representation of the past.

Studying this body of work as a genre is enlightening in itself. It helps to identify why certain devices are broadly aiming to do the same thing: offer entertainment while also providing information. But it also has a greater goal, that of identifying how the genre evolved, as defined by its overall structure. This is confirmed by scholarly work on the various 'stages' of generic development, as Neale notes in his discussion, in *Film and Theory*, of Schatz's theory of generic development. Neale observes that 'citing film theorist Christian Metz and art historian Henri Focillon, Schatz puts forward the view that genres pass through a number of stages'.[12] The first two stages are the ones that best inform this chapter, since the genre here is in the early stages of evolution. Metz defines these two stages in his book *Film Language: A Semiotics in the Cinema* (1974), arguing that 'once a genre has passed through its experimental stage where its conventions have been established, it enters into its classical stage. We might consider this stage as one of formal transparency'.[13] This analysis can be used to illuminate the films listed above, and it will be useful to look, in the first instance, at what is *experimental* and what is *classical* in the very first dramatised history documentaries of 2000: *A History of Britain* and Starkey's *Elizabeth*.

A History of Britain would be considered experimental since, as a series of films, it approached the earliest known history of this island with a stylistically novel approach in which impressionistic dramatisation was utilised, albeit sporadically. Even within the series, the individual films were heterogeneous (to use Bruzzi's term) in that they were various in their approaches, in part because they had different directors. Series 2 and 3 would not be properly considered experimental, on the other hand, since, to follow Metz's criteria: 'its conventions have been established' and the series 'has entered into the classical phase'. This is also true of Starkey's Tudor series. *Elizabeth* is a very experimental approach to the visual and aural narrative of history and represents a stylistic revolution in comparison to Starkey's earlier *Henry VIII* from the 1990s, which had no dramatisation at all. *Elizabeth* introduced the candle-lit royal portrait, an imagining of what it was to be in the glow of the royal presence. These dramatisations evolved into *Henry VIII and his Six Wives*, which introduced dialogue in the form of brief quotations from primary sources, and therefore would still be considered 'experimental'. But by the time Starkey had been commissioned to tell the tale of the journey of *Monarchy*, the series had become 'classical' in the extreme. The dramatisations, instead of becoming more actor-led and quoting more primary sources, returned to a less expensive, non-speaking impressionism. These two examples show that the Metz structure applies well to this new genre: an encouraging start from which to proceed. By the end of this chapter, one should be able to return to the list of films from 2000 to 2005 and differentiate the experimental from the classical. This will enable this book properly to chart where the aesthetic evolutions have occurred.

So, to this chapter's case studies, which it is hoped will chart both stages of Metz's genre development, and also the number of variants on offer. I shall begin with one series on Channel 4 that is a particular prism through which to see the non-dialogue, impressionistic variant settled into the classical phase: Channel 4's eighteenth-century season, known as *The Georgian Underworld*, which includes the film *Bareknuckle Boxer*.

The Georgian Underworld (Channel 4, 2003)

Brief summary: *Four-part series about the seamier end of life in Britain's eighteenth century. Using predominantly impressionistic drama alongside expert interviews and documentary techniques, the films told the narratives of thieves, bare-knuckle boxers, orphans, and the emerging industrial working class.*

From a genre perspective, it is useful to note that Janice Hadlow, by now Head of Specialist Factual at Channel 4, commissioned this series of films in an *ad-hoc* fashion, before drawing them into a 'Long Eighteenth Century' season. The producers themselves were making the films as stand-alone projects and Hadlow herself admits that she had commissioned each one thanks to her own predilection for the eighteenth century and for bottom-up history. She later realised that films sell better to the viewers as seasons and so always looked to pool films together. In an interview with the present writer, she confessed: 'I love the 18th century and believe it to be the forgotten period of British history' (Hadlow, 2019). The eighteenth century, according to Laurence Brockliss, Professor Emeritus in history at Oxford and a specialist in the period, is seen in general as an 'under-valued area of the curriculum somewhere between the Tudors, Civil War and the Victorians' (Brockliss, 2019). Yet to Hadlow, the eighteenth century is when recognisable Britain emerges: language that is recognisably modern; the rise of money, trading, coffee houses; the reading of newspapers; the enlargement of cities due to the agrarian revolution, which meant more city dwellers could be fed; and the rise of trade in India, Canada, the Americas, and the Far East. Compared to the religious fanaticism of the seventeenth century, which is so alien to modern, mostly secular Britain, the eighteenth century stands up to being explored and inspected in detail. As a side note, it must be stressed that much of the emergence of modern Britain in the eighteenth century derived from the unholy trade in human beings under the aegis of men like the now derided Edward Colston of The Royal African Company, whose legacies, when he died in 1721, created the financial foundation for many of Bristol's educational establishments. Since the Black Lives Matter demonstrations of the summer of 2020, these origins have been newly exposed, and it is a mark of how recent progress has been that issues such as these little troubled the history filmmakers of the early 2000s.

These matters will be further explored in the first case study of this chapter, *Bareknuckle Boxer* (Channel 4, 2003), a single film in *The Georgian Underworld* series. Hadlow was not insistent that the subject of history should be told exclusively through the prism of drama documentary. Her remit was to bring history to the widest viewership possible, whether it be through presenter-led programming, such as Starkey's work, or through living history, such as *Edwardian Country House* (Channel 4, 2002). But she was aware that audiences seemed to appreciate the introduction of drama into her commissions. *The Great Plague* and *The Great Fire* (Channel 4, 2001) had been a considerable hit with critics and viewers alike. '*The Great Plague* and *The Great Fire* was an experiment that paid off', says Hadlow, 'so we were prepared to try it again. In many ways, what became the 18th Century season was made up entirely of drama documentaries. It just happened that way.' This commentary gives a behind-the-scenes glimpse at the *ad hoc* development of what could one day be recognised as part of an evolving genre.

Ad hoc or not, there are consistent characteristics in the films that are worth noting, not least the reliance on primary sources – following the approach of *The Great Plague*, with its intimate detail of Cock and Key Alley's church finances. Hence the reliance on Captain Coram's lists of orphans, journals smuggled out of Newgate Jail, and the court transcript of an inquest above a pub. The use of such sources is also reminiscent of the details emanating from the 'regimental orders' utilised to such effect by *Culloden* back in 1964. Indeed, when one comes across the records of boxing newspapers, drawn upon in the first film to be analysed, it is as if the ghosts of Peter Watkins and his team were guiding the distinctive evolution of this new possible genre.

Hadlow commissioned *Bareknuckle Boxer* and *Invitation to a Hanging* from Samir Shah's micro-indie Juniper TV, with *The Peterloo Massacre* and *The Man who Saved Children* from a former colleague at the BBC, Martin Davidson, who was now at the fast-growing indie RDF. What is immediately evident in this series, beyond the individual films' lack of iconography, is the absence of royalty in these narratives, for history under Hadlow was moving away from 'Henry, Hitler, and Hieroglyphics' (although Starkey's *Monarchy*, commissioned by Hadlow, was perhaps sufficient fodder for the endemic appetite for anything royal).

Bareknuckle Boxer showed a rare awareness that British history was not just for, and about, the white, middle-class literati. It was a story of Black experience at the end of the eighteenth century, focusing on a freed enslaved person, Bill Richmond, who came from the United States to Britain, fought his way to a British boxing title fight and progressed through society with a business acumen that brought him to being honoured by King William IV on his coronation day. David Dabydeen, author of *Hogarth's Blacks* (1985), claims that 'Britain was a good place to be for a Black man at the end of the 18th century, since the abolition movement was in full flow.'[14] The film begins with a Black man begging on the streets of London. The narrator, Black actor Hugh Quarshie, comments that 'there were more than 15,000 Black people in London at the end of the 18th century. Many were in poverty, runaway slaves.' In vision, a beggar receives a donation. It is then revealed to the audience's surprise that the beggar is white and the donor is Black, as the narrator continues: 'but some Blacks were in a different class'. A Black man such as Bill Richmond was, according to the editor of *Boxiana*, a sporting journal, 'a pugilist of colour, but not incapable of discourse on other subjects, an extraordinary man'. Under the patronage of Lord Percy, Richmond apprenticed to be a cabinetmaker, and learned to read before revealing his fighting prowess. 'He was not a large man', says Philippa Gregory, author of *A Respectable Trade* (1995): 'Bill was only 10 stone, 12 lbs, far less heavy than his opponents, but like Mohammed Ali, he was agile and exhausted them before landing his right and left.' Steve Martin, another Black author, suggests that Richmond 'was not a serious threat to the nation's identity' (because he loses to the white champion), but Thomas Molineux, another Black boxer and Richmond's groomed replacement, 'really was' a threat. The film is not just a very strong narrative of two Black men vying for the title against white boxers, but a social commentary on how Britain regarded this possibility – one that acknowledges that when Molineux takes the fight to the wire, there is a riot in the auditorium, in which the Black challenger's hand is conveniently broken.

It is asserted by Juniper TV that the British as a nation have always been progressive, but that progressiveness has its periodic limits. The story nevertheless marks this episode as a step forward in race relations, albeit a brief and singular one. But then one should remember that the (traditionally white and male) working-class movement was barely in evidence in this period. Peterloo, which voiced the arguments of the factory workers of the north, was still almost twenty years off and, even then, it was another thirteen years before a suffrage extension was granted in the Great Reform Bill of 1832, and that only for middle-class men of some property. What is more pertinent to this book is that *Bareknuckle Boxer* was such a singular film in the history boom of the 2000s. It was not followed by a slew of films about the Black experience in Britain's past. It was not until 2010 that Channel 4 broadcast another film about the Black experience, *Bloody Foreigners*

(Channel 4, 2010), focusing on the Battle of Trafalgar, and it was another four years after that before the BBC broadcast David Olusoga's *Forgotten Soldiers of Empire* (BBC, 2014). In 2008, the BBC's drama department did also commission *Walter's War*, the true story of Walter Tull, a Black man who fought in World War I, but it was subsequently side-lined to BBC Four.

It is hard to imagine, from the perspective of 2024, how under-represented the BAME viewership must have felt, watching this island's history with little or no inclusion of BAME experiences. Samir Shah, the executive producer of *Bareknuckle Boxer* is, and was not, surprised. Shah came to Britain aged six from Mumbai, where his father still lives, and after an education that culminated with a PhD in Geography at St Catherine's, Oxford, he joined the BBC on Panorama, which was edited at that point by the future BBC Director-General, Tony Hall. Shah made protestations about being the only non-white journalist on the news and current affairs show but did not make much progress with his campaign under Hall. Shah made more headway at LWT under John Birt, who was apparently more progressive in outlook, promoting Trevor Phillips as well as Shah. 'It was never special pleading', says Shah in two interviews conducted in London over 2019 and 2020, 'but if you are not white, you don't see the history of non-whites'. However, Shah does not believe that there was institutional racism in the media in the 1990s and 2000s, with many of his peer group being white middle-class liberals. Shah also asserts that many South Asian families did not want their brightest and best children going into the media, as opposed to medicine or accountancy, and Afro-Caribbean culture broadly did not 'favour going to university, the entry point for the media' until quite recently. Shah finds it a shame, though, that Dabydeen did not have more opportunity on television, during what was the boom in his subject. He was on the race-relations think tank The Runnymede Trust when Shah was chairman, and his book, *Hogarth's Blacks*, was well received, but a television presence remained elusive despite his great success as an ambassador for UNESCO from 1997 until 2010.

Bareknuckle Boxer was a brief but enlightened moment for the representation of history in historical drama documentaries, but it was not so important in terms of aesthetic evolution. It was a very well made but classical rendition of the impressionistic variant. So too *The Man Who Saved Children* and *Invitation to a Hanging*. Only the fourth film of the series, *The Peterloo Massacre*, could be considered to fall within the category of Metz's 'experimentation', since it contained fuller drama, more dialogue, and professional actors assembled in a semi-theatrical courtroom setting, and it had a script derived from the transcripts of the inquest into the Peterloo Massacre of 1819. According to *The Sunday Times* TV critic, John Dugdale:

Instead of trying to recreate the massacre itself, it restages the inquest into the death of one of the victims, John Lees, with Lees's ghost – apparently looking back from the present – providing the commentary. Along with the BBC's Other Boleyn Girl, history television has rarely been so dynamic.[15]

John Dugdale acknowledges the strengths of imaginative solutions increasingly provided by this foray into fuller drama. It is interesting to note that he associated the film with *The Other Boleyn Girl* (BBC, 2003), given that this was a film that was a very different conceit: it was based on a popular novel and commissioned by the drama department but filmed as if in the documentary mode, and it did not employ documentary modes such as a narrator or captions. In view of all this, *The Other Boleyn Girl* cannot be considered for inclusion in our potential genre, since it is a docudrama (a drama based on fact, but commissioned by a drama department, which favours above all, the drama structure), but it is worth discussing here to offer context, as it is evidence of the blurring boundaries of the genre under discussion.

The Other Boleyn Girl (BBC, 2003)

Brief summary: *This BBC drama adaptation of Philippa Gregory's novel was considered unusual for its documentary shooting style, made as if it were a 'fly on the wall' observation of romantic intrigues at the Henrician court.*

This film is worth studying because it helps to establish another of the genre's edges. It is essentially a rather unusual and certainly experimental period drama, and its aesthetic makes it feel a part of the movement towards blurred boundaries. It is shot handheld, for instance, and every time a member of the royal court steps outside, the camera's iris blows out and the sky goes completely white, giving an amateurish sense of home-video recording at King Henry VIII's court. Philippa Lowthorpe, the co-writer and director, must be acknowledged here not only for this brave, new, documentary-style adaptation, but also for her leadership in encouraging more women directors into television.

Again, it seems trite to mention it in 2024, but twenty years ago women were almost never seen at the helm of a drama film crew. Lowthorpe has carved an exemplary career, mostly in dramas based on true stories that we can usefully term *documentary dramas* (better than docudramas) as opposed to *drama documentaries*. In both cases, the primary driver for the film is dictated by the final word in the phrase. Lowthorpe specialises in making dramas for the drama department. But she shoots them in a documentary *verité* style; hence she makes documentary dramas. Her films have included *Five Daughters* (BBC, 2006), a fact-based drama about the murders of Ipswich prostitutes from the perspective of their family lives, and she followed this with *Three Girls* (BBC, 2017) about the Rotherham abuse rings.

The Other Boleyn Girl was based on Gregory's in-depth research but driven entirely by the drama department and its dramatic imperatives. It was produced by the very experienced Ruth Caleb and executive-produced by the Head of BBC Films, David M. Thompson. The film appeared to blur every boundary between drama and documentary. Lowthorpe was a documentarian moving into drama and brought a distinctive innovation – of making a BBC drama look and feel like a present-day observational documentary. She is credited as the writer, with Gregory, and yet the drama department had brought in period-drama expert Andrew Davies to offer his skillset.[16] It is interesting to see that Davies is reduced to the title of script consultant. This may be explained by Lowthorpe's decision to encourage her cast to *ad lib* their way through the domestic story with which all historical viewers are deeply familiar, that of Henry and Anne's affair. Adopting an *ad-hoc* approach with well-trained actors like Natasha McElhone, Jared Harris, Jodhi May, and Steven Mackintosh is unusual, a style normally reserved for the likes of Mike Leigh and his team's contemporary realism.

This was an unusually radical approach for a period film at the BBC, and the experiment was not repeated. Drama debasing itself to look like documentary was not to be encouraged, and period drama at the BBC soon retreated to its silo. But, as mentioned above, lack of immediate impact or rapid imitation does not render a film irrelevant, any more than *Culloden* and *The War Game* were inconsequential. Many observers from the television community saw the value of lending *cinema verité* techniques to a piece of history that was, after all, considerably researched and steeped in verifiable truth. Actors enjoyed the process, as confirmed by Steven Mackintosh in a 2017 interview: 'actors don't enjoy spending hours waiting for the lighting to be completed and being restricted in their movements by a focus puller, adapting their lens' reach with tape measures, every time they respond naturally to the performances around them' (Mackintosh, 2017). Whilst Mackintosh accepts that there are technical aspects to making films that are important for certain kinds of films, he recalls that: 'the documentary-style approach, where both restrictive scripts and movement on set have been loosened, [is] welcomed by actors whose first love is, and will always be, the immediacy of the stage and the playfulness of rehearsal'.

It is perhaps instructive to compare this curious and unrepeated documentary-style version of the novel to the film version, which appeared a few years later. *The Other Boleyn Girl* (BBC Films, 2008), the movie, was written by (documented) drama specialist Peter Morgan and starred Nathalie

Portman and Scarlett Johansson. It is arguably deadened by its three-act structure and its drama-mode shooting style. The camera flows smoothly, actors hit their marks, and the film sinks under the weight of its own contrivance. The *New York Times* called it 'More slog than romp',[17] confirming that the viewer is simply not there, in the past, on a girl's shoulder, as she watches her sister play the most dangerous game of all, that of capturing a king. If ever a film was a traditional drama, and a 'classical-stage' rendition of an excitingly 'experimental' but cheaper forebear, this is it.

In considering the Metzian 'classical' stages of a genre, it is useful at this point to return to the BBC's drama documentary output from this period. When dealing with the commemorative subjects for which the traditional public pay their licence fee, there was little room for experimentation, it seems. But given what Shah calls 'a traditional audience of predominantly white males, aged over 50', the 'classical-stage' approach was no doubt appropriate for the subject matter, and its evocation of hallowed public memory. This was certainly the case for the ambitious *D-Day 6.6.1944*, a well-funded but traditional variant of the proposed drama documentary genre.

D-Day 6.6.1944 (BBC, 2004)

Brief summary: *A national commemoration, in drama documentary form, of the D-Day landings. Interviews, archive, CGI and some scripted drama reconstruction are combined to create a television spectacle that drew a huge UK audience.*

Just as Channel 4's *Georgian Underworld* was broadly in the 'classical' stage in its repetition of impressionistic dramatisation, so too there were further examples of the classical stage over at the BBC. The History Department was making a small number of drama documentaries, usually very big coproductions and often honouring the anniversaries of the Second World War: *D-Day* and *Dunkirk* were the BBC offerings of 2004, one made by a boutique indie called Dangerous Productions and the other by Inhouse at BBC.[18] In aesthetic terms, they were both fairly traditional, intercutting short, spoken vignettes with interviews of older men remembering the landings, alongside archive film.

One striking innovation was in having the documentary speaking to the drama. A British veteran recalls being captured on the beaches and hauled into the German defensive HQ, fearing for his life. The veteran was filmed walking into the empty room – the production having found the exact location the interrogation took place – and then had the German Kommandant, played by an actor, look up and ask some questions, politely, as if he knew the game was up and it would be ungentlemanly to interrogate and torture his enemy. The old man stands there, as if he is hearing this extraordinary exchange, recalling the actual adversary sixty years earlier. Finally, he turns on his heel and walks away. It is a most unnerving and underused cross-pollination of two modes and explores a public memory in an intimate way. The veteran gives a pin-sharp performative interview, his face expressing his inner memory, and the intercut with the drama works seamlessly. It is just one of those moments which confirmed that the mix of performative documentary interview and performed drama reconstruction was not just 'the only way to tell it', but the best way to tell it.

A contained amount of drama set amid traditional archival sources and interviews characterised the majority of drama documentaries during this period, which followed a rule of one third archive, one third interview, one third drama. But another variant was to emerge that would increase the drama content to a much higher proportion of the film, more reminiscent of how *Culloden* or *The War Game*, which had contained almost 100 per cent drama reconstruction, supported by captions on screen and narration on the audio track. This new variant can therefore be regarded as an 'experimental' in terms of the new genre, and it would become enormously influential in the increasingly full immersion of the viewer in the past.

The Trial of the King Killers (Channel 4, 2005)

> Brief summary: *A single seventy-five-minute film on the trial of the regicides who had executed King Charles I at the end of the Civil War in 1649. It was one of the very first fully dramatised history documentaries, with its dialogue drawn from court records.*

Much of the innovation in dramatised history documentary had occurred at Channel 4, on Hadlow's watch. This is primarily because she is genuinely fascinated by historical primary sources, and secondarily because she has no real interest in the 'mode' of a film. Tim Kirby, producer/director of *A History of Britain* and then *The Trial of the King Killers*, confirms this view: 'Janice was always focussed on the source, the story. How we actually realised that story, was of no real interest to her' (Kirby, 2020). This opened the door to considerable innovation in the service of a primary-sourced story.

The Trial of the King Killers was one of those stories and would probably not have been commissioned by anybody else. The problem for Kirby arose when Hadlow left Channel 4 in 2004 to take up her role as the Controller of BBC Four. Hamish Mykura, her deputy at Channel 4's Specialist Factual, took up the reins, and was also keen to promote drama documentaries, but his taste in subject matter was not quite as esoteric as Hadlow's and, more to the point, Mykura had been a well-regarded director in his own right and was very interested in how a film was constructed. *The Trial of the King Killers* did not meet his sense of what a drama documentary should look and sound like. As another trial drama based upon original transcripts, like *Peterloo Massacre* (Channel 4, 2003) and *A Royal Scandal* (BBC, 1996), it lacked action, and was at its heart a philosophical tract on the nature of government that even the most sophisticated Channel 4 audience might not fully appreciate. This was not the very first fully dramatised history documentary of this era, but for the purposes of this argument, it is the most noteworthy and best exemplifies the stuttering moves into a Metzian experimental stage.

The film centred on the trial of the parliamentarians who, having followed Oliver Cromwell to victory on the field of battle, had elected to condemn Charles I to death. Those same killers of the king were themselves brought to trial on the accession of Charles II, a fact that likely encouraged the comparison of the two contrasting trials. The film also boldly, and experimentally, toyed with the arcane language of the seventeenth century, using idioms of religiosity and jurisprudence in a way that added up to an uncompromising attempt to bring the past to life in all its obsessive legalistic detail.

This was not one of the romantic episodes of the Century of Troubles like *Plague, Fire, War,* and *Treason,* films that had done so well with audiences in 2001, who would have recognised the tales from the school curriculum. This was an investigation into which constitutional model England was to follow in a post-republican era. The choice the film underlined was either a royal constitution, with parliament offering support, or a parliamentary model, with royalty exercising appropriate dignitary status. The film showed that this struggle was decided by the Bill of Rights in 1688, in which the constitutional monarchy that Britain has to this day was defined. Thus, historically, *The Trial of the King Killers* was not just a murderous moment, but also another step in the design of British democracy. It was, as such, an episode of *A History of Britain* or *Monarchy* expressed in full drama.

The film could have been couched in what Hayden White called 'presentist' terms, comparing, according to Kirby, 'the English Civil War to the bloody war in Bosnia' which had ended only ten years before the film was made, but, instead, Kirby chose the 'antiquarian' approach, steeping the audience in the past. The budget set by the commissioner, Mykura, was based on 20 to 30 per cent of the programme being filmed as drama, but Kirby proposed that 100 per cent of the narrative be told in this form, within the chamber-piece four walls of a courtroom. The production company,

Mentorn Oxford, was persuaded that this could be achieved for £270,000, and that a full drama with strong casting would lead to more commissions. In interview, Kirby describes the ambition of the film and the clash with Mykura: 'Hamish started questioning everything, the script, the casting. Of course, I believed the film would persuade him in the end.' Kirby believed that the variants of drama documentary were leading inexorably towards much fuller drama, and that this was the way both to dramatise the past and to achieve increased viewership. 'You need the real words', he insists, 'otherwise you have a script made up by a writer, following the three-act structure of Robert McKee.[19] You need authenticity of language. I mean, just listen to Patrick O'Brian on the Royal Navy.'[20]

'Authenticity of language' is certainly on offer here, as never before fully experienced, even in *Peterloo Massacre* or *Ancient Egyptians*, where there is a certain degree of modernisation to achieve presentism. To listen to the words Kirby selected for the film is, as he says, to have another portal opened into the past. The prosecutor, Sir Heneage Finch, opens the teleplay with words that were no doubt spoken very early in the original proceedings:

> The judges, the officers, and the other immediate actors in this black, bloody act were numbered about eighty, and of them about twenty-five are dead, among them the arch usurper, Cromwell, and while some died in peace, be assured that they soon came before a judge more terrible than any here on earth.

Over an hour later in the drama documentary, the judge, Sir Orlando Bridgeman, confirms the sentence as it was handed down:

> You will be led back to the place from whence you came and then drawn upon a hurdle to a place of execution. And there you shall be hanged by the neck, thereupon you shall be cut down and your privy members cut off, your entrails taken out of your body, the same to be burned before your eyes, and your head to be cut off. Your body to be divided into four quarters, and the quarters to be disposed of at the desire of his Majesty the King and may God have mercy upon your soul.

It may well be that the original language contained more 'ye' and 'nay' than this script, but the idioms remain the same. This time and place were courtly, and filled with words intended to be spoken aloud for effect, and their essence was sadistic and terrible. Kirby confesses that when he script-edited the transcripts, he did take a few liberties. He sometimes consolidated paragraphs, and one character, that of John Downes, who claimed he was forced to sign, was a conflation of two persons who offered the same defence. 'But I am a documentarian, and I respect the truth, so I would never allow a conflation that perverted it', Kirby insists. The trial of the king himself had a less good source, he admits, but plenty of secondary source material. 'Our real coup was the regicides' transcript', recalls Kirby. Throughout the film, the 'sense' of research was evident, the narrator according each of the people who killed the King a number on a list. Oliver Cromwell, interestingly, was *Number Three*. Statistics have a habit of suggesting truth more dependably than literary records. Ultimately, as we have noted throughout this book, history is made up of a series of random events that resists the shaping of narrative structure. *Wisconsin Death Trip* was a similar compilation of recorded events that James Marsh allowed to be free of a three-act structure. The same is true of Kirby's approach here. Yes, the film came to a climax of sorts, with the conviction of the lawyer who believed in constitutional reform, but, otherwise, it was a tale told without the contrivance of dramatic shape.

But is it a mongrel? For a critic, perhaps: Jason Deans of the *Guardian* damned it with the faint praise of 'niche appeal'.[21] The script was written by a documentarian, Kirby, not advised by the well-known Andrew Davies, and critics prefer genres they can fully understand – drama people doing separate drama jobs, like writing and directing, for films that have drama stars playing parts that are drawn from writerly imagination, not half-poached from documentary records. I find this attitude frustrating in the extreme. Kirby was doing a brilliant job of covering writing/directing/producing of a documentary *and* a drama – starring top British actors, yet also drawing together whole swathes of the British constitution in its growing pains. Why would one belittle this as a sub-genre that is neither one thing or another, when it is clearly more, much more than a single silo? Yet the critics were not alone …

A lack of more obvious dramatic shape may also have been Mykura's problem with the story, since the construct of a dramatic shape makes for more easily controlled story arcs that keep the audience's attention span in mind, especially over a two-hour film. This in turn makes it easier to sell upstairs in the corporation, and so garner support for marketing, PR, and previews, all of which help to promote a film in a busy marketplace. It may well have been an 'experimental' example of the full-drama documentary genre that lacked commercial clout, but as a representation of history, it was a mature piece of work.

The filming itself reveals a good example of the development of the aesthetic. The shoot began in Harrow School, and the Director of Photography was Doug Hartington, who was another protégé of *A History of Britain*. He had never before devised the lighting scheme as well as operating camera on what was ostensibly a full drama. Hartington gave the present writer an interview in August 2020, in which he observed that drama documentaries are a useful 'leg up' for many in the collective factual and fictional industries, since they act as intensive training grounds for all departments and are more accessible than the heavily contested promotional ladder within the workplace of conventional drama. Hartington recalls that first-time drama director Kirby put himself under immense pressure: 'While the rest of us ate the catering at lunch time, Tim would chew ferociously on a single apple, concentrating on eating every last part of it, then standing up abruptly, ready for the next set up' (Hartington, 2020). This single image confirms the stresses faced by an experienced documentary-maker as he makes a film in an increasingly dramatic mode. The crew grows from three or four to thirty or forty, and the cost per hour of filming rises in parallel. In terms of hours on a film set, every part of shooting a drama is ten times as expensive as shooting a documentary, with every minute being decided by the director. Added to this, a courtroom drama is intense work by any standards of drama shooting, because often one must shoot out of sequence, selecting which shots are in which direction, and maintaining the most effective use of what little crowd one may have. According to Hartington, Kirby filmed the background group shots, which involved forty or fifty impeccably dressed Sealed Knot members, in the first three days.[22] It must have made so little sense to those on the set, and Kirby would have felt very alone in his planning.

In such circumstances, actors cannot maintain a flow of performance because capturing the maximum number of supporting actors in any single shot becomes the priority. Even the camera operator is required to stop shooting fuller sequences. An added complication was the introduction of a jimmy jib. This is a poor man's crane that enables the camera to rise on a 10 or 12-foot arm; it was used to push the camera towards the accused in their pen. 'It could barely fit in the room, and had its rear end sticking through the doorway', says Hartington; 'the huge windows needed a vast amount of light pouring through, but I only had one 6k and it was tied off against the school porch so it didn't blow over'.[23] This is far from the expectations of a traditional drama shoot, where there would be three major lamps on cranes themselves, each with at least 10k of wattage to replicate the power of the sun, and all safely affixed by extra electricians. As it happened, 'we felt blessed', says Hartington, when the jimmy jib set off on its rising motion across the maximum number of attendees, making a convincing case for a trial of this magnitude, and the sun appeared from behind the clouds, streaming what he terms its 'million k' of light through the ancient windows, cutting through the smoke and highlighting motes in the air, aiding the sense of travelling to a dusty past.

Despite having a first-time drama director and Director of Photography at the helm, Hartington notes, the shooting schedule progressed well. The casting was very strong, with the theatre-trained Guy Henry as the prosecutor and the legendary film actor Corin Redgrave as the judge. They anchored the whole piece, their convinced performances drawing the best out of the journeyman actors who played the eight or so accused, whose narratives best reflect the overall story. The king, played by Miles Richardson, was particularly convincing in the scenes that flash back to his own trial. Richardson has gone on to perform in *Outlander* and *The Crown* (Netflix, 2016–), and his performance as Charles I stands comparison with Peter Capaldi in *The Devil's Whore*, Channel 4's major drama of 2008, but it is characteristic of a documentary drama that it does not cast the superstar of the moment – which Capaldi was, off the back of *The Thick of It* (BBC, 2005–2012) – but instead gives a good jobbing actor such as Richardson an opportunity to take a star role.

This point returns the book to the subject of how actors were permitted to work on impoverished dramas of this type. Since the actors' union, Equity, had complained about the use of amateurs in *Culloden* and *The War Game* in the 1960s, there had been very little opportunity for actors to appear on television without an Equity card, and yet there had remained the 'Catch 22' of not being able to get a card without proof of public performance, and no opportunity to perform in public without a card. Actors for years had got around this by performing semi-informally, in fringe theatre, even in street performance. By the 2000s and the emergence of documentary dramas, Equity was under pressure from its own members to allow actors to treat these hybrid productions as quasi 'street theatre' training grounds, places to make their name, learn their craft and build a CV. Acting schools had flourished within university drama departments, and the numbers of unemployed actors pouring onto the market had grown significantly. Actors' agents were also more entrepreneurial, and the whole rigid system began to flex. Casting directors like Louise Cross, who cast *King Killers*, no longer feared asking agents, politely, to release their client-actors, and a new system was created featuring what were called 'favoured nations'.

Favoured nations meant that actors should receive from the production a structured fee that saw Corin Redgrave being paid the same as a regicide in the dock. Everybody was paid the same fee per week. It was an overtly levelling solution that was treated flexibly; Redgrave may well have been paid for one extra day, which effectively amounted to an extra week's fee. But, in general, it meant there was more work for all actors, and soon, the 'named actors' joined in during the gaps in their schedules. Louise Cross, one of the top casting directors in this hybrid field (although she made her regular income as assistant casting director on the longstanding *Midsummer*

Murders (ITV, 1997–)), then devised a system of casting what were called 'actor catchers'. Cross gave an interview in August 2020 in which she explained how it worked: 'One named or respected piece of casting within the theatre realm would often encourage others to join a production, especially when they knew that "favoured nations" was in play. Guy Henry was a respected RSC theatre actor with a period drama CV to fill, and Corin Redgrave was a "name" whose better years were behind him' (Cross, 2020). Drama documentary treated Redgrave well. He had a stroke that seriously affected his short-term memory soon after the *King Killers*, and no drama would either insure or trust him to deliver a performance within their schedule. But the producers of *The Relief of Belsen* (Channel 4, 2007) offered him a role as a general of the British Second Army discovering the Belsen concentration camp and, with patience and the casting of his daughter, Jemma Redgrave, to work alongside him, the viewer was afforded a last look at an actor that television drama would not countenance hiring. This offers another insight into the genre of drama documentary: it embraces a certain degree of rule-breaking to compensate for its financial constraints.

This new kind of history drama documentary observed the rules of traditional drama, but often found its strictures too strict. There is an adage in drama that one needs 'belts and braces to hold up the trousers', that is, that one needs the vigilance of two fall-back positions to work on something as creatively evolving as a drama. Many of these films learned to work with a belt only, and sometimes barely that. This was the case across the board, in lighting, camera, sound, grips, set design, and occasionally health and safety. But actors began to enjoy the process. As *The Other Boleyn Girl* had shown, television drama for an actor could be plodding and overly technical, while drama documentaries were fast and offered actors the opportunity to give an almost 'live' performance, filmed in few takes, keeping up momentum and energy levels. The system had many drawbacks too, inevitably: speed meant the railroading of more nuanced performances, and a lack of camera angles for the editor, but in general, the system was muscular, and the participants, above all, enjoyed the fact that the narratives were about true stories taken from the past – events that were politically relevant, and that could enable actors to undertake deep research. This cocktail of underfunded semi-professionalism, which Watkins would have recognised, brought enormous pressure onto the shoulders of the person driving the set: the director. No wonder Kirby was taking it out on an apple.

The shoot of *King Killers* moved to Oxford for the trial of the king, a change of location to mark the critical difference between this trial and that of the regicides. The film is structurally complex, intercutting between two trials, and the documentary narrator is needed to help make the transitions. But it turned out that one wood-panelled great hall looks much like another, and so Hartington resorted to a post-production colour grade that rendered one court scene as monochrome, the other as colour.[24] Keeping the photography sufficiently high quality was a challenge at all times. Hartington attempted to keep the film moving seamlessly, with moving camera on what is known in the business as 'a wally dolly'. This, he explains, was 'very far from a 50k piece of German engineering, but instead a plastic platform on top of plastic rails. But it gives you the expensive camera move, just in short bursts, before you fall off the end.'

Drama documentaries almost always hit the buffers at some point, a moment when the cracks show in the budget, confirming the unsteady financial underpinnings of the genre, hence the criticisms that films like this belong to a 'mongrel genre'. Yet this was also accompanied by the creative solutions of people working within the genre, something normally little known and un-chronicled. According to Hartington, *King Killers* hit the buffers with the scripted arrival of the king in his royal carriage. Carriages are authentic real-world props, and from a professional provider can cost £2,000 a day upwards.

King Killers did not have this line in the budget, and the armourer/stunt director/costumier Hamish McLeod provided the problem-solving attitude so often evident in the drama documentary culture. He scribbled a design on a beer mat, Hartington reveals, and the next day camera and director arrived at a farmyard to inspect their royal carriage. 'I don't know what we expected for under a hundred quid, but it would have not looked out of place in a kids' fete.' It was a cardboard cut-out made of MDF, and Kirby despairingly pronounced he had 'finally reached the very epicentre of amateurdom'. After a bout of mutual recriminations, it was the camera assistant, Audrey Aquilina (a rare camerawoman at that time) who chose to look at the scene as scripted in a different light. There could be no shot of the carriage sweeping by, but there could possibly be a reverse shot from inside the carriage of the *world* sweeping by. McLeod put the carriage shape on a hay bale and hung some curtains on the window edge shapes. When backlit by a bright sun, it could have been a carriage interior. They put the King in front and shook the structure so the curtains moved. 'How is that?' asked Hartington. 'Like an earthquake in a photobooth', despaired Kirby. Aquilina made another suggestion, this time balancing the carriage on a hay cart, pulled by a local shire horse, and with two outriders in costume beyond the window frame – and, according to Hartington, 'amazingly, it just about worked. Film making, especially drama documentary, is after all, about smoke and mirrors.' This problem-solving attitude is at the heart of the variants of this canon, and stories like this could be elicited from every one of the films where cinematic ambition overwhelmingly exceeded budget.

The Trial of the King Killers is a major step forward in the aesthetic of the canon. *King Killers* recreated a time and place where national fates were being decided by what appears to be up to a hundred people, and thus, the film attempts to recreate the scale of the seventeenth-century event. There is also a significant usage of material that can make best use of the expensive locations on offer, usage that a conventional drama would not have identified. The evocative carvings of names and a hangman in wood that wraps around the title sequence comes from the centuries of schoolboys' graffiti in that first Harrow School location. Kirby could not shake them out of his head and returned, with his own camera, to reinspect the names. 'So many of our names were there, purely by coincidence, but also because they are standard English names. The hangman itself was a typical schoolboy marking', he recalls. So, the available device here is not the actual truth, but it is the spirit of the truth: a sensuousness that etches itself in the viewers' memory. The music too, composed inexpensively by Tony Burke, has the same resonance: without the money to hire an orchestra (drama's default), he used recorded bells from Harrow School, clanging discordantly until they forged a tune. Bells of course were a sound far more common in Christian societies in the past.

To return to the institutional context, *The Trial of the King Killers* was not received favourably at the channel. The two-hour cut of the film was deemed far too long, and the choice of narrator was rejected. This was a blow too many for Kirby, who, like Watkins before him, exited the project, leaving the edits in the hands of his executive producer – 'so the film', Kirby adds with good grace, 'was at least in good hands.'

Thus, the edit went on without him, as often happens in television, and the cut that was aired on Channel 4 was a seventy-five-minute version that begins in the drama mode, with a regicide being dragged behind a horse through cobbled streets; over this scene, and in the documentary mode, the film pre-explains a great deal of information that could have been disseminated more subtly throughout its course. It was often a mark of UK commissioners that they would brutalise the first five minutes to keep the viewer's attention, a nervousness inherited from the multi-channel United States. Opening establishers that make explicit the deal between the channel and its viewers can work well, but it is better if the underlying filmmaker is crafting that introduction. When it is done, hurriedly, by the broadcasting authorities, whose purpose is to explain all, without appropriate recourse to the holistic style of the person who has lived with the film for months, even years, it can be a blunt tool indeed. Kirby comments that 'the Mykura menu' became legendary but admits that it wasn't just Mykura who perpetrated this pre-title spoiler alert. All commissioning editors were determined to wrestle back some commercial control over their commissions.

They feared to let these drama documentary mavericks run away with their new-found opportunities to be slow-paced drama directors.

Kirby was allowed to make one more drama documentary, *The Badness of King George* (BBC, 2004), a clever idea which used (fictitious) opium-induced flashbacks to deliver a two-handed narrative featuring George IV facing the 'Hellhound', who was a composite of all his critics as revealed through primary sources. Oliver Ford Davies played the King, and Robert Glenister the Hellhound – again, excellent casting. But the budget was perilously low, and even though Kirby would like to have made more drama documentaries, he maintains that television tends to a monoculture, a term that brings to mind Peter Watkins' accusations of the prevalence of 'monoform', and the failure to appreciate his own pluriform approach. Watkins would no doubt have recognised Kirby's frustrations with what must always appear to be an ungrateful broadcaster, and hence such experimental films must be regarded as the fragile and rare creations that they are.

Meanwhile, drama documentary was to make another experimental leap in the same year, 2005. It was also commissioned by Mykura at Channel 4 and was a deliberate attempt to represent a historical event through a fully scripted drama, which actually structured the narrative according to drama's rules of engagement. This might be considered an example of pushing documentary drama to the end of the spectrum, beyond the reach of *Culloden*. In terms of audience satisfaction, it enabled entertainment to sit in ideal harmony with information, all packaged within an ideal three-act structure, and containing a hero facing both dilemmas and his own demons before emerging triumphant.

The final case study of this chapter is another one from Channel 4's stable of what Mykura calls 'my genre-busting films': *Trafalgar Battle Surgeon* (Channel 4, 2005).

Trafalgar Battle Surgeon (Channel 4, 2005)

Brief summary: *A film to commemorate the death of Nelson, told through the first-hand accounts of the surgeon who was faced with the dilemma of whether to attempt to operate on the admiral's wound or just keep him alive long enough to hold up the sailors' morale through to victory.*

This section aims to explore the evolution of a film that comes close to the edge of the drama documentary genre, asking whether the increased dramatic imperative promoted the viewers' enjoyment over the delivery of verifiable historical information. The institutional narrative behind the making of this film will go a long way to answering this question. It should be noted that this case study is the product of first-hand involvement by the present writer. As a member of the production team (co-writer and director), my access will enable me to reveal the extent of the challenges faced when developing a drama documentary on the subject of a historical event of such public importance, and when shaping the narrative in a way that makes the fullest use of the drama mode.

The idea for the surgeon's story aboard *HMS Victory*, Nelson's flagship, had scholarly foundations: it originated with Laurence Brockliss, an academic historian who in 2005 was teaching modern history at Magdalen College, Oxford. He had attracted the support of the Wellcome Trust for two studies of surgeons in the armies and navies of the Napoleonic wars. His research partner, Michael Moss of Glasgow University, had discovered, in the Public Records Office, a form that surgeons were required to fill in at the end of their career that gave a great deal of information on their education, their placements, and even their work after retirement. As Brockliss recalled, in interview: 'Surgeons in the army and navy were the merchant bankers of their day, there was a great deal of booty to be had, and taxation was funnelled towards the enterprise of establishing whose Empire would predominate in the world order – Britain or France' (Brockliss, 2019). With retrospective forms such as those filled in by retiring surgeons, computers in the early 2000s were able to create a database that had previously not been available to the historian, or indeed the interested public. A post-doctoral researcher, John Cardwell, thus discovered that a certain William Beatty, surgeon on board the *HMS Victory*, had written an account of the death of Nelson in October 1805. It was one of many accounts, for there were many eyewitnesses, but this account had been absorbed into secondary sources and folklore as being the one that delivered intimate last-minute farewells and an enduringly heroic narrative. Brockliss himself believed this to be most likely an untrustworthy account, filled with sentimentality as it was ('Kiss me, Hardy ... I trust I have done my duty ... remember me to Lady Hamilton' etc.), but he believed that cross-referencing accounts would be a useful act for posterity. Following the experience of the surgeon, meanwhile, might shed light on how the health of the British navy might have enabled the battle to go in favour of the British. Brockliss knew that Wellcome was also interested in funding not just books on the history of medicine, but also museums and television programmes, since it too was aware of the history boom in the television medium. So, he approached two former undergraduate historians at Magdalen: producer Sue Horth, who specialised in historical drama documentary, and the present writer. If Brockliss and his team were to write the book, would Horth and the production team make the film for television, and would Wellcome lend support to both ventures concurrently?

Wellcome agreed, and Mykura at Channel 4 greenlit the film. Mykura could see that the primary source was not only a strong document but that the dramatic possibility afforded by such an unusual take on an iconic subject would create an exciting televisual event. Many documentaries had been made on Nelson and the battle, but they invariably involved a presenter and table-top maps of the battle lines. Mykura wanted a blood-and-guts drama to immerse the audience in the hull of a man of war while it was rocked from each broadside of fifty guns firing.

It was clear that, despite his role as a documentarian, Mykura was intent on the film containing 'as much drama as he could get', and that meant following many of the tropes of drama. The hero must be conflicted, the set-up should be brief, the battle should be the extent of the chronology, and Nelson should be brought down into the surgeon's deck at the halfway point in order to add to the conflict for the surgeon-hero. The ending should be tragic, with Nelson's death, yet uplifting, to resolve the drama. This was a structure that Peter Morgan would be proud of and, amazingly, it was a structure that fit not only the agreed narrative of the battle, but also the microcosm of the surgeon's log. Even the untrustworthy narrative fitted the drama mode well, since it was agreed by the documentary team that, reading between the lines, the surgeon must have considered operating on the admiral before allowing him to live long enough to encourage the men to fight on to victory. (This was not explicitly written in the log, but it was implicit from the reading of the log.) So far so good. Rarely does a document truly fit a dramatic narrative like this one, and hence the drama did not need to detract from the veracity of the document.

This was until Mykura asked for one more imperative of the drama mode: the surgeon should have a tragic secret in his backstory, something that gave him a truly conflicted hero/villain essence. That secret would drive his motivations onwards through the plot, and would be revealed at a critical moment, ideally at the climactic death of Nelson, resolving the surgeon's personal journey. To quote Steven Lipkin's *Real Emotional Logic* (2002), this piece of history would need to be narrativised to enhance the character at its centre: 'the strategy of employing the classic Hollywood narrative mode privileges character desire'.[25] Mykura was already being offered, by the film's producers, that 'we share the character's desire for time' and he was even being delivered a 'pivotal moment strategy'.[26] Mykura had what Rosenstone calls 'a closed story, a notion of progress, emphasis on individuals, heightening of emotional stakes, the focus on surfaces'.[27] But Mykura desired a dramatic alteration that threatened to do something that Rosenstone would refer to as to 'create a past different from the one provided by written history'.[28] The documentary team resisted the request. It risked the film becoming 'melodramatic', they argued, and why risk that, when so much else was true? Rosenstone might have suggested that Mykura, now a commissioner with a developing taste for Hollywood, was simply following what in *Visions of the Past* (1995) he called dramatic imperative: 'melodrama has been the dominant mode of the Hollywood historical film, thus a major source of criticism of the historical film'.[29]

Trafalgar Battle Surgeon was at a crossroads. 'History books emanate from the discovery and shaping of micro-details, not the other way around', comments Brockliss, and, as a historian, he could not create drama from a micro-detail that was not there. It was not the first drama documentary to face the fact-altering instincts of drama, but in this evolving potential genre, it may well have been a pivotal choice, because the genre had added more and more layers of drama from 2000 until 2005, until it was becoming indistinguishable from commissioned drama.

In a moment of serendipity, however, the project's historians, Brockliss, Moss, and Cardwell, announced that they had found a backstory for the surgeon, Beatty, and it was truly derived from the micro-detail of the surgeon's earlier career. Beatty had been court-martialled, years before Trafalgar, for disobeying an officer who wanted his sick patient returned to active service. According to Brockliss, it was 'the most surprising and significant discovery that we made. Nelson must have known that he had been court-martialled. It fits our idea of Nelson as a chancer', he recalls. This was an ideal backstory for the man caring for the sick admiral, mid-battle. And more interesting still, Beatty had been acquitted by none other than Admiral Bligh (of HMS *Bounty* fame).[30] It was a two-part backstory that could be set up to add conflict to his dilemma as to whether or not to operate on Nelson, and then be paid off later, when Nelson lives long enough to hear that the battle has been won. It was an extraordinary solution to a drama commissioning request that could have severely compromised the sincerity of both the book and the filmmaking teams, and yet was a brilliant request that made the most of both drama and documentary modes.

In *Trafalgar Battle Surgeon*, the drama and the documentary modes found themselves in surprising balance, a very rare event in the 'bastard genre'. A pure drama on the same subject matter would have introduced extraneous dialogue and required a star to play Nelson, perhaps implausibly. A pure documentary would have missed out on the emotional power of watching an ex-military amateur actor, playing Nelson, having his shirt removed and revealing the stump of his arm where it had been blown off in the Iraq War. Even A. A. Gill acknowledged in his *Sunday Times* review (2005) that the film team was beset with good fortune to have found not only an amputee, but one where the correct arm had been lost.[31]

In the finished film, Brockliss is impressed by the degree to which the surgeon's background story was drip-fed through the present-time action.

In addition to the court-martial, the researchers had discovered that the surgeon's best friend, also from Ulster, was on board HMS *Victory* and, as this lucky film would have it, died on the surgeon's table in mid-battle. Thus, in the first five minutes, the dramatic narrative has the surgeon patrolling the decks, meeting his best friend, who reminds him they 'should have run away to America when we had the chance'. Critical characters are revealed: the Master Gunner and his son, who would later play a central role in the emergency room. The viewer is taken from the stage set, past the antagonistic Loblolly Boy, onto the actual gun deck, and looks up to glimpse Nelson standing proudly on deck, surrounded by his red-coated marines. The chief source of anxiety is that the wind has dropped, and hence Nelson's unconventional plan to drive straight at the opposing fleets, and to absorb their incoming fire without being able to return it, is rendered an act of suicide. Nobody would have known this more than the surgeon, for whom the casualties would soon be piling up.

The only documentary decision over which Brockliss still agonises is the surgeon's prevarication over the decision to try and save Nelson's life by removing the ball from his back. Medical evidence suggests his spine had been shattered and hence there was nothing that could have been done to save him, but that is a hindsight point of view. Yet Brockliss insists that the surgeon must have questioned his own decisions; he must have agonised over the dilemmas. This is the moment in which Brockliss thinks that the film team created their own history: when the surgeon chooses to turn Nelson onto his side, thus filling his lungs with blood and effectively putting an end to his life. None of this was in any of the formal accounts of Nelson's heroic death. Yet Brockliss says that he does not feel the spirit of the truth had been materially altered. He also admits that 'writers of history books look for their subjects to be proactive', giving the biography cohesion and greater purpose, reminding the viewer that all of history is interpreted through the prism of the historian, as E. H. Carr asserted in *What is History?* (1961).

In terms of the drama documentary mix, *Trafalgar Battle Surgeon* is full of the tropes of drama while offering a limited but crucial amount of documentary. Where *A History of Britain* was 10 per cent dramatisation, *Elizabeth* 25 per cent, *Henry VIII* 40 per cent, *The Great Plague* 60 per cent, *Smallpox* 75 per cent, and *George Orwell* 80 per cent, *King Killers* and *Trafalgar* were 90 per cent told through the mode of dialogue-filled drama. The remaining 10 per cent was documentary mode: through narration or captions, but continuing sufficiently through the film enough to feel balanced between sense and sensuousness. Ultimately, a drama documentary would not contain 100 per cent drama for that would render the film a period drama, no matter how well researched. It clearly remains very important for the viewer to know that the drama they are watching is confirmed in its proximity to known truths. Inserting a simple caption 'this is based on a true story' is not enough to confirm that the whole film is rooted in research. It is soon forgotten, and one senses that the drama has taken hold, without the confirmations of further assertions of truth. Much of the pleasure derived from these drama documentaries during this period was in being educated at the same time as being entertained – in enjoying a curated combination of sense and sensuousness. When dealing with a national hero such as Nelson, it is important for the viewer to know the sources that warranted the film to be made. Hence, there are confirmations through caption as to which of the dramatic characters have been taken down into the emergency room, and why. A lieutenant is brought down with a fractured arm, and a caption confirms it is the same lieutenant who signalled to the fleet the immortal line: 'England expects that every man will do his duty'. The drama mode then picks up where the documentary mode left off, with Surgeon Beatty wondering aloud where that leaves an Irishman like him. 'Beyond the bloody pale', comes the answer. The whole scene is a researched mixture of dramatically laced documentary interwoven with well-informed drama. Thus, drama documentary becomes its own unique style of filmmaking, not just a hybrid performing neither mode very well. The team assembled by Brockliss is quite rightly very proud of this output, and it is not surprising that these films began to attract attention from drama commissioners, well-known actors, and cultural commentators like A. A. Gill.

The shoot of *Trafalgar Battle Surgeon* furthered the aesthetic of the canon. It was another case of budget filmmaking, and reminded the Director of Photography, Doug Hartington, of working on his previous drama documentary, *The Trial of the King Killers*. The production could not afford to use the real HMS *Victory*, and so two sets were used. One was the gundeck of a restored ship in Hartlepool, while the surgeon's deck was built in a warehouse in South London that was not sound-proofed. The cast were, in an indirect image of Watkins' Playcraft, a collection of third-year graduating actors from the Poor School in Kings Cross – they were not amateurs, but nor were they yet professional. As previously hinted, the New History Drama Documentaries also attracted stars of the screen and beyond. While the budget was limited, the authentic storyline offered a rewarding experience. John Castle, whose first job had been acting in the Oscar-winning *The Lion in Winter* (1968) alongside Anthony Hopkins, Peter O'Toole, and Katharine Hepburn, signed up to play the Master Gunner, whose son was known to have undergone a leg amputation during the battle. Meanwhile, the role of the Loblolly Boy, a retired sailor who aided with the amputations, was played by Roger Daltrey, lead-singer of The Who and an experienced actor, having starred in *Tommy* (1975) and *McVicar* (1980). Like

Corin Redgrave in *King Killers*, both of these actors could be said to have been past their peak, but drama documentaries were good routes for a return to the prime-time screen; for the Poor School graduates, they were access points to a first legitimate performance. The lack of structure was the strength of this new form.

These unstructured filmmaking choices were consistent with the *vérité* shooting style. Authenticity was at the heart of the production, and hence it is not a surprise that the Master Gunner's son's amputation scene was to be filmed in real time, recalled by Hartington, who remembers the rehearsal: 'it delivered a reality that made me shiver, even on a run through' (Hartington, 2019). Again, here, the sense and the sensuousness worked hand in hand. The narrator explained that the surgeon was far from being the butcher of popular imagination and was a highly skilled professional working under very constrained conditions. The amputation would need to take place within two and a half minutes or the patient would die of blood loss or shock. This meant cutting the skin, peeling it back like a sock and then sawing through the bone before tying up the exposed arteries with silk ligatures, and folding back the sock over the stump. This meant spending two and a half minutes working in the semi-gloom, with the ship tilting one way then the other, depending on the rolling guns up above. At this point the drama kicks in. The surgeon indicates to his surviving assistants that the saws they will need to hand him are called 'Bone and Apart', a naval joke, causing looks of horror on the faces of the assistants.

It is made clear that every mistake is potentially fatal and thus the ticking clock is set in train. 'Hold him down' is the last line of dialogue for this fateful scene, as the surgeon desperately works to save the terrified boy's life. The only sound is the Loblolly Boy, who starts up a sea shanty of his own devising, about brave men of Albion (it will not be lost on the reader that this is now an original song ascribed to The Who). The master gunner's son joins in until the saw bites – whereupon he immediately convulses, receives a leather strap to bite down upon, and faints. The pressure on the surgeon mounts as the first two minutes go by, and in the dramatic mode this is expressed via a young woman who has been taken away from her usual job as a powder monkey. The drama brings this woman front and centre, forced to tie off the final ligature in the dying seconds. The documentary mode returns, through the narrator, to reveal that the surgeon's log tells us that of the eleven men who went under the knife that day, nine survived.

The narrative was considered so strong by the cast and crew that no logistical problem was permitted to stand in the way of production. Hartington even found a way to deal with the absence of a gimble, a drama device that shakes the set of a plane or a train as if it were in motion. 'When we called "turn over", every actor was tasked with hitting the lamp closest to them, so it would swing. Then we called "cannon ball left side", when a hit came, and everybody including me, would lurch to the left.' Hartington added to the sense of constant cannon-fire by setting off arc lamps at the tops of the two stairways, literal flashes of electric current like lightning bursting forth. This lighting effect led to the perceived reality of a battle observed in all its chaos, that is, only partially seen – what Horth calls 'the denial of information' (Horth, 2020). The art department, led by Mari Lucaccini and Jo Manser, also contributed to the chaos by dropping sandbags on the roof above the actors' heads, causing dust to fall between the cracks in the wooden planks to simulate a wooden ship in turmoil. Every department was thinking innovatively.

Arguably, the aesthetic was a step beyond *Culloden*, partly thanks to the claustrophobic power of the battle's confinement, which concentrated the historical immersion. The splinters of oak that were protruding from Lieutenant Ram, the surgeon's friend, were convincingly achieved, as was the gush of blood from a special-effects pouch when Ram pulls out his own stitches to accelerate his inevitable death, and to allow another wounded man to be treated. 'But nothing convinced as much as the undressing of Nelson by the surgeon's team, searching for the musket-ball's exit wound', says producer, Lucy Bassnett-McGuire. As the shirt is cut away, the stump of his right arm is revealed, not in CGI, but in reality. Bassnett-McGuire explains 'we found this gentleman in the armed forces, returned from Iraq, where he had accidentally detonated an ammunition cache that had taken off his arm above the elbow. He answered our call on a forces appeal' (Bassnett-McGuire, 2020). Guinness and Horth, co-writers, gave him very little dialogue to carry, but it was taken on trust that he would understand the nobility of pain under fire and leave the performance to his devoted officers, who then acted on his behalf. 'It was a good apportionment of skills', says Bassnett-McGuire.

Other aesthetics progressed the *Culloden* battle trope. There was a non-diegetic sound score by Richard Blair-Oliphant, yet one could not quite tell whether much of it had been actually performed on the ship, with the repetitive brushing of a snare drum, reminiscent of Cumberland's forces with their battle drums. Time was actively monitored as it had been in *Culloden*, but the narrator was used less heavily in *Trafalgar Battle Surgeon*, and the clock was visualised on the screen in a count-up from commencement of battle to the hurricane that swept in one hour after battle officially ended. Lipkin's point about time was closely adhered to: 'we share the character's desire for time … (all the way to) the pivotal moment'.[32]

The most considerable evolution in the genre's aesthetic derived from the decision not to show the fleet in full sail, another example of 'denial of information'. Instead, the VFX provider, Jon Underwood, operating not from a grand post-production house in Soho, but from his spare bedroom, designed a series of underwater images – a solution copied by the History Channel's *Vikings* (2013–2020).[33] *Trafalgar Battle Surgeon* opens under water, with the prow of the ship cutting through the Atlantic, bubbles forming in the wake; that takes the viewer to the wooden expanse below the waterline, with a cross fade into the floor being mopped. The shot rises to reveal a view of the surgeons' tables with implements laid out neatly, while the narrator, actor Peter Guinness (also the co-writer), establishes the records from which the film is derived. The underwater view is repeated throughout the film, as flashes of cannon-fire are shown refracted through deep water, accompanied by muffled sound. The climax of this device, at the moment of greatest crisis, is when HMS *Victory* is pounded by broadsides on all sides. Where the film objectively fails is in the recoil of the cannon, filmed on board the surviving frigate HMS *Trincomalee*. David Chater wrote in *The Times* that the 'cannons recoil with all of the conviction of a shopping trolley'.[34] Another problem is the CGI explosions, when men were thrown backwards by cannon balls bursting through the oak walls. Films such as *Master and Commander* (2003) or dramas like *John Adams* (HBO, 2008) were able to depict the fire and fury of battle to a much more visceral extent.

Brockliss saw the film when it aired on Channel 4 and bemoaned the dissection of the film with four sets of advertising slots, each time breaking the portal into the past, but he was carried back in time by the underwater shots, the intimacy of the amputation, and the realistic death of a heroic admiral. He was also reassured that the filmmakers had shown the presence of women on board, a reality that was then too little understood. This was, again, a late arrival in research: a letter to *The Times* had been written in the 1840s by a woman who had been present at the battle. She was not on board HMS *Victory*, but confirmed that there had been women (wives, girlfriends, prostitutes, powder monkeys) on board British naval ships, albeit not recorded in navy documentation. Oddly, as we now know, the number of non-white people was recorded down to the last 1/8 of their bloodline if they were 'mulatto', 'creole' etc., but only if they were male. This presence was more readily expressed four years later in Channel 4's subsequent drama documentary on *Trafalgar: Bloody Foreigners* (Channel 4, 2009).

Conclusion

Trafalgar Battle Surgeon 'moved the dial', to use a television industry term, of dramatised history documentaries, in part because it showed that in forty-five minutes of tightly hewn narrative, this style of programme could provide considerable sensuous action, emotion, and information, and at a lower cost than drama. It could also provide fresh angles on well-known historical subjects, bringing to mind Rosenstone's comment in *Revisioning History* regarding the close relation of drama documentary, that of docudrama: 'Docudrama can have historical value if it offers motivated truthful invention, close proximations and analogies and contributes constructively to the debate surrounding efforts to visualise and understand the past'[35] (1995, p. 7). As a film, it also helped to define the edges of the new potential genre, one that could fully occupy the same corpus as *Culloden*, the progenitor.

Recalling *Culloden*'s ten generic identifiers, it is worth considering whether or not *Trafalgar* can be considered to satisfy each in turn:

1. Narrative drawn from primary source records (as well as secondary source context) – *Yes*
2. Scripting derived from production team (researcher/director/producer) – *Yes*
3. Performance of dramatic construction by actors, whether amateur players, re-enactors, or subsequently professionals – *Yes*
4. These actors looking into the camera, reaching across time – *No*
5. Embracing the pluriform (in this case the hybrid of documentary, drama, and action film) – *Yes*
6. Constructing action sequences that are theatrical conceits that are forgivable to the audience – *Yes*
7. Captions establishing a contract with the audience; a countdown of time within the narrative – *Yes*
8. Narrator as voice of God, or a character within the drama (in this case, Henderson) – *Yes*
9. Constructing the image so it performs as possible archive (in this case, B/W footage) – *No*
10. Sound design that brings the reality of the image to life (in this case, diegetic music exists only as it would have been – marching drums is the only soundtrack) – *Yes*

Trafalgar Battle Surgeon follows eight out of ten of the generic identifiers of *Culloden*. Many of the other films in the case studies satisfy the other two: re-creating a sense of archive (represented by *D-Day 6.6.1944*) and looking into the lens (represented by *The Great Plague* and *Smallpox 2002*). Thus, it has now been shown that a series of variants exist, ranging from impressionistic dramatisation to full-blown drama, which could be classified as belonging to a new genre. In parallel, two of Metz's four stages have been identified: experimental and classical.

The final data set in this chapter will organise the list of films under discussion in terms of Metz's experimental and classical stages, in the judgement of the present author, based on which programmes were known to have been influential as progenitors of future variants. In the data set that follows, films judged to be 'experimental' are shown underlined, those deemed 'classical' not so.

The data set (2000–2005) according to Metz's experimental and classical stages:

1999 – <u>People's Duchess</u>/C4
1999 – <u>Station X</u>/C4 (x4)
1999 – <u>Wisconsin Death Trip</u>/BBC

2000 – <u>A History of Britain</u>/BBC (x6)
2000 – <u>Holocaust on Trial</u>/C4/PBS
2000 – Escape from Colditz/C4
2000 – <u>Elizabeth</u>/C4 (x4)
2000 – Joan of Arc/C4
2000 – <u>When Money Went Mad</u>/C4
2000 – The Day the World Took Off/C4 (x6)

2001 – <u>Smallpox 2002</u>/BBC
2001 – Egypt's Golden Empire/BBC (x3)
2001 – History of Britain 2/BBC (x6)
2001 – <u>Six Wives of Henry VIII</u>/C4 (x4)
2001 – <u>Plague, Fire, War, and Treason</u>/C4 (x4)
2001 – <u>Neanderthal</u>/C4
2001 – The Crusades/History (x2)

2002 – <u>Pyramid</u>/BBC
2002 – <u>A History of Britain</u>/BBC (x3)
2002 – The Battle of the Atlantic/BBC (x3)
2002 – Christmas under Fire/BBC
2002 – Cleopatra/C4
2002 – Spartans C4/PBS (x3)
2002 – Luther/C4/PBS (x2)
2002 – Dambusters/C4
2002 – Charge of the Light Brigade/C4
2002 – Hitler's Britain/C5/History/PBS

2003 – <u>Leonardo</u>/BBC (x3)
2003/5 – <u>Days that Shook the World</u>/BBC (x16)
2003 – Colosseum, Rome's Arena of Death/BBC Discovery
2003 – <u>Seven Wonders of the Industrial World</u>/BBC (x7)

2003 – _George Orwell: A Life in Pictures_/BBC
2003 – _The Day Britain Stopped_/BBC
2003 – _Walking with Cavemen_/BBC (x4)
2003 – _Pepys_/BBC
2003 – _Redcoats and Rebels_/BBC (x4)
2003 – _Ancient Egyptians_/C4 (x4)
2003 – _Georgian Underworld; Invitation to a Hanging, Peterloo Massacre, Coram's Children, Bare Knuckle Boxer_/C4 (x4)
2003 – _Royal Deaths and Diseases_/C4 (x5)
2003 – _Lawrence of Arabia_/PBS/C4 (x2)
2003 – _Witchcraze_/C4
2003 – _Lionheart_/C4
2003 – _Touching The Void_/Film Four

2004 – _Dunkirk_/BBC (x3)
2004 – _Agatha Christie, A Life in Pictures_/BBC
2004 – _The Man who broke Britain_/BBC
2004 – _Wren, the Man who Built Britain_/BBC (x3)
2004 – _D Day 6.6.1944_/BBC
2004 – _Terry Jones' Medieval Lives_/BBC (x4 TBC)
2004 – _Seconds from Disaster_/BBC/Nat Geo (x19)
2004 – _Days that Shook the World_/BBC (x20)
2004 – _If …_/BBC (x5)
2004–6 – _Monarchy_/C4 (x10)
2004 – _Medici, Godfathers of Renaissance_/C4/PBS (x4)
2004 – _Princes in the Tower_/C4
2004 – _Dragons_/C4/Animal Planet (x2)
2004 – _Agincourt_/C4
2004 – _D-Day (ultimate conflict)_/C5/Nat Geo

2005 – _D Day to Berlin_/BBC (x3)
2005 – _Ian Fleming: Bondmaker_/BBC
2005 – _Days that Shook the World_/BBC (x20)
2005 – _Seconds from Disaster_/BBC (x25)
2005 – _Hiroshima_/BBC
2005 – _Auschwitz: The Final Solution_/BBC (x6)
2005 – _If …_/BBC (x7)
2005 – _Trafalgar Battle Surgeon; Rum, Sodomy and the Lash_/C4 (x2)
2005 – _Trial of the King Killers_/C4
2005 – _Helen of Troy_/C4
2005 – _Guns Germs and Steel_/C4/Nat Geo (x3)
2005 – _The Year London Blew Up 1974_/C4

2005 – *E=MC2*/C4
2005 – *Great San Francisco Earthquake*/C4
2005 – *Blitz, London's Firestorm*/C4
2005 – *The Somme*/C4
2005 – *Monarchy*/C4 (x10)
2005 – *The Flight That Fought Back*/C4
2005 – *Blood on our Hands: English Civil War*/C4
2005 – *Ape to Man*/History
2005 – *Vic Reeves Rogues Gallery*/Discovery (x9)
2005 – *Oil Storm*/FX

As can be seen in broad strokes, above, the experimental stage tends to predominate earlier in the chronology, to be replaced by the classical stage later in the era. There is overlap, where some variants default to the classical stage more quickly than others, especially those with multiple formulaic episodes, such as *Days that Shook the World* (BBC, 2003–2005). While some films blur the edges, most are clearly distinguishable as either the originator of a variant, such as *A History of Britain* and *George Orwell*; or as classical, that is, they broadly follow a template already established, such as *A History of Britain Series 2*. Some films, such as *Witchcraze*, may been experimental but were too individualistic to become a template for future commissioning. Yet, like any evolutionary tree, there are strains that spawn many descendants and strains that do not. It is also useful to note that 2005 sees considerable continuing experimentation, five years after the prospective genre had begun.

It is now appropriate in the next chapter to analyse the variants of dramatisation during the height of drama documentary's commercial success, which occurred between 2006 and 2008. The argument for a new genre can now be considered to have been fully made. It will be necessary in the next chapter to find an appropriate name for it.

Notes

1 These statistics are from the data set compiled especially for this book. They have been derived from the key commissioning and producing interviewees, covering the spectrum from Channel 4 to the BBC, both in-house and indie production houses. They have been checked by Martin Davidson (formerly BBC Head of History) and Hamish Mykura (formerly Channel 4's Head of History).
2 David Cannadine (ed.), *History and the Media* (London: Palgrave Macmillan, 2006), p. 1.
3 Steve Neale, *Genre and Hollywood* (London: Routledge, 2000), p. 27.

4 Rick Altman, *Film/Genre* (London: British Film Institute, 1999), p. 160.
5 *Ibid.*, p. 161.
6 Tzvetan Todorov, 'The Origin of Genres', *New Literary History*, 8:1 (1976), p. 163.
7 Neale, *Genre and Hollywood*, p. 165.
8 *Ibid.*, pp. 165–195.
9 Alan Williams, 'Is a Radical Genre Criticism Possible?', *Quarterly Review of Film Studies*, 9:2 (1984), pp. 121–122.
10 Stella Bruzzi, 'Making a Genre: The Case of the Contemporary True Crime Documentary', *Law and Humanities*, 10:2 (2016), pp. 249–280 (p. 249).
11 *Ibid.*
12 Neale, *Genre and Hollywood*, p. 197.
13 Christian Metz, *Film Language: A Semiotics in the Cinema* (New York: Oxford University Press, 1974), pp. 148–61.
14 This and the following quotations are all from the film *Bareknuckle Boxer* (Channel 4, 2003).
15 John Dugdale, Review, *The Sunday Times* (2003).
16 Andrew Davies is best known for his adaptation of *Pride and Prejudice* (BBC, 1995) and more. He would never be considered a mongrel writer, yet this is exactly as his skill was treated with this hybrid film.
17 Manohla Dargis, 'Movie Review: "The Other Boleyn Girl"', *New York Times* (9 December 2008).
18 Inhouse at BBC is the production arm within the BBC.
19 Robert McKee is an influential American touring lecturer/author in story structure.
20 Patrick O'Brian, *Master and Commander: The Far Side of the World* (2003, 20th Century Fox) is notable for his authentic-sounding maritime and eighteenth-century idioms.
21 Jason Deans, 'Appetite for slimming drama remains healthy', *Guardian* (18 February 2005).
22 Sealed Knot – a reenactment society specialising in the English Civil War.
23 A 6K light is one that produces 6,000 watts of light.
24 Colour grade is the correction of tone and colour to an image in post-production.
25 Steven Lipkin, *Real Emotional Logic: Film and Television Docudrama as Persuasive Practice* (Carbondale, IL: Southern Illinois University Press, 2002), p. 40.
26 *Ibid.*, pp. 41–42.
27 Robert Rosenstone, *History on Film/Film on History*, 2nd ed. (Abingdon: Routledge, 2013), p. 65.
28 *Ibid.*
29 Robert Rosenstone, *Visions of the Past: The Challenge of Film to Our Idea of History* (Boston, MA: Harvard University Press, 1995), p. 240.
30 William Bligh was captain of HMS *Bounty* in 1790 when there was a mutiny, and he and half the crew were set adrift in the East Indian seas.
31 A. A. Gill, Review, *Sunday Times* (2005).
32 Lipkin, *Real Emotional Logic*, p. 41.
33 VFX is an industry term for visual effects.
34 David Chater, Review, *The Times* (2005).
35 Robert Rosenstone, *Revisioning History: Film and the Construction of a New Past* (Princeton, NJ: Princeton University Press, 1995), p. 7.

6

2006–2008: Confirming a new genre

Introduction

Genres are best understood as processes. These processes may, for sure, be dominated by repetition, but they are also marked fundamentally by difference, variation, and change.¹

In the two years after 2006, dramatised history documentaries flowered in a variety of directions, especially internationally, a dynamic situation usefully described by Neale (above). The 'variation' of dramatised history documentaries was a sign that the corpus was now fast becoming a potential genre. At the same time, this putative genre was reaching its zenith in terms of production spend per hour and its international reach. It is accepted that the number of hours of programming declined dramatically, from ninety-eight in 2005 to thirty-eight in 2006 and twenty in 2008. These statistics are misleading, however. The huge and relatively inexpensive series of *Days that Shook the World* (BBC, 2003–2005) and *Seconds from Disaster* (BBC, 2004–2005), at £250k/hr, had been replaced by smaller series, such as *Ancient Rome* (BBC, 2006), at £1.25M/hr, that were more highly scripted and, as the drama mode increased, much more expensive. The years 2006–2008 should be regarded, therefore, as the most ambitious period yet.

This chapter aims to show the international growth of the corpus, as the co-production market grew beyond the traditional American, Japanese, and European markets and expanded into China, with *The First Emperor* (Channel 4) transmitting in 2006, followed by *The Great Wall* (Channel 4) in 2007. But the most highly decorated film of the canon was made for the BBC in 2008 by Wall to Wall TV: the Oscar-winning cinema-event *Man on Wire*. This film confirms Bruzzi's notion that every genre has a 'most notorious example to date'.²

By the end of this chapter, it will have been shown that this body of dramatised history documentary can be confirmed as a bone fide genre, even before completing an analysis of Metz's stages of generic decline (which will be saved for Chapter 7). I hope, therefore, to complete a definition of the characteristics of this genre and to attribute to it an appropriate title derived from research that has covered the almost fifty-year period from 1960 to 2008, from *Culloden* – Bruzzi's 'touchstone or foundational text'[3] – to the apotheosis of the genre, *Man on Wire*.

To progress into the case-study analysis, I propose an overview of the data set from 2006 to 2008, drawing attention to the increasing spend per hour on many of these productions. The international co-productions will be underlined.

2006 – *Casualty1906*/BBC
2006 – *The Power of Art*/BBC (x8)
<u>2006 – *Ancient Rome: Rise and Fall of an Empire*/BBC/Discovery (x6)</u>
<u>2006 – *Terry Jones' Barbarians*/BBC (x4)</u>
2006 – *Aberfan*/BBC
<u>2006 – *Blackbeard*/BBC/Discovery (x3)</u>
2006 – *Beau Brummell*/BBC
2006 – *Badness of King George IV*/BBC
2006 – *Elizabeth David: A Life in Recipes*/BBC
2006 – *H.G. Wells: War with the World*/BBC
<u>2006 – *Surviving Disaster*/BBC/Discovery/Pro Sieben (x7)</u>
<u>2006 – *The First Emperor*/C4/Discovery</u>
2006 – *Harlot's Progress*/C4
<u>2006 – *Challenger Countdown to Disaster*/C4/NGC</u>
<u>2006 – *9/11 Twin Towers*/BBC/Discovery</u>
2006 – 38 episodes/spend on average £300k–£1.25 million/hr

2007 – *Casualty 2007*/BBC (x3)
2007 – *Diary of Anne Frank*/BBC (x5)
<u>2007 – *Lusitania, Murder on the Atlantic*/BBC/Discovery/M6/NDR</u>
2007 – *Filth: The Mary Whitehouse Story*/BBC
<u>2007 – *Kamikaze*/C4/Smithsonian</u>
2007 – *City of Vice*/C4 (x5)
2007 – *The Relief of Belsen*/C4
<u>2007 – *Hindenberg*/C4/Smithsonian/ZDF</u>
<u>2007 – *Terracotta Army*/C4/Discovery</u>
<u>2007 – *The Great Wall*/C4/Discovery</u>
2007 – 20 episodes/spend on *The Great Wall* – up to £1.5 million/hr

<u>2008 – *Man on Wire*/BBC/Discovery/UKFC</u>
2008 – *A Medieval Heist*/BBC
2008 – *Hanged Man and the Saint*/BBC
<u>2008 – *Heroes and Villains*/BBC/Discovery (x6)</u>

2008 – _The Unsinkable Titanic_/C4/Nat Geo/Discovery Canada
2008 – _Stonehenge Decoded_/Nat Geo/Disney+
2008 – _True Horror_/C5/History (x3)
2008 – 14 episodes/spend on _Man on Wire_ – budget over £1 million for global cinema release

It is evident from the data set above that much of the increase in spend per hour derived from the increased internationalism of the productions. The year 2006 saw the substantial spend by the BBC and Discovery on _Ancient Rome: Rise and Fall of an Empire_, a full-scale location drama which cost over £1 million per hour. In 2006/7, there were three huge co-productions between Channel 4 and China on its history, which cost £1.5 million per hour. In 2008, the BBC's _Heroes and Villains_ took production crews round the world, like the Oscar-winning _Man on Wire_, whose story ranged from France to Australia and then the United States.

Channel 4's international perspectives

The battle between Channel 4 and BBC over their historical drama documentary content has been discussed in terms of its domestic implications, but one of the factors in this period that led to the boom, in terms of spend, was the rise of co-productions. This is particularly the case in the production of dramatised international history. There was demand for British expertise in this field of programming, which was seen to combine copper-bottomed sense with 'value for money' sensuousness. The foremost company in this regard was the indie production company Lion TV. Its co-managing director, and Head of History, Richard Bradley, gave an interview to me in which he explained the company's thinking: 'We had been looking to make history less like teacher and more like entertainment from the beginning' (Bradley, 2020).

Lion's programming was commercially led and very ambitious in terms of scale, and it was occasionally, in Metzian terms, experimental. During the early years of the history boom, 2000–2005, Lion followed the experiments in impressionistic, non-speaking dramatisation in series such as _A History of Britain_, continuing to utilise the key identifiers of the prospective genre: a narrator, captions throughout, and a blend of interviewees, general views, and drama vignettes. All of Lion's films mentioned in this section fit the generic model. They are all dramatised history documentaries, commissioned by documentary departments and always balancing sense with sensuousness.

By 2002, Lion was producing the first of a number of international commissions from a middle-man broker, Devillier Donegan Enterprises (DDE), which would raise part of the money from PBS in the United States and make their profit on international sales. Through this new international distribution system, Lion produced a three-parter on *Egypt's Golden Empire* (PBS, BBC) in 2001, and *Luther* (PBS) in 2002, a two-parter about Martin Luther and the Reformation, starring Timothy West as an older Luther looking back over his transformative life. Both dramatisations were almost entirely impressionistic, along the lines of Starkey's Tudor series, but the production values were much higher. In *Luther*, director Cassian Harrison's imagery was exquisite, and despite the apparent dourness of the subject matter, the package was deeply sensuous and made history evocative and appealing to PBS audiences first, and international audiences thereafter.[4] The success of *Luther* was quickly followed by *Lawrence of Arabia* (PBS), a two-parter set in the Jordanian desert; and *Medici: Godfathers of the Renaissance* (PBS/Channel 4), a four-parter set in Florence, documenting three centuries of the banking family as they patronised artists, scientists, and thinkers including Brunelleschi, Botticelli, Galileo, Leonardo, Michelangelo, and Savonarola. Sensuousness, quite understandably, hit a high point, as images of paintings, sculptures, and buildings were interlaced with dramatic vignettes of murders in cathedrals, family weddings in olive groves, book burnings in town squares, and internecine warfare. As Bradley recounts, 'international programming needs stories everybody has heard of, and they need to be a rich tapestry to look at' (Bradley, 2020).

When the DDE business model foundered on lower-than-expected international sales, Lion found other international partners for their brand of greatest hits of world history. *Days that Shook the World* (BBC/History Channel, 2003–2006) offered up a three-series greatest hits package, including Hiroshima, the Wright brothers' first flight, the assassination of JFK, the death of Princess Diana, the Apollo moon landing, and the declaration of the state of Israel, often in half-hour bite-sizes, mixing archive with impressionistic dramatisations. *Days that Shook the World* 'put you in the minute-by-minute perspective of an event', explains Bradley; 'the assassination of JFK was seen from the assistant press secretary, the surgeon, a family on the Grassy Knoll. It was on the shoulder view, not helicopter view. We wanted to get people watching history who wouldn't otherwise come, and to get them talking.' In 2005, Lion produced *The Crescent and the Cross* for The History Channel, a vivid account of a time when East met West, seen from both perspectives (and this was many years before Peter Frankopan's acclaimed 2015 book and 2017 documentary *The Silk Roads*). Bradley recalls *The Crescent and the Cross* as having had 'amazing interviews with Muslim scholars, bringing to life ancient Islamic sources', and he maintains that the producer/director Mark Lewis 'worked incredibly hard on his research'.

All of Lion's productions to this date had made a considerable contribution to the evolving historiography, and in Metzian terms, had been in the classical stage of the newly evolving genre. They were using the processes already established by experimental indies such as Wall to Wall and Juniper TV. Following the point of view of JFK's surgeon was reminiscent of how, two years before, *Battle Surgeon* had followed Nelson's surgeon. Yet the company's geographical reach was impressive, unlocking the histories of Egypt, the Middle East, and much of Europe.

There was one area of the world that was entirely unexplored by Western television, however: China. This was a territory that the prolific global salesman, Bradley, wished to unlock. 'No documentary or drama had been made on China's history for Western consumption, and it took a time to gain the confidence of Chinese participants', he explains. 'China has a partial history, there are big gaps in the 20th century for example, and although they clearly have a rich dynastic past, it all depends on how the current Communist party regime sees the merits of their history. Confucius, for example, has not always been popular', Bradley adds. Hence, China's past had until the mid-2000s been globally undersold. Bradley recalls, 'Once we displayed our understanding that China sees itself as Middle Earth (and not as an outpost of our colonial story, or Japan's expansionist story), Chinese co-production opened up to us.'

Bradley constructed unprecedented international financing from Hamish Mykura at Channel 4, Star TV in China, Discovery in the United States, and a French channel, enabling an epic three-part series of China's greatest hits: *The First Emperor* (Channel 4, 2006), *the Terracotta Warriors*, and *the Great Wall* (Both Channel 4, 2007). *The First Emperor* follows the rise, reign, and fall of Chin Shi Huang Di in the third century BC, employing what is described in the publicity as cutting-edge science to unlock the secrets of his tomb. The emperor is compared to Alexander the Great and Julius Caesar for the way in which he commanded disparate populations, united China, and built the Great Wall.

Filmed on location in China, Lion's crew were granted unprecedented access to Emperor Chin's legendary seven-square-mile underground burial complex, which is filled with more than eight thousand figures, including the terracotta army with which the emperor planned to celebrate his political and military power and achieve continued glory in the afterlife. As Lion's publicity states: 'Two thousand years after his death, ground-penetrating radar combined with CGI illustrate for the first time on-screen, the shape, layout and design of the largest unopened tomb in the world.' The film contained impressionistic drama, interviews, and narration, again confirming its inclusion within the genre.

Reviews for the first film were very encouraging: The *Hollywood Reporter* called it 'A two-hour television program that combines high-level documentary techniques with engaging drama to tell the story of the monster who created China more than 2,000 years ago.'[5] The *Guardian* acknowledged the 'exploration of a potentially fascinating subject ... this film contains some stunning footage of Qin's tomb ... spectacular scenes enacted in gorgeous locations ... as a five-act tragedy, it was near enough perfect.'[6] This praise reinforces the dramatic imperative of structuring a complex history into a five-act structure. It is zenith-worthy praise indeed. It also shows great critical self-awareness that the *Guardian* should have so overtly referred to the 'five-act structure', as if history would always best fit into audience-friendly dramatic narrative structures. After six years of evolving drama documentaries, it appears that the 'product' of Paget's 'cultural tourism' was now so fully understood by the audience that television critics saw fit to describe the dramatic structures within which they were presented. It was only one step away from confirming that this five-act structure existed to service five advertising breaks.

The First Emperor is a piece of highly manufactured and mature genre filmmaking. The producers knew what the audience (particularly in the West) expect to see of the Orient, although Bradley admits that China's rulers dictated the version of their history that they wanted the world to see. In terms of the Metzian four stages, *The First Emperor* inhabits the classical stage as a dramatisation that follows previously articulated modes – *A History of Britain* reworked as a history of China. Its sensuous scale was achieved, according to Bradley, because 'China has quite a tradition of historical drama, so there was a resource of costumes, and riders on horseback. There's even an 80% scale replica of the Forbidden City made of stone, which is both a film set as well as a tourist attraction.' This history of China was following the model of the tourist's Ancient Egypt. Paget ties these tourist models together nicely: 'cultural tourists, then, visit unfamiliar territory over which they hold economic power, and they go for specified periods in order to consume "ways of life" different from their own'.[7]

The First Emperor, according to Bradley, was a ratings hit on Channel 4, watched by 3.5 million viewers. It was a considerable success in the United States too. 'Using the English language in dialogue made something alien really work', explains Bradley. 'One or two television critics were sniffy. But it worked! Ralph Lee [the future Head of History at Channel 4] called it his favourite B movie.' A 'B movie' is a low-budget commercial variant of a successful genre, and while *The First Emperor* has some scale in its production, it does contain a degree of cinematic epic on a television budget. The term 'commercial' is the key here. Lee was recognising the nakedly commercial 'product' for sale, the creeping cynicism of pre-packaged history for the masses. It must be made clear that this is not the fault of the Chinese partners per se, but is due to the growing maturity of the genre, which by 2006 had forged a certain 'knowing' shorthand within the television history industry. Bradley knew what Lee at Channel 4 would buy, and Lee knew what Bradley was selling. The *Guardian* critic referred to earlier knew what was being offered to the public in its satisfying package, and UK viewers duly imbibed it – all 3.5 million of them.

The Great Wall followed in 2007 – a feature-length dramatised history of increased ambition and scale. The two-hour film traced the story of the building of the Great Wall of China, which was intended to defend the Ming Dynasty from Mongol attacks in the mid-sixteenth century – apocalyptic, terror-inducing attacks that Bradley calls 'the Ming dynasty's own 9/11'. The narrative follows the founding of the nation's first professional army and its testing in battle all the way to the building of the wall. The drama documentary brings the viewer face-to-face with the descendants of the wall's builders, a very novel 'proximity' to have achieved. The film also takes the audience to the remotest reaches of the wall itself and into the heart of China's legendary People's Liberation Army – which, according to Bradley, was the first time a Western film crew had ever been allowed such access. This film is, arguably, an evocation of a monumental and exotic history, combining the sense of politically crafted information with the sensuousness of epic television entertainment.

With regard to the aesthetics of *The Great Wall* (2007), the international market had moved on from impressionistic silent dramatisations to the fuller drama variant, requiring Bradley to use words derived from original primary sources. Lion TV cast actors from LA's Chinese community and out of Hong Kong, but the international partners could not agree on the language format. Discovery wanted the actors to speak in English, while Hamish Mykura at Channel 4 wanted to hear the original language with English subtitles. 'It was ironic that drama doc was getting a bad name here in Britain by now', recalls Bradley, 'and there were accusations of unknown actors being risible, especially when acting in a foreign language.' Despite the spoken drama, the film still retained a narrator to guide the viewer through the documentary evidence.

Lion TV was, by 2007, a very mature salesroom for international dramatised history, having practised for seven years on the glamorous histories of Egypt, the Middle East, the European Renaissance, the Reformation, and now China. Lion TV had increasingly realised that strong but simple storytelling, interwoven with visceral battles, ornate palaces, and costumed heroes and heroines, was very marketable the world over. The downside of this development in the genre was hinted at by Lee and Mykura at Channel 4. They suggested that some of the translated dramatic dialogue, although broadly well achieved, would not pass muster for every territory, especially the United Kingdom, where the audience's appetite for translated cultural tourism was evolving; it was felt that viewer might want a sense of local authenticity by hearing the dialogue in the original language, rather as Wall to Wall's *Ancient Egyptians* had attempted in 2003.

The decision was not for the United Kingdom alone, however, because the film was co-owned by a series of international partners. It was soon revealed that each country's appetite for the genre was at a different stage. In the period 2005–2010, for example, France was known to want more philosophical ideas, and thus they were strong on 'sense', while Germany favoured the gloss of the drama and were strong on 'sensuousness'. Japan appreciated the latest technology on screen, be it HD or 4K super-clear image rendition, while the United States repeatedly required frequent use of the hyperbole of the 'greatest epic story ever told …', without much recourse to the complexity of the sources or the culture under consideration.

A mongrel genre is hinted at here. It was not the first and nor would it be the last time. But this was increasingly a genre that was still going strong for a whole decade. It must be further acknowledged that the internationalisation of this unique generic product represented a great commercial success for drama documentary, bringing a great deal of work and currency into Britain's production base. The next film to be studied also brought great critical acclaim – as well as that rare achievement, an Academy award.[8]

Man on Wire (BBC/Discovery/UKFC, 2008)

> Brief summary: *This feature-length dramatised documentary tells the story of a Frenchman walking a tightrope across the Twin Towers and the international adventures that led to this single high-wire performance.*

Alex Graham, executive producer of *Man on Wire*, describes it as a fairly traditional reconstruction/interview/archive film that abides by the five generic identifiers. It combines history, drama, and documentary; it sets out its pact with the audience; it uses captions and interviews to maintain the documentary mode; it has actors; and it is commissioned from the documentary departments. Indeed, it was a film that was so successful at merging what Paget would refer to as 'playful' drama with its French documentary subject that it became worthy of a cinema release.[9]

Graham had met Simon Chinn, the producer of *Man on Wire*, when Chinn produced *Smallpox 2002* for Wall to Wall. According to Graham, Chinn had wanted to succeed as a movie producer from the outset. 'Chinn had been struggling with his feature film company, Red Box, when he had heard the Desert Island Discs with Philippe Petit in 2004', explains Graham, adding, 'I had heard it simultaneously and loved the story, but Simon chased it.'[10] Petit was a Frenchman who had illegally walked a high-wire between the World Trade Centre's Twin Towers in 1974. Chinn, according to Graham, had been 'given the run around' by both Petit and Nick Fraser, editor of BBC's *Storyville*. Chinn had optioned Petit's book *To Reach the Clouds* (2002) for £15,000 but was shocked to only be offered £25,000 for a BBC *Storyville* slot. Chinn had then presented it to Graham and Hewes at Wall to Wall, when Hewes proclaimed that 'this is a fantastic film – a heist movie. If the Twin Towers were still standing this would be a one-hour Discovery show, but 9/11 makes this a feature film, a love letter to the Twin Towers.' Wall to Wall was at the peak of its confidence at this point, according to Graham, and its franchises were making money, 'so I told Chinn what do you need? An option, research, a treatment? Would £25k cover it?' Chinn said yes and Graham wrote him a cheque. There were two versions possible: a TV version, meaning 90' UK/2 hr US at £750k per hour, and a movie version, at £1 million per hour. Wall to Wall went for the movie option. Graham recalls, 'We went on a two-pronged attack. £375k out of BBC, £375k out of Discovery. No need for a patchwork movie approach with 14 different territories.'

Graham approached Richard Klein at the BBC (Head of Documentaries, and later to be Controller of BBC Four after Hadlow's departure), who offered £25k from *Storyville* on BBC Four and £150k from the network (BBC 2), totalling £175k. Graham refused the offer and took the project to Channel 4, where Angus McQueen, a distinguished documentary director, was temporarily installed. He said yes to £375k, straight away. 'But there was a problem', recalls Graham, 'Simon Chinn did not want to piss off the BBC, since for a documentary producer, they were so important to his future, and he insisted that we give them a chance to match it. Channel 4, after all, was not felt to be as enduring as a market.' Graham argued that the BBC had had their opportunity to be involved, and did not want McQueen to feel used, simply to bump up the price. According to Graham, Klein began shouting 'you can't do this!' which caused Graham to retort: 'yes, I fucking can, and I will. I have something you really want. You have all the power normally, and just for once, I've got the opportunity to tell you what to do!' Graham adds, 'the arrogance of the BBC!' Klein relented and agreed to the terms, and John Ford, Commissioner at Discovery, matched the funds. The UK Film Council came in, and Graham assembled the feature-film budget of £1 million per hour. 'It was such hard work raising this budget. I could tell that the drama documentary bubble was almost over', explains Graham, as he reflects on beginning of the end for the genre.

Aesthetically, the Petit film (as it was known during production) was a heist movie without a victim, the artistic crime of the century, and *Oceans 11* (2001) was the inspiration. The film was a mix of impressionistic drama vignettes, interviews with the key protagonists, and captions that confirmed the veracity of the various stunts. The drama element was considered essential because although the events had occurred within living memory, footage of the stunts was not forthcoming. 'He scratched around for less than twenty not very good photographs of the actual day of the walk, and only six on the wire. But then found footage of him practising in France, which was an incredible discovery.' Graham returns to the actual New York walk; 'We considered utilising CGI to fake the imagery but knew that we would be breaking the contract with the audience.' Graham admits that one shot was faked, the actual stepping of Petit's foot onto the wire, which stimulates the viewer to believe that what they see next is action footage of the walk, but it is a subtle trick. Graham credits director, James Marsh, director of *Wisconsin Death Trip* (BBC, 1999), for this sleight of hand.

Marsh and his editor, Jinx Godfrey, constructed a lyrical, acrophobia-inducing and deeply sensuous montage made up of footage of passers-by watching in horror and the police arriving at the top of the building and ordering Petit to get off the wire. This combination is linked breathlessly by the haunting soundtrack (of Satie's '*Gymnopedie*'), which makes the audience feel as if it will end inevitably in tragedy. 'Most people believe they have witnessed live, action footage of Petit walking the wire as the climax to the film, but they haven't', says Graham, 'it is a trick of the mind', He adds that 'the whole film worked better than we could have hoped: the heist preamble was so wittily reconstructed, so playfully done, we should really have credited ourselves as producers (Graham and his right-hand man, Jonathan Hewes) because then we would have picked up the Oscar!'

The title came later in the process than the shooting. The provisional title, *To Reach the Clouds*, 'sounded very Douglas Bader', recalls Graham; 'then we found the police report, written by a New York cop, and there in capital letters it said: MAN ON WIRE'. Serendipity arose from all that planning and then throwing the plans away, according to Graham, who quotes the golfer Gary Player: 'the harder I practice, the luckier I get'. Graham, to this day, is visibly moved by the memories of the film: 'We didn't expect the film to be so philosophical, so French. Petit's friends strove to help him make something extraordinary happen, and then when it was done, the best friend bursts into tears at the loss, and his girlfriend woefully accepts that Petit is having sex with an American fangirl. It is over, the magic is gone' (Graham, 2020).

Yet the magic remained within this extraordinary feature film, an example of the genre quite unlike any other. It was a story that could not be easily repeated, and hence it could not be copied or franchised. In *Man on Wire*, it is arguable that the proposed genre reached its zenith in terms of a confluence of aesthetics, storytelling, history, and ambition. Certainly, the film remains the most popularly known of the genre in terms of name recognition.

Conclusion – and a new genre defined

In six chapters of analysis, covering eight years of films, the body of work has been explored, codified, and taxonomised thoroughly, case study by case study, from progenitors and foundational texts to works belonging to the experimental and classical stages. It only remains, in Chapter 7, to explore the decline and fall of the works under consideration through the lens of Metz's generic final two stages, what have been termed the stages of parody and deconstruction.

But it is appropriate that this chapter, which deals with the zenith of the prospective genre, should assert that a new genre has indeed been defined, and a name for it can therefore be given. The genre has been identified as full of variants – although two key variants have been fully discussed: the impressionistic non-speaking dramatisations and the fuller, scripted dramas. But what unites them is that they *all* retain narration and/or captions as representatives of the documentary form. It is worth reiterating the five characteristics of the corpus, described earlier in the chapter, here:

1. All the films contain drama, history, and documentary.
2. There is a pact with the audience, in the form of a disclaimer at the front of the film.
3. Historical truth is established by a narrator and/or captions throughout the film.
4. The drama is performed by actors, whether speaking or not.
5. The films are commissioned by documentary departments (if not specifically history) that prioritise the telling of truth alongside drama.

These are the key characteristics that define our genre, and which are applicable to over four hundred films over the ten-year period of 2000–2010. These films have been discussed in Chapters 1–6 of this book, beginning with *A History of Britain* and its competitors in 2000–2001, looking back to *Culloden* and *The War Game* in the 1960s, then continuing with *Ancient Egyptians* and *George Orwell: A Life in Pictures* in 2002 and *Bareknuckle Boxer* and the fuller dramas of *Trial of the King Killers* and *Trafalgar Battle Surgeon* in 2005. Finally, the zenith of the genre has been reached in 2006–2008, with expansion into the international marketplace, especially China.

So what name should be attributed to this genre? It is proposed that as the three key terms are 'drama', 'documentary', and 'history', then all three words should be incorporated into the genre's name. But in what order? Are these films documentary dramas or drama documentaries? While Paget debates this point in *No Other Way to Tell It* (1998), where the United States tends to use one term, the United Kingdom the other, it is worth noting that Paget admits that very few people in the industry (still less viewers) regard this subsidiary question as significant. Nevertheless, precision and consistency in terminology are important, so it is suggested that because the films are almost entirely commissioned from the documentary departments, the family to which they belong is therefore documentary. What kind of documentary, then? They are drama documentaries, as opposed to presenter-led or 'living' documentaries like *1900 House*.

The term should be hyphenated better to link them with what Paget calls 'a grammatical umbilical cord',[11] confirming the mutual interdependence of their sense and sensuousness, hence drama documentary. *Culloden*, and to a lesser extent *The War Game*, are the key progenitors, so our genre is the 'new' version of an older mini-genre. Hence, with all of this in mind, the name proposed for this new genre is:

New History Drama-Documentary.

This admittedly less-than-concise moniker is nevertheless clear: it defines what lies within the scope, and what falls without. It also establishes distance from Paget's (and Lipkin's) title for the genre including *Band of Brothers* and the fact-based dramas of the 2000s, the New Docudrama.[12] Their considered writing on this drama-led genre has often guided the present writer through the research, albeit on a different but related corpus of films.

As with all genres, the boundaries of New History Drama-Documentary are blurred for filmmakers, academics, and viewers alike. *Conspiracy* (BBC, 2001), starring Kenneth Branagh, by way of example, belongs to Paget and Lipkin's New Docudrama, but it is notable that it contains a narrator at top and bottom and offers photographic evidence, positioned in direct relation to the cast. It is also set in a single location, and Loring Mandel drew the script from the stenographer's notes of the meeting to determine The Final Solution. All that notwithstanding, the majority of the film is pure drama, and Mandel admitted to the present writer that the stenographer's record was fragmentary and much of the script came from his imagination (Mandel, 2009). Crucially, there is no confirmation of truth throughout the film, either in caption or narration. This is New Docudrama, then, but of a kind that New History Drama-Documentarians can appreciate for its considerable proximity to historical events and characters. What remains important is that practitioners who wish to create history documentaries in the future, using the powerful combination of sense and sensuousness, of drama and documentary, can rely on the analysis and definitions offered in this book as a partial guide for whatever storytelling devices they use, even those that are still to be conceived.

Now that the genre under consideration by this work is defined and titled, it is appropriate to turn to the final two years of the New History Drama-Documentary. The next chapter will describe the decline and fall of the genre between 2008 and 2010, and asks whether the generic final two stages of parody and deconstruction can shed light on this descent.

Notes

1 Steve Neale, *Genre and Hollywood* (London: Routledge, 2000), p. 165.
2 Stella Bruzzi, 'Making a Genre: The Case of the Contemporary True Crime Documentary', *Law and Humanities*, 10:2 (2016), pp. 249–280 (p. 249).
3 *Ibid.*
4 Cassian Harrison – director of *Luther*, about Martin Luther and the Reformation.
5 Review, *Hollywood Reporter* (December 2006).
6 Review, *Guardian* (15 December 2006).
7 Derek Paget, *True Stories: Documentary Drama on Radio, Screen and Stage* (Manchester: Manchester University Press, 1990), p. 89.
8 *Man on Wire* won the 2009 Academy Award for Documentary Feature.
9 'There is also a heightened awareness in difficult times of the ability of docudrama (especially in the hands of a Frears or a Kosminsky) to be playful, provocative, questioning and critical in its representation of events.' Derek Paget, 'Making Mischief: Peter Kosminsky, Stephen Frears and British Television', *Journal of British Cinema and Television*, 10:1 (2013), pp. 171–186 (p. 174).
10 *Desert Island Discs* is a long-running BBC Radio 4 programme featuring a single weekly interview with a significant public figure.
11 Derek Paget, *No Other Way to Tell It: Dramadoc/Docu-drama on Television* (Manchester: Manchester University Press, 1998), p. 93.
12 'The maximising of the act of witness both in performance and reception [is] evident in the New Docudrama' (Derek Paget and Steven Lipkin, '"Movie-of-the-Week" Docudrama, "Historical-Event" Television, and the Steven Spielberg Series *Band of Brothers*', *New Review of Film and Television Studies*, 7:1 (2009), pp. 93–107).

7

2008–2010: Decline and fall of a genre

Introduction

In a 2020 interview, Hamish Mykura, former Head of History at Channel 4, and more recently Head of UK Production at National Geographic, made an important reference to his perception of the decline of what is now termed the New History Drama-Documentary. Mykura commented that 'there was time between 2000 and 2007 or 2008, when one could commission dramatised documentaries in the history space and know there were audiences for the increased cost of these programmes. But after that period, it became a lot harder' (Mykura, 2020). This chapter will argue that Mykura's memory of the decline of this genre within the industry is indeed accurate, despite the endurance of some strong programming and a complex statistical picture showing an uneven decline in programmes made. Between 2007 and 2008, there was a fall in commissions of what shall now be termed New History Drama-Documentary from twenty to fourteen per year. In 2009, this rose to twenty-two, an unexpected and unexplained rise, but by 2010 there had been another fall to ten programmes per year. The blip in the smooth statistical arc is not easily explained, but it has been previously noted that some programmes were commissioned two years before transmission, and often the development time is even longer. It is also notable that genres are 'loose' structures and are not necessarily well represented by statistics.

What is more helpful is the application of the model of a genre's development proposed by Christian Metz in the 1970s and Henri Focillon in the 1940s, and in particular its last two stages, refined by Schatz and Jauss in the 1980s and Kingsley-Jones in 2015. They identified the decline of a genre in terms of films moving from the classical stage to becoming parodic of themselves. Steven Schatz describes the French theorists' model:

> [Once] the genre's straightforward message has 'saturated' the audience … the genre evolves into what Focillon terms the age of refinement. As a genre's classic conventions are refined and eventually parodied and subverted, its transparency gradually gives way to opacity.[1]

In this chapter, it is argued that the conventions of this genre become, in several ways, 'parodied and subverted'. There were certainly, by 2008, some very ambitious and internationally co-produced drama documentaries that were pilloried by the critics and can justifiably be termed 'parodic' examples of the genre. These films attracted considerable negative attention to the whole genre and shall be described in their detail, since it is also arguable that the parodic stage led inexorably to what has been described by Kingsley-Jones as the fourth stage of a genre's arc, that of 'deconstruction'. This deconstruction involved a return to silos, in particular the drama documentary mode being absorbed by drama departments.

The genre's decline and nadir will be charted within this one chapter, covering the period 2008–2010. The end-date is approximate, and partly offered to conveniently contain the rise and fall of the genre within a decade, but it is also broadly supported by quantitative research, as the volume of New History Drama-Documentaries had fallen away dramatically by that date. It is useful here to return to the list of New History Drama-Documentaries, which attempts to illustrate the decline of the genre in terms of the numbers of episodes commissioned:

2008
2008 – *Man on Wire*/BBC
2008 – *Heist*/BBC
2008 – *Hanged Man and the Saint*/BBC
2008 – *Heroes and Villains*/BBC/Discovery (x6)
2008 – *The Unsinkable Titanic*/C4/Nat Geo/Discovery Canada
2008 – *Stonehenge Decoded*/ Nat Geo
2008 – *True Horror*/C5/History (x3)
2008 – 14 episodes

2009
2009 – *Cleopatra, Portrait of a Killer*/BBC
2009 – *Casualty 1909*/BBC (x6)
2009 – *Garrow's Law*/BBC (x4)
2009 – *Blitz, the Bombing of Coventry*/BBC
2009 – *The Execution of Gary Glitter*/C4
2009 – *Fighting the Red Baron*/C4
2009 – *Bloody Foreigners*/C4 (x3)
2009 – *1066*/C4 (x3)
2009 – *The Crescent and the Cross*/History (x2)
2009 – 22 episodes

2010
2010 – *Garrow's Law*/BBC (x4)
2010 – *Secret Diaries of Miss Anne Lister*/BBC
2010 – *First Light* (BBC)

2010 – *Operation Mincemeat*/BBC
2010 – *Belfast Blitz*/BBCNI
2010 – *The Taking of Prince Harry*/C4
2010 – *Untold Invasion of Britain*/C4
2010 – 10 episodes

It is worth reiterating here that in 2005, ninety-eight episodes were commissioned, while in 2006 this had dropped to thirty-eight and in 2007 to twenty. Hence, apart from the increase in 2009, there is a steady rise from 2000 to 2005 and a less steady but clear fall from 2006 to 2010.

As in earlier chapters, the decline of the genre will be charted with a series of case studies, beginning with the BBC's international co-productions, which were already attracting negative notices from critics; as noted in chapter 6, Richard Bradley of Lion TV had heard the word 'risible' being used.[2]

Ancient Rome: The Rise and Fall of an Empire (BBC/Discovery, 2006)

> Brief summary: *In this dramatised documentary, CGI is mixed with drama to tell the dramatic stories – the great battles, rivalries, rebellions and momentous achievements – that shaped the Roman Empire.*

The co-production partnership between the BBC and Discovery was known as the JV (joint venture) and was a five-year rolling deal. This section will cover two series that were produced by an in-house BBC department specially created for such New History Drama-Documentaries, with Discovery providing much of the funding. The first series, *Ancient Rome: The Rise and Fall of an Empire* (BBC/Discovery, 2006) pre-dates the rest of the films covered in this section by two years but is included on the grounds that it is thematically relevant.

Ancient Rome is not to be confused with the HBO 'sex, sand and sandals' docudrama series, *Rome* (HBO/BBC, 2005–2007), although both featured television stars: *Ancient Rome* starred Michael Sheen and Geraldine James, among others, while *Rome* starred James Purefoy and Polly Walker. The difference was, as ever, in the origins of the commissioning. *Rome* was a much larger *drama* commission, written by American dramatists and focused on the theme of corruption and the battle for power between Julius Caesar, Mark Anthony, and Augustus. It follows the careers of two imagined soldiers. *Ancient Rome* was more of a high-level documentary commission, and the film charts the rise and fall of an empire. The series was intended to run chronologically, starting with the destruction of the rival, Carthage, and moving on to the creation of the empire with the military success of Julius Caesar. This was followed by imperial instability, crystallised in the reign of Nero; the threats to the Empire brought about by the Jewish Revolt; the unification of the empire caused by Constantine's conversion to Christianity; and the decline of a militaristic society epitomised by the literal Fall of Rome. The series producer, Mark Hedgecoe, was quoted in *The Times* as saying that he made the series in response to previous films that 'have tended to ignore the real history and chosen to fictionalise the story'.[3]

Hedgecoe was responding to the success of the drama series *Rome*, whose producers at HBO had decided to include significant fictional elements. The sights and sounds of ancient Rome were recreated in exterior scenes that invariably pre-empted the speaking drama. This recreation was, in Hayden White's terms, 'antiquarian' in its proximity to a foreign world: many gods are on show, bathhouses spill out onto the streets, and naked men admire the slaughter of a bull in view of the *populus*. Dialogue is often inaudible, drowned in the audio of a city on the edge. When the editor cut away to the interiors, by contrast, the drama immediately became 'presentist'. Characters speak to each other in modern comprehensible English, albeit laced with idiomatic references to power, politics, and plenty of sex. If this is fictionalising the story, as Mark Hedgecoe claimed, then this type of fiction was a true modern crowd pleaser. It is interesting to note that the history consultant for *Rome* was Jonathan Stamp, the BBC director of *Pyramid* (BBC, 2001), discussed in Chapter 2. This present writer would argue that HBO's *Rome* balanced drama with its historical responsibilities very well, and rather better than Hedgecoe's *Ancient Rome*, which made claims to historical fidelity but, from the very outset of the series' transmission, failed, arguably, to deliver on its claims and hence slid towards the parodic stage.

Ancient Rome brings to mind the third stage of genre previously discussed, which refers to conventions being 'subverted' and transparency giving way to 'opacity': 'As a genre's classic conventions are refined and eventually parodied and subverted, its transparency gradually gives way to opacity.'[4] Thus, parodic opaqueness here means an imitation of the genre's surface without its underlying values. This begins to define what is meant, for the purposes of this work, by parody or parodic. This definition will include notions of the drama being 'risible', which will be dealt with in more detail shortly.

To return to historical novelist Lindsey Davis in the same *Times* article on *Ancient Rome*, she criticises the decision to broadcast the episodes out of chronological order as 'if they stick with their eccentric programming, we'll be jerked about maniacally'. She continues, 'this is history on the Eric Morecambe principle: all of the moments – but not necessarily in the right order!'[5] Why did the BBC choose to show *Nero* before *Julius Caesar* and delay *The Fall of Carthage*, one thousand years earlier? The answer lies in the hands of the television schedulers, who lacked confidence that an audience would materialise for the less iconic tale of Rome's early conquests. According to Nick Murphy, who wrote and directed the episode *Nero*, the schedulers were also playing the drama game of presenting their biggest stars first. Murphy had attracted Michael Sheen to play Nero, much the biggest star of the series, who, as Murphy observed, 'had indelibly played Tony Blair in *The Deal* and *The Queen*' (Murphy, 2020). Nancy Banks-Smith in the *Guardian* was complimentary of Michael Sheen's 'storming performance' as Nero, adding that she found it 'slightly disturbing' that he 'reminded you subliminally of Tony Blair'. Banks-Smith was critical of the drama documentary format of 'spicy drama sandwiched between simple slices of narrative' which she compared to 'watching a play with someone who insists on explaining the obvious'. Of Episode 2, *Caesar*, she remarked that 'the historians have got their chilly mitts on', pointing out that it 'was so painstakingly dull that *Nero*, always a crowd pleaser, had to be shown first'.[6] Sam Wollaston, also of the *Guardian*, compared it to the drama series *Rome* (HBO, BBC, 2005–2007), postulating that this series 'came about in response to all the mutterings from cross historians about factual inaccuracies in the BBC's grand romp (*Rome*) last year'. He states that 'after some extensive research' (he looked up Gracchus on Wikipedia), 'I declare this one to be historically accurate, but also a grand bore'. Highly critical of the drama documentary format, he states that 'they never work, either as dramas or as documentaries', continuing 'there's no proper character development, and you don't care about any of them', before concluding that this 'goes to show that sex is more fun than the truth'.[7]

Davis compliments the producers, who avoided the 'talking-heads style, though they use literature and the advice of modern historians' (in the opening captions), but she criticises the series in that 'once they fill up with battle and crowd scenes, the formula of one-hour dramas doesn't give enough scope'.[8] The ratings began well enough, with *Nero* attracting 4.2 million viewers (a 21 per cent audience share), but by Episode 6, this had fallen to 3 million viewers (and an audience share of 13 per cent). Three million viewers on BBC One is a low number indeed and suggested to the commissioners that the experiment with a full-drama-and-locations variant of the New History Drama-Documentary genre was not worth the money.

Murphy argues that the problem lay with the joint venture with Discovery that had guaranteed financial support for non-fiction output for five years. He believes that the American executive influence in the series led to muddled decision-making at the BBC. 'I have huge respect for Mark Hedgecoe, he is a very good documentary maker', recalls Murphy, 'but he is certainly no dramatist, and the American execs were not respectful of the rules of the drama documentary dilemma' (Murphy, 2020). Murphy argues that 'drama and documentary pull in different directions. Drama provides motive, decision and action, whereas documentary wants explanation.' The Discovery executives, according to Murphy, 'wanted commentary. The documentary version would be, for example, "convinced he was right, Caesar went South". The drama version would have Caesar kill a sheep and have its entrails checked for signs, then interpret them the way he has already decided'. Murphy points to Peter Morgan's dramatic moment in *The Queen* 'when the stag appears and Elizabeth decides to deal with Diana'. This follows the rules of drama where the outcome, if not the event, is documented.

Murphy would agree that *Ancient Rome* contains elements of the parodic stage of the genre. Each of the six episodes is written and directed by a different team, and Nick Murphy's episode of *Nero* is one of the few successful examples, by his own modest admission. It was promoted from third position in the chronology to being transmitted first, and it received the best reviews of the series and the highest viewing figures. Murphy looks back on this, the first of three New History Drama-Documentaries for the BBC in 2006–2007, and believes that he 'navigated the drama/documentary divide with reasonable balance'. He spoke extensively to Mary Beard, the consultant on the series, and sought out 'authenticity' derived from research in a way that would have made Alex Graham proud. He wrote a script that focused on the microcosm of Nero's household and told a thrilling tale of his descent into madness, aided, naturally, by the 'storming performance' identified by Nancy Banks-Smith. The rest of the series falls well short of the *Nero* episode and becomes worthy of the criticism levelled at it by Sam Wollaston: 'they never work, either as dramas or as documentaries … there's no proper character development, and you don't care about any of them.'

Drama documentaries had been criticised since their earliest conception, so none of this was new. What was new was the ambition of these drama documentaries of 2006–2007. They were competing with period drama, proudly asserting that they would put the record straight and identify the factual through-lines, as well as provide battle scenes and star actors.

It was all perhaps too tall an order. But did this make them parodic, in terms of the development of the genre? In a strict sense, the series was not trying to find a parodic or opaque approach to a well-worn genre. They became parodic and 'opaque', however, in that they were 'risible' – to use the word chosen by Richard Bradley to describe critical responses to some drama documentaries. (Bradley's comment is discussed more fully in Chapter 6, but it is worth quoting again here: 'It was ironic that drama doc was getting a bad name here in Britain by now, and there were accusations of unknown actors being risible.')

Martin Davidson returned to the BBC as Head of History Commissioning just as *Ancient Rome* was being transmitted. While accepting that the *Nero* episode was well done, he looks back on the series as being 'risible in places' (Davidson, 2019). Although risibility is only part of what makes something opaque/parodic, it represents a further step along the arc of the genre's development.

Davidson then received the rushes of the next joint venture series, already commissioned, and made by the same team, including Mark Hedgecoe as series producer and Nick Murphy as one of the directors. The intention of the series was to take the world's most iconic warriors and deliver all-action biopics for an international audience. Davidson gave this present writer an interview in which he recalls being embarrassed by the series 'as the worst kind of "how now from the North" kind of historical dialogue, placed in the mouths of inappropriate actors, in ludicrously simplistic storylines, where action scenes were a few dodgy set pieces, fleshed out by some poor made up at home CGI'. The series was *Heroes and Villains* (BBC, 2008), and the word 'ludicrous' rings out in addition to 'risible' as proof that the genre has moved into the generic third stage.

Heroes and Villains (Discovery/BBC, 2008)

Brief summary: *Focusing on six of the most powerful and magnetic leaders of all time, the stories examine the motives, the personal strengths, and often the weaknesses that drove them to achieve what no one else dared.*

The series that subsequently transmitted as *Heroes and Villains* followed the same six-part commissioning structure as *Ancient Rome* but had an even more global reach in terms of content, bringing together Attila the Hun, Spartacus, Richard the Lionheart, the Shogun, Cortés, and, in the final episode, Napoleon. Murphy confesses that his *Napoleon* was poorly received by the documentary commissioners at the BBC, yet he thinks of it as being, as he recounts, 'the most accomplished drama of the two series in terms of the solutions provided for a one-hour film on the motivations of a future icon'. While *Nero* was about a 'man who believed he was a god because he did terrible things without a consequence, *Napoleon* was a man in a culture without kings who realised that there will always be a king and it might as well be him'. Murphy did not want the film to begin with the New History Drama-Documentary trope of a commentary that introduces the pact with the audience (i.e. a caption or narration), instead he wanted to begin with a gritty depiction of an execution. Murphy fought the Discovery executives all the way to the final mix until the narrator was inserted, pronouncing:

'welcome to the bloody age of the revolution'. Murphy is still furious about this betrayal of his drama: 'I fucking hate that line. It is the antithesis of drama. The viewer should be asking where am I? Who's he? Oh Jesus!' Murphy would admit that his sensibility with *Napoleon* was more heavily weighted towards drama over documentary than with *Nero*, and that he was to find the balance best of all with his third film, which will be extensively discussed later in this chapter – that of Murphy's *Surviving Disaster: Chernobyl* (BBC, 2006). But he would also agree that *Heroes and Villains* was a series whose writers and directors did not know what it was attempting to achieve – true stories well evoked, or simply as much action as could be fitted into a forty-five-minute show. The result, therefore, is often 'ludicrous', another sign of parodic opaqueness, which refers to a series imitating the genre's surface without assuming its underlying values.

Taking the point of view of an executive producer, Martin Davidson references *Attila the Hun* as one of the 'ludicrous' films of this series. Its origins as a documented piece of history are so poorly signposted that the film does little to persuade the viewer that it is based on evidence at all. None of the dialogue contains period idioms. If the film is rescued, it is by the casting of physically imposing, wild-haired Scottish actor Rory McCann, better known for his role as The Hound in *Game of Thrones* (HBO, 2011–2019). It also displays some oddly convincing CGI, often pulling focus from the eponymous hero to a massed army in the distance, rather than just cutting to 'the CGI shot', which is the default of the other episodes of the series. This deft handling of the aesthetic technique was being mastered by Gareth Edwards, the director – 'in his bedroom', according to Davidson. It is little wonder that Edwards went on to make his own micro-feature film, again utilising technology to serve the story: his film *Monsters* (2010) was described by the *Guardian* as 'the bedroom blockbuster that is anti-Avatar', and while made for an apocryphal sub-£100,000, grossed around $5 million, and earned Edwards the helm of the studio movie *Godzilla* (2014), which grossed $500 million, as well as the lavishly budgeted *Star Wars Rogue One* (2016).[9]

Davidson's implication that the *Heroes and Villains* series was entering the parodic stage rests especially on the *Spartacus* episode (BBC, 2008). A close textual analysis of the opening scenes illustrates how the film mishandles the tropes of New History Drama-Documentary with unintentional parodic effect. Written by Colin Heber-Percy and Lyall B. Watson (who had together written the very good *Casualty 1909* [BBC, 2009]) and directed by Tim Dunn, the combination, in this specific case, neither respects the past nor is able to elicit it. The following excerpt charts a scene as it is actually spoken and captioned (in italics), alongside the present writer's commentary:

The film opens with a shaft of light revealing a gloomy cell. The narrator speaks with an East End growl:

> No one even knows where he came from. Some say he came from Thrace in Greece, but he never said. All I know is he was in the army, and his wife was stolen from him in a slave market in Rome. And that's where the story began.

The visual is of a generic faux-period market scene, where the clean-cut stones are evidently made of papier-mâché. Spartacus is white, English, from the twenty-first century, with make-up smears on his unmuscled body (Anthony Flanagan, a jobbing actor continuing his performance as a police constable in *Wild Bill* (ITV, 2019). He is inspected by a 'Slave Master', played by Mark Wingett, keeping his accent from *The Bill* (ITV, 1983–2010).

> Slave Master: All right, all right, I'll pay two sesertii, but what do I want with the woman?

Spartacus looks to his wife, who bursts into tears. A fight breaks out. Spartacus fights with various stuntmen but is defeated by overwhelming odds. His wife laments.

> Narrator: Spartacus will be known as the man who fought back. He was a hero, he was my friend, and most of all he was a slave who took on the might of Rome [portentous pause] to be free.

Captions follow:

> This film depicts real events and real characters.
> It is based on the accounts of writers of the time.
> It has been written with the advice of modern historians.

To read this scene back is to imagine a parody. This could be a *Carry On* film.[10] The viewer has no idea when in time the film is set, or where it is located: in Italy, North Africa – or a studio in Merton, where *The Bill* was shot. The film is, after all, using the London gangster idiom. Perhaps it was intended that it be a televisual interpretation of *Gladiator* (2000), in which case why were the actors not cast to feel like they came from a more muscular age, as Russell Crowe evidently was? It was certainly purported, by series producer Hedgecoe, to be the true story of the legendary 1960 film starring Kirk Douglas, but if that was the case, where was the information, where did the story emanate from, what was the source being utilised?[11] It is clear that establishing what Lipkin refers to in his book *Real Emotional Logic* (2002) as 'proximities and warrants' was not in the minds of those associated with the Joint Venture. It would be wrong just to blame the American partners at Discovery Channel, even if its viewers are admitted by one of their executives, Charlie Foley, to be 'white bread and circus' types (Foley, 2007). According to Davidson, 'the BBC history department suffered a loss of confidence under the JV. The fault was too much money that came with too many stipulations.' These two glossy BBC New History Drama-Documentaries were caught between two modes. Returning to Sam Wollaston's review of *Ancient Rome*, his observation might refer to any drama documentary from this particular joint venture: 'they never work, *either* as dramas or as documentaries' [my italics].

Cut to a CGI shot of a colosseum. Robert Glenister plays the local governor, in a toga, watching Spartacus' first public fight. Rupert Vansittart steps up beside him. Two very English actors.

RG: What a pleasant surprise, Senator, more than we deserve I am sure, or at least expected.
RV: People appreciate seeing the future consul I always think.

Cut to second CGI shot of an oddly static crowd. Cut to mid shot of crowd, full of Moroccan supporting artists. Hence, the film mixes its racial idioms. A supporting artist leans into Glenister:

SA: What the hell is he doing here?
RG: He'd turn up for the opening of a shithouse if he thought there'd be a vote in it.

There follows a limp gladiatorial fight between Spartacus and a Moroccan extra (not even a stuntman) who looks genuinely confused as he falls backwards. The Moroccan crowd meanwhile cup hands to mouths, shouting the English idiom '*BOOooo*'.

The further into the film one goes, the more unintentionally parodic it becomes. As Schatz puts it, drawing on Metz and Focillon, 'As a genre's classic conventions are refined and eventually parodied and subverted, its transparency gradually gives way to opacity.'[12] It is argued here that *Heroes and Villains* subverts its subject and makes it opaque.

It is clearly not an easy task to tell a story from a foreign place and in a foreign time, and to make it sufficiently 'presentist' for a modern audience, especially if the story has been marketed for its heroism, villainy, and all-round entertainment mixed with a dash-of-truth confirmation. It could also be argued that the fault lies less with the drama documentary divide and more with the expectations aroused by transposing of epic history to film. Even blockbuster movies struggle with the scale of representing the great battles, sieges, and conflicts of the past. *Troy* (2004) and *Alexander the Great* (2005) are contemporary cinema renditions of epic narratives that, according to critics, fail to deliver emotionally satisfying narratives as well as action sequences. There are, of course, great epics that succeed. *Saving Private Ryan* (1998) and *Schindler's List* (1993) are epic in scale and ambition, but certainly the latter has that ingredient that is at the heart of many historical films' successes: a microcosm. The New History Drama-Documentary is at its most focused when it contains its narrative within a microcosm: *Culloden, Pyramid, George Orwell: a Life in Pictures, Neanderthal, Bareknuckle Boxer, Trial of the King Killers* – all tell their stories within microcosms. They utilise primary sources that illuminate the microcosm, and they keep the audience informed at the same time as engaged.

These films feed sense and sensuousness into the viewer's consciousness with a subtle mix of education and entertainment. HBO, as a provider of drama (often based on truth), is a production company and distributor that frequently understands that delicate balance, as if it were a public service broadcaster. In *Rome* (HBO, 2007) and *John Adams* (HBO, 2008), a combination of exterior and interior devices offers information about the time and place as well as emotional intrigue. Whether or not this interior/exterior division works for every film, *Rome* and *John Adams* were resounding successes as drama series for HBO and continued the interest in offering authenticity through the drama mode. *Heroes and Villains*, by contrast, damaged the New History Drama-Documentary format, which at this point was now being perceived by viewers as well as critics to have entered a 'tired rehash' stage, or what we would know as the 'parodic' stage. Suffice it to say, Davidson's embarrassment about an expensive series that represented the tail end of a British/American co-venture was confirmed when the British schedulers aired the series after 11pm. It was, effectively, buried by the BBC.

In scholarly terms, *Heroes and Villains* is a series that especially blurs the boundaries between fact and fiction, recalling Derek Paget's observation in *No Other Way to Tell It*:

> The increasingly popular idea is that the boundary between fact and fiction is becoming dangerously blurred and that fact and fiction are now harder than ever to distinguish is at the heart of such phrase making as: 'blurring the boundaries, the truth of fiction is stranger than facts, friction over faction, dubious drama, drama out of suffering, fact or fiction, true to the facts, an unsuitable case for television treatment?'[13]

While this critical approach was taken to an earlier consideration of documentary dramas, in the 1990s, it is useful to apply it to the drama documentaries of the 2000s. As a documentary scholar, Bill Nichols comments in Lipkin's *Real Emotional Logic* (2002) that 'telling stories and representing history are fundamentally distinct tasks'.[14] Lipkin himself confirms this unbalance in his notion that 'docudrama stories are told through the melodramatic staging of documentary material'.[15] While the word 'melodramatic' is not being used in a derogatory sense here, a problem nevertheless lies with melodrama being too foregrounded. Robert Rosenstone agrees: 'Melodrama has been the dominant mode of the Hollywood historical film, thus a major source of criticism of the historical film.'[16]

Rosenstone goes on to define the rules of melodrama in true stories, noting that they should contain a:

1. Closed story
2. Notion of progress
3. Emphasis on individuals
4. Heightening of emotional states
5. Focus on surfaces

History, based on documents, welcomes the closed story, the notion of progress, the emphasis on individuals, and the heightening of emotional states, as have been seen in the earlier years of the genre, but *not* when they are overly wrought. In the case of *Heroes and Villains*, the genre, arguably, had become *too* melodramatic. The genre had also lost touch with its proximity to its sources, a practice that had served the genre well. In Lipkin's words: 'the closer a work's proximity to its referents, the greater will be its effectiveness as discourse, as persuasive argument'.[17] Conversely, the more distanced a work's proximity from its referents, the less will be its effectiveness as discourse, as persuasive argument, indeed even as entertainment.

The unintentional parodic stage of the genre is a very useful exercise in defining the determinants of making successful New History Drama-Documentary. First, the subject matter of *Heroes and Villains* is perhaps too epic in scale to be attempted by a documentary department, even one with an uplifted budget of over £1 million/hr. The episode *Spartacus* seeks to reconstruct ancient Roman city exteriors, riots, and battle sequences in the same way that the Kirk Douglas film had done years before. This is the wrong perspective from which to successfully reconstruct the past. We have identified, in earlier chapters, that microcosms need to be identified to work well with a televisual budget. *Trafalgar Battle Surgeon* or *Trial of the King Killers* (Channel 4, 2005) are better-sized approaches, having identified a more closed section of a microcosm amid a cataclysm.

The second determinant of making successful New History Drama-Documentary is to identify the historical primary source from which one is deriving one's film. This is often closely allied to the choice of a microcosm. A single trial record or a personal diary in the cases of *King Killers* and *Battle Surgeon* sets the scene for a slice of history to be reconstructed, rather than an entire swathe. *Heroes and Villains* too often covers entire rebellions that spread over vast territory and considerable periods of time. This means that a televisual hour is broken down into representing a few years every ten minutes, and the historical source becomes derived from an approach that is based upon generic 'coffee-table book' secondary sources. *Spartacus* does not identify which source or which historian is the basis for the dramatisation. The film simply employs a caption at the front indicating that 'it is based on the writings of contemporary historians'. Ultimately, the sense of having witnessed the past is diminished without proximity in the form of a proper identification of the source from which the film is derived.

A third determinant of making successful New History Drama-Documentary is to identify where creative solutions might enhance the aesthetic rather than allowing budgetary constraints to limit it. *Spartacus* attempts to reconstruct the past by utilising CGI to multiply the numbers of warriors on screen and to enhance the available architecture to a point where it feels appropriate to its time. This is a very tall order for most studio movies, let alone producers working on a televisual budget. The better solutions that have emerged from the evolving genre are the result of imaginative choices by production teams. *Battle Surgeon* was advised by its historical advisor, Professor Brockliss, to chart the amputation of a limb in real time. It is consistent with the surgeon's log to know that the surgeon performed eleven amputations during battle and saved nine of the patients. The operation, as has been outlined in Chapter 5, was timed at two and a half minutes, after which the patient would die from loss of blood. Hence, the team filmed this scene, uninterrupted, in real time.

Another example of a creative solution is to be found in a night scene in *1066: Battle for Middle Earth* (Channel 4, 2008). A night shoot would ordinarily have required an expensive set of arc lamps to light up an entire woodland. Doug Hartington, the Director of Photography, decided to employ night-scope technology, which enables a lens to see into the dark using a device pioneered by the military. The effect is to make the screen become green, and eyeballs flash with light. Adopting this for Harold's night attack on William of Normandy's camp, the night before the Battle of Hastings, evokes what Stella Bruzzi calls the 'jouissance' of audience recognition of an SAS raid in a contemporary theatre of war.

These aesthetic choices represent considerable risks by the production teams, and are dependent upon the support of a fourth determinant of making successful New History Drama-Documentary: sympathetic patronage. Janice Hadlow, Martin Davidson, Hamish Mykura, and Ralph Lee are examples of patrons who inherently understood that in New History Drama-Documentary, the drama mode is a big-budget item compressed into a lower-budget framework. This requires considerable experimentation, some of which works, and some of which does not. The critics were very quick to identify those risks that did not deliver a plausible result, hence the term 'risible' attached to some drama documentaries. Poor performances, unconvincing CGI, and other inadequate drama techniques are very easily exposed in the cold light of a television transmission. But the patrons named above continued to allow experimentation in their pursuit of a greater sensuousness in the reconstruction of the past. *Heroes and Villains*, by contrast, was a series that was guided by unsympathetic patrons from the Discovery Channel. According to Nick Murphy, the drive for more cinematic scope on screen caused the distributors to pay less attention to the creative decision-makers at the BBC. Martin Davidson was one of those commissioners caught in the middle between creatives and distributors. He recalls that 'we simply were trying to tell the wrong stories in the wrong way and for the wrong clients' (Davidson, 2019).

The fifth and final determinant of making successful New History Drama-Documentary in the first decade of the twenty-first century can be grouped under the heading of production professionalism. Broadly speaking, this refers to good decisions being made by filmmaking teams at any given juncture. The production teams surrounding Watkins, Schama, Starkey, Juniper TV, Wall to Wall TV, Lion TV, and others, including BBC in-house, across this ten-year period often made strong and successful professional decisions to take an audience on a journey into the past. There were many errors of judgement along the way, and some, as in the case of *Heroes and Villains*, were expensive and very damaging to the genre. But overall, the past *was* indeed reconstructed in a way that both entertained and informed at the same time. The ideal drama documentary has been identified as well sourced, microcosmic, aesthetically challenging, and sympathetically transmitted to the viewer. It might be impressionistic, with no dialogue, or it might be fully dramatised, but the ultimate accolade must be reserved for those that, for many viewers, evoke what Rosenstone calls 'the traces of the past'.[18]

Horrible Histories (CBBC, 2009–2014)

Brief summary: *A group of British comedians show the sides of history they do not teach you in school. From the 'Savage Stone Age' to the 'Troublesome 20th Century', history is revealed in musical comedy.*

It is worth mentioning that another example of historical filmmaking emerged at this time that would lend support to the argument that the genre had reached the parodic stage, and which might be worthy of further discussion beyond the scope of this book. The dramatised history documentary series *Horrible Histories* is better known for being a children's historical and musical sketch comedy television series, but it also brings together the key components of our genre: history, documentary fact, and drama (represented by comedy and music). It also links to this book because it was produced by Lion TV, and executive produced by none other than Richard Bradley.

The franchise's style was to take an irreverent but broadly accurate view on scatological and often gruesome aspects of British and other Western world history, spanning from the Stone Age to the late twentieth century. This irreverent view would be best described as parodic, not because it was, like *Heroes and Villains*, so poorly achieved that it was 'risible'; it was intentionally risible, and therefore reminds us once again of Schatz's notion that 'as a genre's classic conventions are refined and eventually parodied and subverted, its transparency gradually gives way to opacity'.[19] Many, especially children, would disagree that *Horrible Histories* made history opaque. On the contrary, it made it transparent, revealing history for what it really is in modern representation – a series of blood-thirsty characters who fit the celebrity culture of the second decade of the millennium.

Laurence Brockliss takes up this theme: 'It is possible, and certainly worthy of consideration, that *Horrible Histories* was responsible for the decline of taking history seriously on television' (Brockliss, 2019). Once history is subverted by the parody of effective comedy, he maintains, it is hard to look at historical characters in costume without the porous effect of irreverence. Once seen as a rock star, is difficult to return Henry VIII in the viewer's mind to the complex and academically sourced figure of David Starkey's tale of intrigue and power. In further support of this point, Brockliss wonders if the earlier parodies of Monty Python may have helped to render less popular the Early History Drama Documentaries of *Culloden* and *The War Game*. *Monty Python and The Holy Grail* (1975), a satirical spoof on the Arthurian legend, was a considerable cinema hit in 1975, ten years after Watkins had left Britain. The time lag of ten years is a long one, however, and it is more likely that the BBC team responsible for *Culloden* and *The War Game* did not repeat the drama documentary process for the reasons offered in Chapter 3 – notably BBC drama returning to its silos, and Equity refusing amateur actors permission to work on screen. But the timing of *Horrible Histories*, which transmitted from 2009, does coincide intriguingly with the decline of the New History Drama-Documentary genre. Further research into Richard Bradley's suggestion of a connection would be welcome.

Deconstruction of the genre

In the last two years of the genre, 2008–2010, even the titles of the films made might suggest that the genre had begun to run out of steam and was headed towards the last of this work's generic stages: deconstruction. This is interpreted as meaning the breaking up of a genre into either another genre or a series of smaller parts that no longer constitute an entity worthy of note. It is proposed that New History Drama-Documentary deconstructed in both of these ways. Meanwhile, as discussed previously, the volume of programmes had dropped from their height in 2005, with ninety-eight programmes, to fourteen in 2008 and less than ten in 2010, albeit with a rise in 2009.

Further evidence of decline can be found in the kinds of stories being told and how much was being invested in them. *Heroes and Villains* was the last of the joint venture deals between Discovery and the BBC, with very few productions at this scale following in its footsteps. National Geographic TV had entered the fray but with smaller budgets for unoriginal shows such as *Stonehenge Decoded* and *Unsinkable Titanic* (Nat Geo, 2008). Smaller but experimental indie fare still existed: *The Execution of Gary Glitter* (Channel 4, 2009) and *The Taking of Prince Harry* (Channel 4, 2010), which was a parodic mimicry of *The War Game, Smallpox 2002*, and other 'what if' films. *Bloody Foreigners* (Channel 4, 2009) was a commission that would previously have been in full drama documtenary mode, but instead returned to non-speaking impressionistic drama reconstruction, mixed with interviews and CGI. In many regards, the deconstruction of the genre took the form of a return to its less ambitious origins.

Arguably, the genre's decline was partly due to the financial crisis of 2008. It was not solely responsible for the contraction of funds in drama documentary, but it was certainly a contributing factor. The impact of this macro event on the industry is best examined through the prism of the institutional guide for much of this book: Alex Graham, CEO of the influential indie Wall to Wall TV. Graham's story of the sale of his company in late 2007–early 2008 completes this book's study of the indie companies that made so much dramatised documentary possible. As Graham admits, after the 'consolidation', as he describes it, much of the company's creativity was lost, replaced by the drive to make money, hit targets, earn out and milk franchises.

Graham recounts how 'consolidation happened quickly, since we had assets that were making money: *Who Do you Think You Are* and *The House* series were rolling on nicely, we were still doing bijou dramatisations such as *Filth, The Mary Whitehouse Story* (BBC, 2008) and along came Shed.' The buyer, Shed Productions, was run by Brian Park and Eileen Gallagher, who learned their business and creative crafts on *Coronation Street* (ITV, 1960–) and set up a business model in prime-time drama. 'Wall to Wall was relatively slow to sell, partly because the hit shows came from 2003/4 onwards, and even then we didn't have enough value till 2007', Graham adds. Buyers had mooted a purchase through the 2000s – even Channel 4 had suggested it under Michael Jackson – but Graham was conflicted about selling the business. 'I didn't want the money, I wanted to keep making interesting programmes', he insists. But by 2006, he recalls, 'I thought we can't afford to stay outside the consolidation process, we'll get squeezed and crushed. I was in my early to mid 50s, I had a body of work I was fucking proud of, how much longer could I go on?'

Graham also reflects on whether his creativity had run out: 'Did the money really damage creativity? I'm not sure I really agree. The real problem was the risk aversion of the broadcasters. They, like indies, have a bell curve.' Graham's theory, which might, mischievously, be titled the 'Alexander Graham Bell Curve', is that if competition is too slack, the risk of creativity is low, but when it is intense, the risk of creativity increases, and when the competition becomes too intense, the willingness to risk falls again. Graham sees pre-1998 as a period of slack competition and low risk-taking, and post-2007–2008 as a time when competition was too intense (with digital channels coming on stream). But in between, he sees 1998–2008 as a sweet spot, a period of controlled competition between Channel 4 and BBC, two organisations that competed for audiences, but not for revenue, or at least not the same sources of revenue.

This unique ten-year period enabled the freedom to take creative risks, and it was this freedom that, arguably, created the genre under consideration. Channel 4 under Hadlow and Mykura took risks to compete with the BBC, with its greater resources and automatically larger audience share. By taking money across the board from traditional history and other specialised documentaries, they funded more sensuous, exciting, visceral approaches to history, with costumes, locations, actors, and scripts, and the audience responded – viewing figures went up. The critics argued about whether the dramatisation was good or not, but the genre was given the oxygen of discussion. The BBC responded to this onslaught by its more nimble, innovative competitor by poaching Hadlow, forging BBC Four, and ultimately outbidding Channel 4 for top level drama documentaries such as *Man on Wire* in 2008.

But Graham had seen that 2008 was a turning point, and he recalls clearly how risk averse the BBC had been, initially, with *Man on Wire*; he had to be strong-armed into the partnership, as discussed in Chapter 6. Graham notes that the BBC's risk aversion grew steadily worse after 2008. With the growth of cable and the pressure on audience share, the BBC lost its boldness, which Graham bemoans as an unnecessary response. 'The BBC should be in every genre', he argues, 'and it should be setting the gold standard as an innovative powerhouse'. He believes firmly that if the BBC is to survive with its licence fee justified, this is the narrative that should be put forward: 'innovate in drama, in documentaries and in dramatised documentaries in particular, which is perfect Reithian material'. Documentaries and drama should not return, as they have done, to being separate silos; they should continue to interlock in places, and to find progression through interdisciplinarity, as academia is learning to do. Graham adds that, 'sadly, Channel 4 has also lost its cross-pollinating hybridity. Ralph Lee at Channel 4 commissioned less and less dramatisation in history', as can be seen in his final New History Drama-Documentary commissions of 2009–2010, *Bloody Foreigners* (*Great Fire*, *Trafalgar*, and *Battle of Britain*).

Graham sold Wall to Wall to Shed in 2008, and Graham considers himself lucky that the deal was concluded four months before Lehman Brothers collapsed.[20] The 2008 crash brought an end to much of the consolidation of the indies, but with good timing, the deconstruction of Wall to Wall's drama documentary output coincided, for Alex Graham, with the making of considerable profit.

In the last years of New History Drama-Documentaries, between 2008 and 2010, it is possible to identify another form of deconstruction taking place. In this period, several examples of the genre are absorbed into what are essentially period drama series, based loosely on fact: *Garrows' Law* (BBC, 2009), for instance, and *Casualty 1909* (BBC, 2009). By 2010, however, this strand of the genre disappears. Over the next decade, some films appear that might superficially appear to be New History Drama-Documentaries. *37 Days* (BBC, 2014), for instance, tells the story of how the world in 1914 fell into world war in just over a month; *The Eichmann Show* (BBC, 2016) is a film about the televising of the Eichmann trial in Israel. Both are impeccably researched, and the dramatic shape bows to the will of the documented evidence. But neither has a documentary narrator or captions confirming research throughout, and so they do not possess all the core generic identifiers. Hence, it is argued that by this time, the genre had been absorbed into drama – dramas based on true stories and commissioned by drama departments.

It was *Wolf Hall* (BBC, 2015), *The Crown* (Netflix, 2016–), and *Chernobyl* (HBO, Sky 2019) that were to be the inheritors of the New History Drama-Documentary genre, with their welding of developed research culture to the prime-time drama mode. These films are also based on primary sources, which provides for great drama. As Martin Davidson (who retired from BBC History in 2017) puts it: 'History rescues drama, and then drama rescues history.' Davidson had seen it all first hand at the BBC, when his wife,

Janice Hadlow, originated *A History of Britain* in the late 1990s and then, in 2015, fought an uphill battle to get *Wolf Hall* commissioned for BBC Two. 'She saw the authenticity of history in Hilary Mantel's book', says Davidson, 'and so too did the audience through the authenticity of Mark Rylance's performance, and the sincere direction of former documentarian, Peter Kosminsky'. But in general, there was not a boom in these period dramas, since commercial success requires returning series, and history, as Davidson recalls from *Heroes and Villains*, does not naturally offer such a return.

However, history does provide for tent-pole event television drama. In this light, Davidson points to one of the most successful drama series of recent times, the multiple award-winning *Chernobyl* (HBO/Sky, 2019), as confirmation that drama based on true stories, as a form, has its roots in the New History Drama-Documentary period of 2000–2010. He claims, controversially, that director Johan Renck and his writer, Craig Mazin, do not entirely deserve the credit for their admittedly brilliant rendition of the true story, and that narrative choices made in two particular BBC New History Drama-Documentaries that were *directly copied* for *Chernobyl*. These films will be discussed in detail as part of the analysis of *Chernobyl* that follows here; they offer considerable and previously undiscovered evidence that New History Drama-Documentary deconstructed almost frame for frame into the top-rated drama of recent years.

Finally, this book has come to the key questions: does the link to dramas like *Chernobyl* underline the relevance of New History Drama-Documentary to the modern day? What connection is there with recent, global period-drama successes, and why should we care about an obscure genre that is at least ten years old? The answer is that, arguably, *Chernobyl* would *not have been made* without its drama documentary forebears. And *Chernobyl* matters, not least because it has been lauded by many as the best depiction of the past on television: IMDb gives it the highest rating in television history, ranging from 9.5 for the first episode to 9.9 for the final one.

Chernobyl (HBO/Sky, 2019): heir of the genre

> Brief summary: *A historical miniseries that revolves around the Chernobyl disaster of 1986 and the clean-up efforts that followed. It played in five parts to resounding critical praise.*

Although many viewers might not necessarily have chosen to watch five episodes of an appalling nuclear disaster in 1980s Ukraine, the word-of-mouth quickly indicated that they were required to 'bear witness' to the event, such was the power of the series. Who can forget the compelling documentary-drama tropes of the series? (In this case, it is a responsible drama that feels utterly factual). The casting of Jared Harris, Stellan Skarsgård, and Emily Watson as convincing players in a Soviet-era tragedy was a master stroke, providing the series with actors of the highest quality but not 'stars' who might undermine the subject matter with their fame. The decision by Craig Mazin (writer), Johan Renck (director), and the British production company, Sister Pictures, along with Sky and HBO, to present an English-speaking cast in an authentic Soviet setting mixes the idioms very effectively. Derek Paget and the producer of *Hostages* (ITV, 1990), Sita Williams, would appreciate the difficult decisions involved in dramatising a well-known, recent historical subject. *Chernobyl* is full of such dramatic decisions, such as the choice to follow the aftermath of the explosion at reactor number 4 through the microcosmic characters of Legasov, the official investigator (Jared Harris), supported by the composite character of Ulana Khomyuk (Emily Watson).[21] The production design, achieved on a shoot in Vilnius, Lithuania, is detailed, nicotine-stained, and leaves Robert Rosenstone's 'traces of the past' smeared all over the screen. The series is filled with iconic moments, such as the hanging of Legasov in the first five minutes, exactly two hours and one minute after the explosion (as the captions confirm, drawing directly from New History Drama-Documentary); or the explosion seen over the shoulder of a fireman's wife as she passes a window in her high-rise apartment, cleverly suggesting that events randomly happen to people, and are being captured fortuitously by an observational, documentary-mode camera. A traditional drama would have seen the explosion through the eyes of a protagonist, a classic drama conceit; not *Chernobyl*.

The first act is followed by equally memorable moments of documentary-style observation filmed in drama-style contrivance. Documentary-mode research and technique is evident in the use of translations of actual phone recordings from those first few minutes – 'What's that burning?' 'Hello, 353, the roof of Chernobyl reactor 4 is on fire' – accompanied by imagery of actual radio transmissions, as if from a documentary. Yet the pregnant wife of the firefighter must watch her husband walk towards the fire – a drama-mode conceit if ever there was one. Sense and sensuousness, through documentary and drama modes, are therefore walking *side by side* throughout the evolving narrative. The critical mismanagement of the first week, in which the surrounding citizens are needlessly exposed to radiation, does not have the sense of a Rosenstone 'closed' drama structure, but an 'open' documentary one. The narrative, like real life, is messy. The shooting of the dogs that roam an abandoned area for miles around takes almost a whole episode, a diversion worthy of the unconstructed nature of history. The narrative could be following the template of Hayden White's *Annals of St Gall*, or the open structure of *Wisconsin Death Trip* (BBC, 1999), a documentary heavy on primary sources.

There follows the somewhat random depiction of the miners who accept a short lifetime of agony in order to dig a tunnel under the reactor and prevent more damage to the area and, ultimately, the whole of the Eurasian landmass. Throughout the series, some key characters carry the emotional weight of melodrama – as opposed to the very real meta-drama of the population – and yet the culture of this film is not to create melodrama as other (Hollywood) dramatists might. The culture of the Anglo/American production, shot in Lithuania, and concerning a Ukrainian tragedy, is instead one of documentary and drama modes existing in respectful balance. By the final episode, the science is explained – and the revelation is made – that the Soviet nuclear industry made a series of shortcuts that caused the reactor's boron rods to be tipped in graphite to save money, and that this caused the fatal surge in power. This explanation is made by the key characters in a relay, a device that speaks of drama, but the series has surely earned the right to make comprehensible something that in a documentary would risk being too technical. Finally, the deconstruction of New History Drama-Documentary into popular drama is confirmed by the presence of captions that run at the end of the fifth episode, for minute after minute (over five minutes – so many captions that could have spread throughout the series), the documentary mode uncompromisingly evident.

It is suggested by Richard Bradley of Lion TV that one of the legacies of the era of New History Drama-Documentaries is that 'dramas like *Chernobyl* would not have been made with such attention to authenticity, *without* drama-docs. Particular attention to the detail of *The Great Plague*'s Cock and Key alley shows drama writers that the devil truly lies in the detail, not in imagined scenarios.' Bradley also confirms that 'on certain subjects, audiences crave information as well as entertainment, documentary authenticity as well as the packaging of expensively reconstructed drama'. This present writer would agree that *Chernobyl* is an exemplar of sense and sensuousness existing in consistent and brutal harmony; it is as if *The War Game* had come out of its slumber and brought the horrors of nuclear war to the screen all over again. It is striking, though, that HBO's version of this narrative has been discussed online by many more viewers than a New History Drama-Documentary would have been, at least judging by the 550,000 viewers who gave the film its IMDb rating.

Underlining the direct connection between New History Drama-Documentaries and *Chernobyl*, *not one but two* such documentaries have been made on the subject of the Chernobyl nuclear meltdown, in 2004 and

2006. This book is the first to analyse them in detail and describe their similarities with *Chernobyl*.

The 2004 series, *Seconds from Disaster: Meltdown in Chernobyl*, was produced for National Geographic by British indie Darlow Smithson. It was one of many films that counted down the minutes and seconds until the moment of disaster, rather as *Culloden* had counted up the minutes through the horror of battle. The same key characters seen in the HBO drama are in the control room – Akimov, Toptunov (so young, at only twenty-six), and Dyatlov (it is important to hear his background, the son of a Siberian fisherman, who left home at fourteen and became the deputy chief nuclear scientist in the most prestigious power plant in the Soviet Union). Suddenly, the comparison between this £200k/hour drama documentary and the lauded drama makes a shift. This drama documentary provides more documentary 'sense', represented by the addition of critical information to enhance the narrative, and makes one reflect on how little sense the HBO drama actually provides until the five-minute intertitles. Early in its forty-five-minute length, for instance, the 2004 film explains the background to the two critical faults in the test: the science regarding the boron rods and the personal factors behind Dyatlov's decision to operate the test, against the rules, below 700/1000 mega-watts. (Dyatlov wants promotion to get him away from the shop floor, where he has been upbraided by the party for insulting his workers. When he was younger, he was present at a nuclear failure on a submarine. He received massive amounts of radiation, and his son died of leukaemia. There is plenty of dramatic information in that documentary research.)

The viewer is also led to understand why the test is necessary: a Russian-made reactor was blown up by an Israeli airstrike in Iraq in the early 1980s, aggravating the fear of attack on the mother country's nuclear prizes. Reactor 4 had been built quickly, ignoring advice, to trigger bonus payments for a number of the characters in the narrative. The roof was supposed to be made of fireproof materials, but cost-cutting prevented it. The film provides crucially informative CGI animation of the hard-to-understand and invisible core – and its unseen increased heat that underpinned so many of the mistakes subsequently made in a dramatically unexciting control room. The director, Maninderpal Sahota, had found recently declassified KGB footage of the core, imagining how the film crew had fared under such intense radiation. Some of the footage had flashes on it, which is chilling evidence of radiation revealed on the silver nitrate of film. The dramatisation is underfunded, in a typical drama documentary way, but always arises from research: the control room characters are exactly replicated, with their moustaches, beards, glasses, and cigarettes squashed at the filters, and they are all Russian speakers, subtitled in English. One of the control worker's wives is in her apartment when the explosion occurs, and it is seen over her shoulder (the same narrative device replicated by HBO), and suddenly the viewer is aware, perhaps for the first time, that the HBO version is standing on the shoulders of previous drama documentary incarnations.

Specifically, the drama also uses the documentary footage of the real phone calls: 'what's that burning? Hello, 353, the roof of Chernobyl reactor 4 is on fire'. The 2004 version ends where the drama begins, concluding with an extraordinary and previously unknown interview with Dyatlov, ten years after the incident (and shortly before he died of radiation poisoning), in which he blames the atomic authorities, who had lied so frequently to their own staff: 'The reactor marched straight to its doom', Dyatlov says, his now skeletal head bowed.

The 2004 drama documentary takes a different approach to the drama, as one would expect from the title: *Seconds from Disaster*. It has concentrated on the lead up to the disaster, not the aftermath, and while the drama has used some of the research and documentary techniques, it would be more surprising if it had not. But then the present writer came across another New History Drama-Documentary on the same subject, one that even better supports the argument that the genre deconstructed into drama. It is again part of a 'disaster' series, entitled *Surviving Disaster: Chernobyl Nuclear Disaster* (BBC, Discovery, Pro Sieben, France 5, 2006), filmed in Vilnius, Lithuania, like the 2019 HBO drama. It features a strong cast, led by Adrian Edmondson as Legasov (the Jared Harris role), who also narrates much of the story of his investigation, some of it in a confessional monologue to camera, mimicking the documentary interview mode. From the first moment, the parallels with the HBO version are startling: Legasov is found hanged in his apartment, exactly the same beat as the drama utilises. Captions confirm: 'In April 1988, the man who led the Chernobyl investigation was found hanged at this home in Moscow. It was two years to the day since the explosion'. Again, the same beat is employed, except that the drama states: 'two years *and one minute* since the explosion'.

The drama documentary cuts not to the wife's apartment, as the drama does, but to the control room, the third scene of the drama, where the same decision has been made to place English voices within Russian visuals. The 'sense' is almost exactly the same in both films, except that Edmondson, within six minutes, increases the viewer's understanding of the situation by explaining in mock interview that there had been accidents before in the Soviet nuclear industry – fourteen accidents, to be precise, and there was always fear of a 'big one'. The story of the explosion is tightly told but, arguably, with just as much dramatic tension as the subsequent and much more expensive drama provides: those same characters with the period identifiers of thick spectacles, moustaches, and filtered cigarettes. The informative mode is also enhanced when Edmondson's Legasov explains what nuclear radiation does – flashing forwards to the control room characters in agony, skin going black, widows in grief, accelerating the delivery of the 'sense' – a decision required by the limitations of a single BBC hour as opposed to HBO's five hours.

The film shows the control room workers coming back from the core, their skin already detaching. Legasov explains that nuclear radiation 'affects your DNA, robbing you not just of your life but of the thing that makes you what you are'. This is curiously poetic writing, and skipping through to the end, it is revealed that the writer is also the director, a certain Nick Murphy. He had made this BBC New History Drama-Documentary just after *Nero* and just before *Napoleon*, where he was also writer/director. In his script, he intuits that Legasov wonders 'how the mind can only tolerate so much horror before it closes down and refuses to acknowledge the facts before it'. In an interview with the present writer, Murphy explains that his occasional poetic flourish emanates directly from research and from primary sources, in particular, the memories of the witnesses. 'The translations of the testimonies were like reading Pushkin', comments Murphy; 'they said things like "the devil would have cried that day".' His biggest problem was finding a clear structure that could be represented in a single phrase. The one he chose would be copied thereafter by HBO as the through-line for the whole series: 'The blind love for the Russian state is what caused the problem, and also what solved the problem', Murphy recalls.

The budget restrictions of the dramatised documentary are in evidence in parts of the one-hour programme, made for what Murphy remembers was £240k. Looking down into the core involves CGI smoke that is not as dynamic as that afforded by the HBO drama. But in other respects, the narrative is well structured, the beats given a low-tech immediacy. In the drama, the physical effects of radiation in the power plant show as pools of blood spreading across white scientific coats. In the drama documentary, the bloodstains are in evidence, with an additional detail of tongue-swelling, which then makes the characters struggle to speak. The two control room operatives sent down to open the water valves, thus hoping to cool the core, are shown with blood spreading on their coats, and they are shown attempting to articulate with swollen tongues. One says, 'I am never going to see my wife.'

The drama documentary shows the Prypiat townspeople spending a nice warm Saturday outside, with no warning that they are absorbing four hundred times the accepted radiation for humans. A man sunbathes on a roof – and when the film cuts back to him, as he tries to get up unsteadily. The narrative is again clear and simply told. The evacuation of Prypiat is copied by the drama directly from the drama documentary, and the iconic shot of a single dog running to catch up the departing buses is *directly repeated*. As Murphy admits, he 'watched the drama with more than a raised eyebrow'. The dog scene emanated from his own imagination – a rare departure from sources – and so he was particularly surprised to see it being lifted wholesale for the drama, as if he had created a fresh source.

In most respects, he ordered the primary sources into a shape that had not really existed before, not even in the 2004 version. He charts the theme of self-sacrifice as the solution to over-reliance on the state. It is when Legasov has to find a solution to the floor melting and threatening a thermo-nuclear explosion that would level two hundred square kilometres that self-sacrifice kicks in in the drama documentary, and once again the narrative is *copied by the drama*. Hence the story of the divers being told by their military superior that it is a suicide mission. From inside the cab of a truck, Legasov watches as each man steps forward, and he voices his new-found respect for his nation: 'I don't believe there are even a handful of nations that can produce such unquestioning self-sacrifice.'

The story of the control room is more tightly woven in the drama documentary, as it runs in parallel to the drama: cue the guilty speech by Akimov (the man who pushed the critical button) to his wife, listening beyond the plastic sheets surrounding his hospital bed: 'I got out of bed yesterday and the skin on my leg slipped down like a loose sock', he whispers. At this point, the drama documentary calls to mind *The War Game* (1965), with its depictions of the aftermath of a nuclear explosion: the peeling skin, the bleeding from the inside, the information that a society must keep in mind when it harbours this destructive force in its midst.

Later in the 2006 film, having covered the key narrative and contextual events (except the role of the miners, and there is no composite character as played in the later film by Watson), Legasov is required to bury his report, and lay the blame squarely on the control-room errors, causing him to reflect that lessons will never be learned; there will continue to be nuclear accidents. Yet the drama documentary provides one more trick that the drama misses: it says that Russia is not alone in suppressing the truth. Windscale in Britain, Three Mile Island in the United States, Fukushima in Japan – all the nations involved only made partial admissions. Hence, the story comes full circle – Legasov is not heard and kills himself. Yet as the drama documentary ends, actor Bernard Hill takes up the narration and confirms that Legasov did not die in vain; his suicide made waves, changes in the Soviet Union were hurriedly begun and, indeed, may even have led to Perestroika.[22]

This is not an exercise in deciding which version tells the story better. But in this very microcosm, it is hard to ignore the narrative structure of a drama that was first used thirteen years earlier in a largely ignored New History

Drama-Documentary. Lee Darwell, a blogger writing in 2019, expresses a feeling of injustice:

> This is a brilliant one hour, hard hitting account of Chernobyl. The recent HBO version of this story seems to have used this as a blueprint ... HBO should be honest and admit that that took this and basically copied it. But this is better. One hour to tell one of the most important stories of the late twentieth century. Full marks to the BBC!

Similarly, a commentator using the handle 'Top Binz' wrote in 2019, 'HBO basically took this and turned it into a brilliant 6-part thriller'.

What matters is not that a true story was repackaged, even closely. What does matter, for the purposes of this book, is that the New History Drama-Documentaries *still have a legacy* that is felt to the present day. The genre, which originated in the 1960s and reached full flower in the first decade of the twenty-first century, was not universally loved by audiences or reviewers, but there are many examples (more than can be discussed in detail here) of films that were strong melders of information and education, of sense and sensuousness – films that were aesthetically innovative and often gave excellent representations of history.

Awaiting the genre's return

History on British television is still extant at the time of writing, in 2024, in a variety of guises. Presenter-led series are quite rightly concentrating on correcting the gender and racial imbalance of Britain's self-reflection. In 2014, David Olusoga's film about the *Forgotten Soldiers of Empire* (BBC) was aired as part of the commemorations for World War I to wide critical praise, and in 2016, Olusoga's *Britain's Slave Owners* (BBC) revealed the existence of forty-six thousand British enslavers, including the ancestors of Benedict Cumberbatch and David Cameron. This made front-page news, won a BAFTA, and changed the direction of the recounting of history, whether presenter led, Living History or dramatically reconstructed.

One of the only recent BBC films to include dramatisation and that fits our genre has been *Suffragettes* (BBC, 2020), the BAFTA-winning Lucy Worsley vehicle, featuring some impressionistic drama vignettes with some excellent performances. It was executive produced by *Trafalgar Battle Surgeon*'s Sue Horth. One or two independents still produce history programmes with the uplift that drama provides: Oxford TV and Elephant House for Channel 5, which has now occupied the market with a return to 'Henry, Hitler and Hieroglyphics'. And it was little surprise to commissioners and historians alike to see the transmission of another variant of New History Drama-Documentary in the well-photographed *The Rise of the Nazis* (BBC, 2019). The History Channel has filled the PSB void with some very high-end drama documentaries like *Washington* (2020), starring British actor Nicholas Rowe, who ages from twenty to sixty in this lavish biopic. It was directed with true visual verve by Roel Reine, who made his mark in the docudrama *Black Sails* (STARZ, 2014). The sense of the show was delivered by Pulitzer prize-winners and, most innovatively, interviews with Colin Powell and Bill Clinton. The History Channel has continued this approach with the most recent *Colosseum* (History/BBC 2023), a blood-and-sand extravaganza. Meanwhile, London producer Raw TV produces non-speaking drama documentaries for the US market, mostly for the channel CNN, most recently *Race for the White House* (CNN, 2019/20) and *The Windsors: Behind the Royal Dynasty* (CNN/Channel 4, 2020). Hence, there are continued variations of the genre in existence as I write. But I must say that the genre is not as vibrant as it was during the first decade of the millennium.

As a genre cycle, the New History Drama-Documentary at its height enjoyed a particularly long life. As BBC scheduler Don Cameron attests, 'Three or four years is the average length of time for most television genre cycles. Ten years is a rare feat' (Cameron, 2020). The decade 2000 to 2010 saw not just a history boom but a dramatised history boom, and at its peak it was innovative, informative, and entertaining, not just to the British audience but global viewers. If there is a renewed interest in TV history, either nationally or internationally, this book will be available to help guide a new generation of historian-filmmakers to embrace the challenges of mixing drama and documentary successfully in one mode. The knowledge outlined here, it is hoped, will help that future generation avoid some of the pitfalls of the genre.

Notes

1 Steven Schatz (1981), cited by Steve Neale, *Genre and Hollywood* (London: Routledge, 2000), p. 195.
2 Bradley (2020) referred to performances in *The Great Wall* and *The First Emperor* being described as 'risible'.
3 Lindsey Davis, 'All Tantrums and Togas', *The Times* (16 September 2006).
4 Schatz (1981), cited by Neale, *Genre and Hollywood*, p. 195.
5 Davis, 'All Tantrums and Togas'.
6 Nancy Banks-Smith, 'Last Night's TV', *Guardian* (22 September 2006).
7 Sam Wollaston, 'Last Night's TV', *Guardian* (6 October 2006).
8 Davis, 'All Tantrums and Togas'.

9 Steve Rose, 'Monsters: The Bedroom Blockbuster That's the Anti-Avatar', *Guardian* (27 November 2010).
10 *Carry On* films – thirty-one comedies (often based on historical subjects) made between 1958 and 1992.
11 *Spartacus* (1960).
12 Schatz (1981), cited by Neale, *Genre and Hollywood*, p. 195.
13 Derek Paget, *No Other Way to Tell It: Dramadoc/Docu-drama on Television* (Manchester: Manchester University Press, 1998), p. 2.
14 Bill Nichols cited in Steven Lipkin, *Real Emotional Logic: Film and Television Docudrama as Persuasive Practice* (Carbondale, IL: Southern Illinois University Press, 2002), p. 32.
15 Lipkin, *Real Emotional Logic*, p. 41.
16 Robert Rosenstone, *Revisioning History: Film and the Construction of a New Past* (Princeton, NJ: Princeton University Press, 1995), p. 240.
17 Lipkin, *Real Emotional Logic*, p. 54.
18 Robert Rosenstone, *History on Film/Film on History*, 2nd ed. (Abingdon: Routledge, 2006), p. 79.
19 Schatz (1981), cited by Neale, *Genre and Hollywood*, p. 195.
20 The collapse of Lehman Brothers in September 2008 is regarded as a low point of the financial crisis.
21 'She's not a real person. She's a tribute to the scientists in her situation.' Emily Watson, cited in Christina Radish, 'Emily Watson on Why HBO's "Chernobyl" Is a Cautionary Tale for Our Times', *Collider* (21 May 2019).
22 A political movement for reformation of the Communist Party in the 1980s.

Conclusion

This conclusion will summarise the findings from each chapter followed by indications of further research to be considered. First, the chapter findings should establish where themes have emerged that help to answer the research questions posed regarding the emergence at the turn of the millennium of a new genre for television, newly entitled New History Drama-Documentary.

To recap, the approach to this book has been multi-disciplinary, combining television studies and (televisual) history. Furthermore, I have indicated, at the beginning of the work, its inter-disciplinary nature, bringing together both theoretical and practical perspectives. This approach is crystallised in the words of Derek Paget, a specialist in documentary drama theory who has interviewed many practising filmmakers:

> I try ... to bridge what is often seen as a gap between the academy and the entertainment industry; people from both worlds have been helpful to me in my attempt to combine theory and practice.[1]

Combining theory and practice remains the key to the particular approach of *A New Genre?* As a writer, director, and producer of television history dramatisations during the period of the history boom years around the turn of the millennium, I have attempted to put my practice into theory, as it were. I hope to have offered a rare insight into the industrial and aesthetic processes of television production.

Covering the period 2000–2010, I have explored the body of work of over four hundred films, most of which have been forgotten. This has required analysis of the emerging canon by selecting case studies, utilising an industrial perspective derived from my primary skillset as a producer within the television arena. The industrial context is answered through institutional insight and first-hand witness accounts. The characteristics of the dramatisations are defined partly on the basis of my experience as a writer/director who has utilised a great variety of aesthetic choices, and partly by means of applying important perspectives derived from theory. The televisual representation of history and the emergence of a genre are, surprisingly to me, heavily dependent on theory. Now I shall summarise my findings:

In Chapter 1, the process of defining the corpus of dramatised history on television begins with the identification of the first adopters of limited dramatisation within the documentary mode, where the dramatisation is impressionistic, non-speaking, and integrated into interviews and other forms of documentary filmmaking. The BBC and Channel 4 of the 2000s are identified as the two public service broadcasters who compete for the growing historical space that is encouraged by a boom in history books. BBC's *A History of Britain* (2000) and Channel 4's *Elizabeth* (2000) are regarded as pioneers for telling history on television in a new way that includes dramatisation.

Chapter 2 combines what this book terms 'sense and sensuousness', a key term designed to indicate the benefits to the viewer of drama being integrated with documentary in a balanced way. *The Great Plague* (Channel 4, 2001) and *The Great Pyramid* (BBC, 2001) are also pioneering films in that they evolved the aesthetic possibilities of taking the audience back in time without recourse to a presenter. One uses CGI to great effect, the other evokes horror – both moving the dial of what sensuousness can offer. Both focus their narratives on well-researched microcosms that proved very popular with audiences and critics alike. Theory supports the adoption of the new terminology of 'sense and sensuousness' for dramas that are based on true stories. It is argued that drama documentaries make prominent both qualities throughout the films, beyond the balder terms of education and entertainment.

In order to understand the origins of the dramatised history phenomenon, it is argued, in Chapter 3, that one should go back to the BBC's innovative films *Culloden* and *The War Game*, from the 1960s. Practitioners in this field have often remarked upon these two films as inspirations, but it is now shown how, precisely, the new genre originated in these films in ways that combine the particular qualities identified here as sense and sensuousness. *Culloden* and *The War Game*, through their use of amateur actors (drama mode) and narration (documentary mode), even helped to establish some of the rules of the genre. The chapter offers a ten-point checklist of the aesthetic qualities of the emergent genre, drawn from analysis of the films; this is offered not as a definitive statement but as a reasonable first step towards more developed definitions. The chapter embraces another production from the late 1990s that challenges our notions of how a historical narrative should operate. This film is *Wisconsin Death Trip* (BBC, 1999) and is in many ways the most honest rendition of a historical primary source from the entire canon under consideration. The film does not abide by the three-act structure normally associated with the dramatic mode. It is a rare choice, supported by the non-commercial remit of public service broadcasting, and this present writer would encourage more histories to follow at least some elements of this approach in the future. While it does not offer the satisfying closure of a melodramatic shape, it allows the primary sources to speak more directly to the present and encourages the audience to take its time to absorb the nuances of the past. 'Slow television' has been evolving since its scandi-noir drama origins, and its principles would be worth reflecting on in the documentary genre. Serious immersion into history through the prism of a slower film narrative would enable more social history to be explored, for example – a slow historical television, if you like.

Chapter 4 explores the innovation of the corpus in its early years through the prism of a single indie company, Wall to Wall TV, and its inspirational CEO, Alex Graham. As close to an auteur as one can get in the producer/production company role, it is shown that he succeeded in catalysing a number of the most striking and well-reviewed films in the new mode, and almost single-handedly boosted the emerging genre as a business. Graham and his team brought in co-production money and innovative funding structures to turn creative ideas into repeatable franchises. The films *Neanderthal* (Channel 4, 2001) and *Ancient Egyptians* (Channel 4, 2003) evolve the aesthetic, while *Smallpox 2002* (BBC, 2001) and *George Orwell: A Life in Pictures* (BBC, 2003) evolve the franchisable model. It is argued that if Graham could have made more profit out of the time-consuming and expensive hybrid approach to storytelling the truth, he would have dominated the market. But instead, he found greater profits and critical success in rival historical modes, in the series *Who Do You Think You Are* (BBC, 2004–) and *The House* (Channel 4, 2000–2004). While he continued to make replicas of some of the earlier films, he admits that the sense of innovation was over for him. The producorial powerhouse leaves a legacy for other drama documentaries to follow, a model that is often more boutique in funding structure and arguably just as innovative in creativity.

This chapter also tests the theory that this kind of historical dramatisation might have been the product of auteurs. Auteur theory is examined, both pro- and anti-auteur camps, and it is concluded that the possible genre was *not* the product of an auteur-led drive. Too many team members contribute to successful films for individuals to be solely credited. I have been consistent in not over-identifying filmmakers like Peter Watkins as the auteurs responsible for their famous films. This is a correction that will hopefully be absorbed into wider scholarship, since from the point of view of a practitioner it is a naïve practice. Still, the consideration of the role of the auteur has been useful in highlighting the characteristics of 'a culture of authenticity' that drove many of the films of this growing corpus.

Chapter 5 investigates the explosion of variants, following Neale's notion that 'genres are best understood as processes. These processes may, for sure, be dominated by repetition, but they are also marked fundamentally by difference, variation, and change.'[2] Through the prism of genre theory, the canon is taxonomised and codified: through its proximity to primary sources, its pact with the audience through captions, its narration to guide the viewer through a dramatic narrative, its hybrid budgets that inspire innovations in the aesthetic. As the history boom takes off in earnest between 2003 and 2005, these films – which include a rare acknowledgement of diversity in *Bareknuckle Boxer* (Channel 4, 2003) – extend their form in a series of alterations while maintaining the same core values. A series of lists is offered so as to clarify the extent of the genre and identify its constituent elements. The genre is then further analysed through this book's theory of the generic stages that accompany a rise and fall. The first two of these stages, experimental and classical, when a genre starts to take hold in the public imagination, are particularly relevant to this chapter. In essence, the case studies offered here, *Trial of the King Killers* (Channel 4, 2005) and *Trafalgar Battle Surgeon* (Channel 4, 2005), represent key aesthetic evolutions in the genre's creativity.

Chapter 6 charts the zenith of the genre's success in terms of volume of programmes commissioned and what Bruzzi terms the 'most notorious example to date',[3] which is *Man on Wire* (BBC, 2008). The film received international recognition and a cinema release, eventually picking up an Academy award. Combine this with the international co-productions of films offering selective histories of China, and it can be argued that the dramatised history form has reached its zenith. This chapter also argues that the canon can indeed be considered as a genre and makes a case for titling it New History Drama-Documentary. While the edges of the genre are blurred, this is a definition that can be referenced for future use.

Chapter 7 identifies the next two stages of generic decline in the years 2008–2010. It is shown that the more international the genre becomes, and the more money is committed to the successful mix of sense and sensuousness, the more parodic or 'risible' the fuller drama variant can become. It is argued that the genre shows signs of becoming unintentionally parodic both at Channel 4, in its co-productions with China, and at the BBC, with its joint venture with Discovery (US). It is further argued that *Ancient Rome* (BBC, 2006) and *Heroes and Villains* (BBC, 2008) are nadirs of the genre and are partly responsible for the decline of the genre towards its fourth stage: deconstruction into other generic forms. Deconstruction is interpreted as a decline of the form, which is evidenced within the context of the financial crisis of 2008 and the withdrawal of funds for this expensive factual genre.

Finally, the legacy of the genre is analysed through the question as to why this obscure genre matters. It is argued that the huge hit of 2019, *Chernobyl* (HBO), could not have been produced without the acquired skill sets of the New History Drama-Documentaries from a decade earlier. This is proven, in part, by the comparison and contrasting of two BBC drama documentaries from 2004 and 2006, elements of which were almost directly copied by the makers of HBO's critical success.

Further research

As a theorist, there are several future research options available to be considered. Now that the New History Drama-Documentary genre has been defined and named, the natural extension is to apply the same procedures and methods of analysis to other kinds of factual drama, especially where they relate to the representation of history. There is no real UK book alternative to Melvyn Stokes' *American History Through Hollywood* (2013), for instance, or Rosenstone's *History on Film: Film on History* (2017), and it might be productive to bring some of the ideas expressed in this book to bear upon the documentary dramas discussed by Paget and Lipkin, while also considering some drama documentaries as useful comparisons.

It would be worthwhile, too, to build upon Paget and Ebbrecht's European survey on documentary dramas to build a growing sense of European history on film and television, again drawing on the drama documentaries of the past twenty years. A further possibility, bearing in mind the work of the Swedish historian-filmmakers Hager and Villius, is to identify other historian-filmmakers around the globe, if indeed they exist.

It remains surprising that there is no other work on this specific area of dramatised documentaries and, to this extent, the book breaks new ground. It is hoped, however, that more writing will follow on the aesthetics of British history on the screen (whether represented as documented drama/drama documentary or presenter-led modes). This might also lead to useful work on the question of how best to tell the historical stories of all nations and peoples – once the financial situation becomes more favourable and a new historiography gains confidence. It is also clear that de-centring history will require the finding of primary sources that have not been written by Europeans.

Speaking personally, as a practitioner, working on this book has reawakened my interest in the question of how to attempt to be a historian-filmmaker – in how to combine the drama and documentary modes in ideal balance. The process of theorising has contributed to a sense that my life's work has now been given a legitimate place as a genre within the greater story of the making of history on film. Furthermore, this genre offers a practical structure to guide the process of balancing information with entertainment. It is now better understood how to begin an informational pact with a viewer that can be sustained throughout a film. It is also clear that too much melodrama can adversely affect the successful sensuousness that is so carefully crafted into a film trying to evoke the nuances of the past.

It is to be regretted that the television industry remains in drama and documentary silos, and there are few signs that the drama documentary mode will be revived any time soon. There is too much reliance on tentpole drama series, between Netflix and its competitors, for the drama documentary to achieve much prominence in the schedules. While one waits for drama documentary to return in the commercial battle for eyeballs, there is a clue as to where the mode might be well received. The clue lies in the word 'commercial'. New History Drama-Documentaries were *never* overtly commercial. They were successful within public service broadcasting, where informational content is prized, especially if accompanied by sincere entertainment. I believe that this cooperation might be offered through a new type of public service broadcaster, one that would include among its various partners the modern global university.

One cannot know what media distribution will look like in a few years' time, but using stories that matter, and applying dramatic techniques to make those narratives popular, will be foundational. Already, at UCL, there are new disciplines in Augmented and Virtual Reality that might well be looking for style-led content. The Bartlett School of Architecture department may have the answer when it uses a term which refers to the 'senography' of a building. It means the affect on the senses as a viewer/listener passes through a 3D space. Senography could offer a new form for the next iteration of history drama documentary. Imagine walking through a sensuous landscape surrounded by sights, sounds, and smells that evoke another time. Imagine, too, being able to absorb information about these sensations, feeding one's curiosity at will rather than being spoon fed. The landscape could be the building site of a pyramid; it could be a plague-infested alley; it could be Chernobyl's nuclear reactor number 4. Such possibilities for future history-telling could be led by the MA in Public History at UCL. It should be noted that Rosenstone points out in Lipkin's *Docudrama Performs the Past: Arenas of Argument in Films based on True Stories* (2011) that UCL hosted a conference on Film and the Historian as far back as 1968. Is it time to revive this tradition?

Meanwhile, what have I learned, as a historian-filmmaker seeking a sophisticated representation of 'the traces of the past'? The answer is surprising. It could be argued that the more full-blown drama, with contrived narratives and employing recognisable actors to mock-up imagined dialogue, is *not* the way to best immerse oneself into the foreignness of history. The brain appears designed to need what producer Sue Horth calls 'the denial of information' (Horth, 2019) to believe that it has plausible access. So, turn off the sound, enable the viewer to catch a fleeting glance of a figure through a crack in the wall, and increase the viewer's need to imagine, to decode what is just beyond grasp. This type of well-sourced yet difficult-to-achieve time travel lies in the discipline of experimental filmmaking, and where better to attempt this than at a global university?

I imagine that the new, immersive experiences of the future will be short-form (ten-minute) vignettes, less burdened by narrative structure and offering a more radical and sensuous glimpse into the past. The experience might follow the kind of senography that filmmaker Steve McQueen believed he attempted in *Hunger* (Channel 4, 2008). He wanted to have the audience feel 'the texture' of the Maze Prison at the time, 'Like walking into a room with the lights off, feeling your way inch by inch'.[4] Feeling one's way, inch by inch, in the dark is another expression of feeling one's way into the past, using imagination to navigate the denial of information. To this current writer, it is a new kind of haptic microcosm, like many of the case studies in this book.

It remains to end with the thoughts of *Wolf Hall*'s author, Hilary Mantel, on the worthy pursuit of dramatising the past:

> The past is not dead ground, and to traverse it is not a sterile exercise. History is always changing behind us, and the past changes a little every time we retell it ... the only requirement is for conjecture to be plausible and grounded in the best facts one can get.[5]

Like McQueen and Mantel, we will need to tread carefully. But we should consider drama documentary as our mode, for as Paget and Ebbrecht wrote in 2016, 'we are convinced that the docudramatic mode has been, is, and will continue to be vital to the representation, narrativisation and understanding of difficult times'.[6] Not bad for 'an impure, mongrel element in an already mongrel medium'.[7]

Notes

1 Derek Paget, *No Other Way to Tell It: Dramadoc/Docu-drama on Television* (Manchester: Manchester University Press, 1998), p. vii.
2 Steve Neale, *Genre and Hollywood* (London: Routledge, 2000), p. 165.
3 Stella Bruzzi, 'Making a Genre: The Case of the Contemporary True Crime Documentary', *Law and Humanities*, 10:2 (2016), pp. 249–280.

4 McQueen, cited by Jerome De Groot, *Consuming History: Historians and Heritage in Contemporary Popular Culture*, 2nd ed. (London: Routledge, 2016), p. 213.
5 Hilary Mantel, 'Booker Winner Hilary Mantel on Dealing with History in Fiction', *Guardian* (17 October 2009).
6 Derek Paget and Tobias Ebbrecht-Hartmann (eds), *Docudrama on European Television: A Selective Survey* (London: Palgrave Macmillan, 2016), p. 5.
7 *Ibid.*, p. 7.

Bibliography

Agnew, V. (2007) 'History's Affective Turn: Historical Reenactment and Its Work in the Present', *Rethinking History*, 11:3, pp. 299–312.
Altman, R. (1984) 'A Semantic/Syntactic Approach to Film Genre', *Cinema Journal*, 23:3, pp. 6–18.
Astruc, A. (1948) 'The Birth of a New Avant Garde: La Camèra-Stylo' in MacKenzie, S. (ed.) (2014), *Film Manifestos and Global Cinema Cultures: A Critical Anthology*. Berkeley, CA: University of California Press, pp. 603–607.
Banks Smith, N. (2006) 'Last Night's TV', *Guardian* (22 September 2006).
Barthes, R. (1967) 'The Death of the Author' in Heath, S. (trans.) (1977), *Image-Music-Text*. New York: Hill & Wang, pp. 142–148.
Beck, P. J. (2012) *Presenting History Past and Present*. London: Palgrave Macmillan.
Bignell, J. (2010) 'Docudrama Performance: Realism, Recognition and Representation' in Cornea, C. (ed.), *Genre and Performance: Film and Television*. Manchester: Manchester University Press, Chapter 3.
Bignell, J. (2011) 'Docudramatising the Real: Developments in British TV Docudrama since 1990', *Studies in Documentary Film*, 4:3, pp. 195–208.
Bignell, J. (2013). *An Introduction to Television Studies*. London: Routledge.
Bignell, J., Paget, D. J., Sutherland, H. A. and Taylor, L. (2011) 'Narrativising the Facts: Acting in Screen and Stage Docudrama', *Narrative in Drama: Contemporary Drama in English*, 18, pp. 21–52.
Billen, A. (2001) 'Refuge in the Past', *New Statesman* (22 October 2001).
Bordwell, D. (1997) *On the History of Film Style*. Cambridge, MA: Harvard University Press.
Bordwell, D. (2005) *Figures Traces in Light: On Cinematic Staging*. Berkeley, CA: University of California Press.
Bordwell, D. (2007) *Poetics of Cinema*. New York: Routledge.
Bradshaw, P. (2008) 'Man on Wire', *Guardian* (1 August 2008).
Branston, G. and Stafford, R. (2010) *The Media Student's Book*. London: Routledge.
Bruzzi, S. (2000) *New Documentary: A Critical Introduction*. London: Routledge.
Bruzzi, S. (2016) 'Making a Genre: The Case of the Contemporary True Crime Documentary', *Law and Humanities*, 10:2, pp. 249–280.

Bruzzi, S. (2020) *Approximation: Documentary, History and the Staging of Reality*. London: Routledge.
Burgoyne, R. (1997) *Film Nation: Hollywood Looks at U.S. History*. London: University of Minneapolis Press.
Burgoyne, R. (2008) *The Hollywood Historical Film*. Oxford: Blackwell.
Butler, J. (2010) *Television Style*. New York: Routledge.
Caldwell, J. T. (2008) *Production Culture: Industrial Reflexivity and Critical Practice in Film and Television*. Durham, NC: Duke University Press.
Campbell, J. (1949) *The Hero with a Thousand Faces*. New York: Pantheon Books.
Cannadine, D. (ed.) (2006) *History and the Media*. London: Palgrave Macmillan.
Carr, E. H. (1961) *What is History?* New York: Vintage.
Champion, J. (2003) 'Seeing the Past: Simon Schama's "A History of Britain" and Public History', *History Workshop Journal*, 56, pp. 153–174.
Chapman, J. (2006) 'The BBC and the Censorship of *The War Game* (1965)', *Journal of Contemporary History*, 41:1, pp. 75–94.
Chater, D. (2001) TV review, *The Times* (January 2001).
Chater, D. (2005) TV review, *The Times* (August 2005).
Collingwood, R. G. (1946) *The Idea of History*. Oxford: Oxford University Press.
Cook, J. R. (2002) 'History-Makers', *Historical Journal of Film, Radio and Television*, 22, pp. 375–380.
Cook, J. R. (2010) '"Don't Forget to Look into the Camera!": Peter Watkins' Approach to Acting with Facts', *Studies in Documentary Film*, 4:3, pp. 227–240.
Corner, J. (1991) 'Public Knowledge and Popular Culture: Spaces and Tensions', *Media, Culture & Society*, 31:1, pp. 141–149.
Corner, J. (1996) *The Art of Record: A Critical Introduction*. Manchester: Manchester University Press.
Corner, J. (2002) 'Performing the Real: Documentary Diversions', *Television & New Media*, 3:3, pp. 255–269.
Corner, J. (2006a) 'Archive Aesthetics and the Historical Imaginary: *Wisconsin Death Trip*', *Screen*, 47:3, pp. 291–306.
Corner, J. (2006b) 'Backward Looks: Mediating the Past', *Media, Culture & Society*, 28:3, pp. 466–472.
Cottle, S. (2003) *Media Organisation and Production*. London: Sage.
Creeber, G. (2015) *The Television Genre Book*, 3rd ed. London: Palgrave.
Dargis, M. (2008) 'Movie Review: "The Other Boleyn Girl"', *New York Times* (9 December 2008).
Davis, L. (2006) 'All Tantrums and Togas', *The Times* (16 September 2006).
Davis, N. Z. (2000) *Slaves on the Screen*. Cambridge, MA: Harvard University Press.
De Groot, J. (2006) 'Empathy and Enfranchisement: Popular Histories', *Rethinking History: The Journal of Theory and Practice*, 10:3, pp. 391–413.
De Groot, J. (2016) *Consuming History: Historians and Heritage in Contemporary Culture*, 2nd ed. London: Routledge.
De Groot, J. (2018) 'Changing the Game: Public History and the Space of Fiction', *International Public History*, 1:1.

Dover, C. (2004) '"Crisis" in British Documentary Television: The End of a Genre?', *Journal of British Cinema and Television*, 1, pp. 242–259.

Ebbrecht, T. (2007a) 'Docudramatising History on TV: German and British Docudrama and Historical Event Television in the Memorial Year 2005', *European Journal of Cultural Studies*, 10:1, pp. 35–53.

Ebbrecht, T. (2007b) 'History, Public Memory and Media Event', *Media History*, 13:2–3, pp. 221–234.

Edgerton, G. (1995) 'Ken Burns – A conversation with Public Television's Resident Historian', *The Journal of American Culture*, 18:1, pp. 1–12.

Edgerton, G. and Rollins, P. C. (2001) *Television Histories: Shaping Collective Memories in the Media Age*. Lexington, KY: The University Press of Kentucky.

Edgerton, G. and Rose, B. G. (2005) *Thinking Outside the Box: A Contemporary Television Genre Reader*. Lexington, KY: The University Press of Kentucky.

Ellis, J. (2000) *Seeing Things: Television in the Age of Uncertainty*. London: Bloomsbury.

Ellis, J. (2012) *Documentary: Witness and Self-Revelation*. Abingdon: Routledge.

Fernández-Armesto, F. (2002) 'Epilogue: What is History *Now*?' in Cannadine, D. (ed.), *What is History Now?* London: Palgrave Macmillan, pp. 148–161.

Gallagher, J. (2014) 'Killers of the King: The Men Who Dared to Execute Charles I', *Guardian* (31 October 2014).

Gill, A. A. (2005) TV review, *The Sunday Times* (31 August 2005).

Godet, A. (2012) '"The West Wing with Wigs": Politics and History in HBO's *John Adams*', *TV/Series*, 1, pp. 61–79.

Goodman, W. (1989) 'The Basic Crookedness of Docudramas', *The New York Times* (2 November 1989).

Gray, A. and Bell, E. (eds) (2010) *Televising History: Mediating the Past in Postwar Europe*. Basingstoke: Palgrave Macmillan.

Gray, A. and Bell, E. (2013) *History on Television*. London: Routledge.

Gray, J. and Lotz, A. D. (2012) *Television Studies*. Cambridge: Polity.

Harding, V. (2002) *The Dead and the Living in Paris and London: 1500–1670*. Cambridge: Cambridge University Press.

Harlan, D. (2003) 'Ken Burns and the Coming Crisis of Academic History', *Rethinking History: The Journal of Theory and Practice*, 7:2, pp. 169–192.

Hughes-Warrington, M. (2009) *The History on Film Reader*. London: Routledge.

Hunt, T. (2006) 'Reality, Identity and Empathy: The Changing Face of Social History Television', *Journal of Social History*, 39:3, pp. 843–858.

Hunt, T. (2007) 'The Time Bandits: Television History is Now More about a Self Indulgent Search for Our Identity Than an Attempt to Explain the Past and Its Modern Meaning', *Guardian* (10 September 2007).

Johnson, N. K. (2016) 'HBO and the Holocaust: Conspiracy, the Historical Film, and Public History at Wannsee' (MA dissertation, Indiana University).

Kerrigan, S. and McIntyre, P. (2010) 'The "Creative Treatment of Actuality": Rationalizing and Reconceptualizing the Notion of Creativity for Documentary Practice', *Journal of Media Practice*, 11:2, pp. 111–130.

Kingsley-Jones, J. (2015) 'Genre Theory: Christian Metz's Four Stages of Genre Evolution', prezi.com, https://prezi.com/ijyiwcfrhvfo/genre-theory-christian-metzs-four-stages-of-genre-evoluti/ (accessed 13 September 2024).

Knudsen, E. (2016) 'The Total Filmmaker: Thinking of Screenwriting, Directing and Editing as One Role', *New Writing: The International Journal for the Practice and Theory of Creative Writing*, 13:1, pp. 109–129.

Landsberg, A. (2004) *Prosthetic Memory: The Transformation of American Remembrance in the Age of Mass Culture*. New York: Columbia University Press.

Linklater, A. (1993) 'Fade Far Away, Dissolve, and Quite Forget', *Spectator* (10 April 1993).

Lipkin, S. (2002) *Real Emotional Logic: Film and Television Docudrama as Persuasive Practice*. Carbondale, IL: Southern Illinois University Press.

Lipkin, S. (2011) *Docudrama Performs the Past: Arenas of Argument in Films Based on True Stories*. Newcastle-upon-Tyne: Cambridge Scholars.

Ludvigsson, D. (2003) 'The Historian-Filmmaker's Dilemma. Historical Documentaries in Sweden in the Era of Häger and Villius' (PhD dissertation, Uppsala University).

Mantel, H. (2009) 'Booker Winner Hilary Mantel on Dealing with History in Fiction', *Guardian* (17 October 2009).

Marlborough, D. (1964) 'To Arms Brothers, They Were Blacklegs at Culloden', *Daily Mail* (22 December 1964).

McElroy, R. and Williams, R. (2011) 'Remembering Ourselves, Viewing the Others: Historical Reality Television and Celebrity in the Small Nation', *Television & New Media*, 12:3, pp. 187–206.

Metz, C. and Taylor, M. (1974) *Film Language: A Semiotics of the Cinema*. New York: Oxford University Press.

Mittell, J. (2004) *Genre and Television: From Cop Shows to Cartoons in American Culture*. New York: Routledge.

Neale, S. (2000) *Genre and Hollywood*. London: Routledge.

Odin, R. (2018) 'Christian Metz for Today' in Tröhler, M. and Kirsten, G. (eds), *Christian Metz and the Codes of Cinema: Film Semiology and Beyond*. Amsterdam: Amsterdam University Press, pp. 91–114.

Paget, D. (1990) *True Stories: Documentary Drama on Radio, Screen and Stage*. Manchester: Manchester University Press.

Paget, D. (1998) *No Other Way to Tell It: Dramadoc/Docu-drama on Television*. Manchester: Manchester University Press.

Paget, D. (2007) '"Acting with Facts": Actors Performing the Real in British Theatre and Television since 1990. A Preliminary Report on a New Research Project', *Studies in Documentary Film*, 1:2, pp. 165–176.

Paget, D. (2013) 'Making Mischief: Peter Kosminsky, Stephen Frears and British Television Docudrama', *Journal of British Cinema and Television*, 10:1, pp. 171–186.

Paget, D. and Ebbrecht, T. (2007) 'Historical Event-Television: Codes and Conventions of "New Docudrama"', Position Paper for Visible Evidence XIV conference, Bochum.

Paget, D. and Ebbrecht-Hartmann, T. (eds) (2016) *Docudrama on European Television: A Selective Survey*. London: Palgrave Macmillan.

Paget, D. and Lacey, S. (eds) (2015) *The 'War on Terror': Post-9/11 Television Drama, Docudrama and Documentary*. Cardiff: University of Wales Press.

Paget, D. and Lipkin, S. (2009) '"Movie-of-the-Week" Docudrama, "Historical-Event" Television and the Steven Spielberg Miniseries Band of Brothers', *New Review of Film and Television Studies*, 7:1, pp. 93–107.

Peck, L. L. (2009) 'Schama's Britannia', *The American Historical Review*, 114:3, pp. 673–683.

Piccini, A. (2007) 'A Survey of Heritage Television Viewing Figures', *Council for British Archaeology* (21 June 2007).

Piper, H. (2015) *The TV Detective: Voices of Dissent in Contemporary Television*. London: I. B. Tauris.

Prebble, J. (2016) *Culloden*. London: Secker and Warburg.

Radish, C. (2019) 'Emily Watson on Why HBO's 'Chernobyl' Is a Cautionary Tale for Our Times', *Collider* (21 May 2019).

Ramsay, D. (2013) 'Television's "True Stories": Paratexts and the Promotion of HBO's Band of Brothers and the Pacific', *In Media: The French Journal of Media and Media Representations in the English-Speaking World*, 4.

Rose, A. (1964) 'Faces of the "45"', *Amateur Cine World*, 8:25, p. 834.

Rosenstone, R. (1995a) *Revisioning History: Film and the Construction of a New Past*. Princeton, NJ: Princeton University Press.

Rosenstone, R. (1995b) *Visions of the Past: The Challenge of Film to Our Idea of History*. Boston, MA: Harvard University Press.

Rosenstone, R. (2013) *History on Film, Film on History*, 2nd ed. Abingdon: Routledge.

Rosenthal, A. (1999) *Why Docudrama? Fact-Fiction on Film and TV*. Carbondale, IL: Southern Illinois University Press.

Samuel, R. (1994) *Theatres of Memory Volume 1: Past and Present in Contemporary Culture*. London: Verso.

Sarris, A. (1963) 'The Auteur Theory and the Perils of Pauline', *Film Quarterly*, 16:4, pp. 26–33.

Schatz, T. (1981) *Hollywood Genres: Formulas, Filmmaking, and the Studio System*. New York: McGraw-Hill Education.

Schrader, P. (1972) 'Notes on Film Noir', *Film Comment*, 8:1, pp. 8–13.

Scott, A. O. (2008) 'Walking on Air Between the Towers', *New York Times* (25 July 2008).

Sexton, M. and Lees, D. (2021) *Seeing It on Television: Televisuality in the Contemporary US 'High-End' Series*. London: Bloomsbury.

Seymour, L. (2017) *An Analysis of Roland Barthes's The Death of the Author*. London: Macat Library.

Shand, R. and Craven, I. (2013) *Small-Gauge Storytelling: Discovering the Amateur Fiction Film*. Edinburgh: Edinburgh University Press.

Shaw, T. (2006) 'The BBC, the State and Cold War Culture: The Case of Television's The War Game (1965)', *The English Historical Review*, 121:494, pp. 1351–1384.

Sills-Jones, D. (2009) 'History Documentary on UK Terrestrial Television, 1982–2002' (Unpublished PhD dissertation, University of Aberystwyth).

Sills-Jones, D. (2016) 'Revisiting UK's History Television Documentary Production', *Critical Studies in Television: The International Journal of Television Studies*, 11:1, pp. 78–95.

Smith, S. B. (2016) *Modernity and its Discontents*. New Haven, CT: Yale University Press.

Solecki, S. (1954) *A Truffaut Notebook*. Montreal, QC: McGill-Queen's University Press.

Sorlin, P. (1980) *The Film in History: Restaging the Past*. Oxford: Blackwell.

Stam, R. and Miller, T. 'Simon Schama: A History of Britain', *The American Historical Review*, 114:3, pp. 684–691.

Stokes, M. (2013) *American History Through Hollywood Film: From the Revolution to the 1960s*. London: Bloomsbury.

Tarrant-Willis, T. (2017) 'Finding an Audience: Evaluating the Production and Marketing of Low Budget British films in the iFeatures Production Scheme, 2009–2014' (PhD dissertation, University of the West of England, Bristol).

Taylor, D. J. (2001) 'David Starkey: The Apoplectic Academic', *Independent* (9 September 2001).

Todorov, T. (1976) 'The Origin of Genres', *New Literary History* 8:1, pp. 159–170.

Toplin, R. B. (1996) *History by Hollywood: The Use and Abuse of the American Past*. Urbana, IL: University of Illinois Press.

Trevelyan, G. H. (1913) *Clio, a Muse: And Other Essays Literary and Pedestrian*. London: Longmans, Green and Co.

Truffaut, F. (1954) 'A Certain Tendency in French Cinema' in MacKenzie, S. (ed.), (2014) *Film Manifestos and Global Cinema Cultures: A Critical Anthology*. Berkeley, CA: University of California Press, pp. 133–144.

Turner, G. (2010) *Ordinary People and the Media: The Demotic Turn*. London: SAGE.

Usborne, D. (2011) '9/11: The Day That Changed My City', *Independent* (9 September 2011).

Watkins, P. (1983) 'The Fear of Commitment', *Literature/Film Quarterly*, 11:4, pp. 221–233.

Wayne, M. (2007) 'Failing the Public: The BBC, The War Game and Revisionist History: A Reply to James Chapman', *Journal of Contemporary History*, 42:4, pp. 627–637.

White, H. (1973) *Metahistory: The Historical Imagination in Nineteenth-Century Europe*. Baltimore, MD: Johns Hopkins University Press.

White, H. (1980) 'The Value of Narrativity in the Representation of Reality', *Critical Inquiry*, 7:1, pp. 5–27.

White, H. (1987) *The Content of the Form: Narrative Discourse and Historical Representation*. Baltimore, MD: Johns Hopkins University Press.

White, R. (2009) 'Send in the Cyborgs', *Film Quarterly*, 62:3, 4–7.

Williams, A. (1984) 'Is a Radical Genre Criticism Possible?', *Quarterly Review of Film Studies*, 9:2, pp. 121–125.

Willis, J. (2001) 'Past is Perfect', *Guardian* (29 October 2001).
Winston, B. (2010) 'Combatting "a Message without a Code": Writing the "History" Documentary' in Gray, A. and Bell, E. (eds), *Televising History: Mediating the Past in Postwar Europe*. Basingstoke: Palgrave Macmillan, pp. 42–58.
Winston, B. (2013) *The Documentary Film Book*. Basingstoke: Palgrave Macmillan on behalf of the British Film Institute.
Wollen, P. (1969) *Signs and Meaning in the Cinema*. London: British Film Institute.
Woollaston, S. (2006) 'Last Night's TV', *Guardian* (6 October 2006).

Interviews

Bassnett-McGuire, L. Producer. January 2020, London.
Beavan, C. Director/producer. March 2020, London.
Bradley, R. Managing director Lion TV (1997–). March 2020, Oxford. Transcript.
Brockliss, L. Emeritus Professor of Oxford University. November 2019, Oxford. Transcript.
Cameron, D. Head of Planning BBC Four (2004–2019). January 2020, London.
Cardiff, L. Director of Photography. January 2020, London.
Cross, L. Casting Director. January 2020, Zoom in Cornwall.
Davidson, M. BBC Head of History (2012–2016). November 2019, Edinburgh. Transcript.
Fielder, M. Producer/director. January 2020, Bristol. Transcript.
Foley, C. SVP Animal Planet/Discovery Channel. 2007, Los Angeles.
Graham, A. CEO Wall to Wall TV (1988–2007). 2020–2022, London. Transcript.
Gray, A. Emerita Professor of Lincoln University. October 2019, Leamington Spa.
Hadlow, J. Channel 4 (1999–2004), Controller BBC Four (2004–2008), Controller BBC Two (2008–2014). November 2019, Edinburgh. Transcript.
Hartford, L. Producer/director. January 2020, London.
Hartington, D. Director of Photography. 2019–2020, Zoom in Manchester.
Holland, P. Controller BBC Two (2017–2021). August 2017, London.
Horth, S. BAFTA-winning producer. 2019–2020, London.
Jackson, M. Controller BBC One (1996–1997), CEO Channel 4 (1997–2001). January 2020, London. Transcript.
Kirby, T. Producer/director. January 2020, London. Transcript.
Mackintosh, S. Actor. 2017, London.
Mandel, L. Writer. 2019, Vienna.
Mitchell, A. Director. February 2020, Zoom in Belfast.
Muir, J. Producer/director. December 2019, London. Transcript.
Murphy, N. BAFTA-winning director. March 2020, Zoom in London.
Mykura, H. Channel 4, Head of Documentaries (2008–2012), SVP Nat Geo UK (2012–2019). February 2020–2021, Sussex. Transcript.
Orr, A. Producer. February 2020, Zoom in Belfast.
Phillips, R. Publisher. 2019, London.
Shah, S. CEO of Juniper TV (1998–). September 2019, London. Transcript.
Toba, J. Writer/producer. August 2019, Zoom.

Index

Aquilina, Audrey 141
Armesto, Felipe Fernandez 7
Astruc, Alexandre 12, 108
Austen, Jane 52

Banks-Smith, Nancy 174–175
Barthes, Rolande 12, 110
Bassnett-McGuire, Lucy 150
Beard, Mary 33, 175
Beavan, Clare 21–31, 56, 102
Blethyn, Brenda 41–42
Blight, David 40–41
Bordwell, David 20–21, 27
Bradley, Richard 5, 41, 87, 159–163, 172, 175, 184, 190
Bradsell, Michael 63, 65, 70
Bray, Simon 41
Brebner, Veronica 41
Brockliss, Laurence 127, 144–148, 151, 182, 184
Bruzzi, Stella 52, 92, 135–136, 157–158, 182, 201
Burgoyne, Robert 9, 51
Burke, Tony 142
Burns, Ken 76, 89, 112, 183, 200

Caldwell, J. T. 43
Cameron, Don 196
Cannadine, (Sir) David 7, 116
Cardiff, Luke 22–23
Cardwell, John 144, 146
Carr, E. H. 147
Castle, John 148
Champion, Justin 19, 24–25, 41
Chinn, Simon 94–95, 112, 164–165
Collingwood, R. G. 20
Cook, John 56, 58–59, 62, 70
Corner, John 20, 47, 52, 72–73

Cranham, Kenneth 86
Cross, Louise 139–140

Dabydeen, David 129–130
Daltrey, Roger 148
Darlow Smithson 78–79, 88, 191
Davidson, Martin 4, 16–19, 22, 24, 26, 40, 49, 71, 73, 87, 118, 128, 176–177, 179–180, 182–183, 187–188
Davies, Andrew 132, 137
Davies, Charles 41
Davis, Natalie Zemon 4, 10–11, 92, 95, 108
De Groot, Jerome 20, 34
Durlacher, Chris 104

Ebbrecht-Hartmann, Tobias 7, 118, 202, 204
Edmondson, Adrian 192
Edwards, Gareth 177
Einstein, Sergei 11

Fielder, Mark 26–32
Foley, Charley 179
Foreman, Amanda 33
Foucault, Michel 12, 110

Gardam, Tim 78
Garnett, Tony 59, 70–71
Gill, A. A. 146, 148
Glenister, Robert 143, 179
Goold, Ben 91–93, 102, 108
Graham, Alex 4–5, 56, 76–80, 82–84, 87–97, 101–112, 116, 164–166, 175, 185–187, 200
Gray, Ann 6, 50
Greenhalgh, Peter 92

Grierson, John 52
Guinness, Peter 26

Hadlow, Janice 4–5, 15–20, 24, 29, 32, 34, 38–42, 49, 78–79, 127–128, 134–135, 165, 182, 186, 188
Hager and Vilius 202
Harding, Vanessa 39–41
Harris, Jared 3, 132, 189, 192
Harrison, Cassian 160
Hartford, Liz 16, 18–19, 21–22
Hartington, Doug 22, 137–139, 141, 148–150, 182
Hedgecoe, Mark 173–174, 176, 178
Henry, Guy 139–140
Hewes, Jonathan 94–95, 112, 165–166
Hitchcock, Alfred 11, 76
Horth, Sue 5, 114, 150, 195, 204
Hunt, Tristram 1, 3, 5, 7
Hutton, Ronald 41

Jackson, Michael 5, 16–18, 24–25, 79–80, 186
James, Geraldine 172
Jardine, Lisa 41
Juniper TV 38–39, 78–79, 128–129, 161, 183

Kershaw, Ian 7, 16
Khan, Yasmin 6
Kirby, Tim 16, 24, 117, 134–138, 140–143
Klein, Richard 165
Knudsen, Eric 12, 111
Kosminsky, Peter 84, 188
Kuehl, Jerome 1

Langham, Chris 103–108
Lees, Dominic 21
Leigh, Mike 32
Lion TV 41, 78–79, 88, 104, 159–161, 163, 172, 183–184, 190
Lipkin, Steven 1, 8–9, 34, 47, 51, 60, 77, 82, 84, 86–87, 90, 93, 145, 150, 168, 178, 180–181, 202–203
Loach, Ken 58, 63, 70–71
Lowthorpe, Philippa 21, 131–132
Lucaccini, Mari 150

Mackintosh, Steven 132
McLeod, Hamish 141

McQueen, Steve 204
Mangan, Stephen 41
Manser, Jo 150
Mantel, Hilary 188, 204
Marsh, James 72, 137, 166
Mazin, Craig 188–189
Mitchell, Tony (Mitch) 82–85, 87–93, 109, 112
Muir, Jamie 22–23, 28, 31, 39, 61
Murphy, Nick 110–111, 174–177, 183, 193–194
Mykura, Hamish 6, 37, 59, 118, 134–137, 142–143, 145–146, 161, 163, 170, 182, 186

Olusoga, David 5, 33, 130, 195
Orr, Alisa 82–85, 87–88, 91, 93, 112
Oxford TV 79, 195

Paget, Derek 1–4, 7–8, 46–48, 72, 84, 90, 100–102, 118, 162, 164, 168, 180, 189, 198, 202, 204
Pennington, Michael 44
Pepys, Samuel 40, 42
Percival, Dan 94–95, 102, 110
Phillips, Roland 33–34
Prebble, John 57–58, 63, 66

Ramsden, Sara 78–79, 84, 89–90, 93, 112
Range, Gabriel 100–101
Rani, Anita 6
Rawcliffe, Carol 41
RDF 79, 104, 128
Redgrave, Corin 139–140, 149
Redgrave, Jemma 140
Rees, Laurence 16–17, 26, 43–44
Renck, Johan 188–189
Renoir, Jean 109
Richardson, Miles 139
Root, Jane 5, 18, 32, 78–80, 93, 95–96, 101, 112
Rosenstone, Robert 10–11, 22, 81, 93, 98, 102, 145–146, 152, 181, 183, 189, 202–203
Rosenthal, Alan 20, 47–48

Sahota, Maninderpal 191
Schama, Simon 7, 15–20, 23–26, 31–34, 37–40, 49–50, 52, 54, 73, 88, 106, 183
Sexton, Max 21

Shah, Samir 4–5, 33, 37, 39–41, 44, 128, 130, 133
Sharif, Omar 44–45
Shaw, Tony 67–70
Sheen, Michael 172, 174
Skarsgård, Stellan 189
Smithson, John 89
Snow, Dan 5
Stamp, Jonathan 43–44, 173
Starkey, David 15, 25–34, 37–40, 49–50, 52, 54, 73, 128, 160, 183–184

Tanner, Caitlyn 108
Thompson, Mark 18
Throssell, Dave 46
Tiger Aspect 79
Toba, John 37, 39–41, 56
Truffaut, François 12, 76, 109, 111

Underwood, Jon 150

Vansittart, Rupert 179

Wall to Wall TV 4, 38, 56, 76–80, 82–84, 87, 89–90, 93–96, 99, 101–109, 111–112, 116–117, 157, 161, 164–165, 183, 185–187, 200
Ware, Derek 65, 68
Watkins, Peter 6, 57–63, 67–68, 70–71, 74, 76, 89, 94, 112, 128, 140, 142–143, 148, 183–184, 200
Watson, Emily 3, 189, 194
Wheldon, Huw 57, 67, 69, 112
White, Hayden 8, 49, 85, 90–91, 97, 135, 173, 190
Willis, Emma 102
Willis, John 31–32
Windfall Films 78–79
Winston, Brian 52
Wollaston, Sam 174–175, 179

EU authorised representative for GPSR:
Easy Access System Europe, Mustamäe tee 50,
10621 Tallinn, Estonia
gpsr.requests@easproject.com

www.ingramcontent.com/pod-product-compliance
Lightning Source LLC
LaVergne TN
LVHW052017230825
819359LV00004B/144